LOUISVILLE GUIDE

AN ATTRACTIVE

LOUISVILLE

PUBLIC BUILDINGS

PARKS

UGLY CURB CORNERS GIVE
WAY TO ATTRACTIVE CURB CORNERS

LOUISVILLE GUIDE

Gregory A. Luhan
Dennis Domer
David Mohney

with essays by
Edith Bingham, Grady Clay, and
Susan Rademacher

A CITYBASE™ ARCHITECTURAL GUIDE FROM
PRINCETON ARCHITECTURAL PRESS
NEW YORK

Published by
Princeton Architectural Press
37 East Seventh Street
New York, New York 10003

For a free catalog of books, call 1.800.722.6657 or visit www.papress.com.
For more information on Citybase™ architectural databases, visit www.citybase.us.

Project Editor: Jennifer N. Thompson
Design: Deb Wood
Copy Editor: Lauren Neefe

Special thanks to: Nettie Aljian, Nicola Bednarek, Janet Behning, Megan Carey,
Penny (Yuen Pik) Chu, Russell Fernandez, Jan Haux, Clare Jacobson, John King,
Mark Lamster, Nancy Eklund Later, Linda Lee, Katharine Myers, Jane Sheinman,
Scott Tennent, Joseph Weston, and Deb Wood of Princeton Architectural Press
—Kevin C. Lippert, publisher

Library of Congress Cataloging-in-Publication Data

Luhan, Gregory A.
Louisville guide / Gregory A. Luhan, Dennis Domer, David Mohney.
    p. cm.
Includes bibliographical references and index.
ISBN 1-56898-451-0 (pbk. : alk. paper)
1. Architecture—Kentucky—Louisville. 2. Louisville (Ky.)—Buildings, structures,
etc. I. Domer, Dennis, 1944– II. Mohney, David, 1953– III. Title.

NA735.L6L84 2004
720'.9769'44—dc22
                    2004013659

CONTENTS

Acknowledgments

Many members of Louisville's design community shared their knowledge, both firsthand and accumulated through a long oral tradition. They include Larry Leis, John H. Bickel III, James Lee Gibson, H. Stow Chapman, Arnold Judd Sr., Arnold Judd Jr., Graham Rapp, Steve Wiser, John Chovan, Clyde Warner, Jim Walters, Carleton Godsey Jr., Jasper D. Ward, Sam M. Molloy, and Larry Melillo. Susan Jacobs Lockhart at Taliesin confirmed a number of points about the three Taliesin Associated Architects' projects in Louisville.

Louisvillians naturally take great pride in their city and understand its particular quirks well. We had the good fortune to discuss these traits in depth with Edith Bingham, Emily Bingham, Susan Rademacher, Ann Hassett, Charles Cash, Joanne Weeter, Richard Jett, Barry Alberts, Judith McCandless, Robin Silverman, Raymond P. McIntyre, Teka Ward, and Michael Ward. Jeff Ziebarth and Janice Barnes of Perkins & Will in Chicago and Michael Jacobs of Lexington also provided assistance. And Kentucky's State Historic Preservation Officer, David Morgan, provided both counsel and inspiration.

Through grant funding from the Kentucky Oral History Commission and working directly with Kim Lady Smith, Teka Ward, Samuel Thomas, and Douglas Stern, the following oral histories were recorded for the guide and are in the process of transcription under a separate KOHC grant (the oral histories will be available online and the tapes stored in the Oral History Program Collection at the University of Kentucky with support from Terry L. Birdwhistell, director of the Ford Research Center and Public Policy Archives and Jeffrey Suchanek of the Oral History Program, Division of Special Collections and Archives at the University of Kentucky Libraries): Norbourne 'Skip' Thorpe, Adele and Leonard Leight, Virginia Stites, Jim Walters, Samuel Thomas, John P. Chovan, Edie Bingham, Anthony Eardley, Graham Rapp, Arthur Tafel Jr., Bill

Weyland, Ed Cooke, Neal O. Hammon, Hugh Bennett, William Morgan, H. Stow Chapman, Fred Joseph, Bob Doherty, Herb Shulhafer, Arnold Judd Jr., Nana Lampton, K. Norman Berry, Frank Burke, John H. Bickel III, Clyde K. Warner, George Schipporeit, Byron Romanowitz, Mark O'Bryan, Grady Clay, James Lee Gibson, Jacqueline Sweet, Arnold Judd Sr., Clyde Carpenter, Carruthers A. Coleman Jr., Larry Leis, Carleton Godsey, Donald L. Williams, Tom Owen, and Herb Greene.

Kevin Lippert and Jennifer Thompson of Princeton Architectural Press have been thoughtful allies in this process. The effort to publish the work through an electronic database, Citybase, is Kevin's; we are hopeful that this will serve as a resource to scholars and others and perhaps set a precedent for a new method of distributing this kind of information. Gregory Luhan and Jeff Turner helped develop the model for the database.

Most of all, we appreciate the enormous assistance of the owners and residents of the properties we researched for this guide. They were supportive of our efforts, even if, in some cases, they first heard about it during a cold call, after a knock on the door. These encounters brought a wealth of knowledge, most of which could not fit into descriptions of 250 words. They include the Merriwether family; the friends of the Farnsley-Moreman House; James C. Anderson, curator of Special Collections, Eastman Library in Rochester, New York; Marsha Burton; Lynn S. Renan; Allan M. Steinberg; Dr. and Mrs. Ben Birkhead; Dr. Elizabeth Alexander; Barbara Basen; Dr. Mark Wetherington; and Andra Deetsch. Thanks also to Mayor Jerry Abramson and the Office of the Mayor, University of Louisville Libraries and their staffs, the Filson Historical Society, the Louisville *Courier-Journal,* the Old Louisville Neighborhood Association, Butchertown, the Kentucky Heritage Council, the Metro Louisville Historic Preservation Commission, and the Jefferson County Fiscal Court.

We also received strong support from our colleagues and students at the University of Kentucky College of Design. Amy Bennett, Nick Winter, Heather Green, Amelia Armstrong, Mary Anne Ocampo, Marissa Tirone, Lyssa Halley, Feng Li, and Jennifer Lucas served as research assistants on the project. They gathered the surveys of historic buildings and National Register forms, which have been completed by many branches of government as well as individuals over the years. Staff support came from Mark Royse, Dana Cox, Patrick Thrush, and Ginny Miller. The University of Kentucky Library system was a great resource, and we thank Faith Harders and Lalana Powell from the Hunter Adams Architecture Library in the College of Design. Thanks to David Mullins and Mary Rezny at the Film Lab, who provided their technical expertise and photographic work, and Jeff Turner, Tom Moreland, and Jeff Levy for their assistance with GIS data. Finally, we thank the individuals and organizations that offered financial support for this project, including the American Institute of Architects Central Kentucky Chapter, Dr. Wendy Baldwin, Executive Vice President for Research, University of Kentucky, John H. Bickel III, Barry and Edith Bingham, Brown-Forman Corporation, The Graham Foundation for Advanced Studies in the Fine Arts, PNC Bank, Louisville and the Al J. Schneider Foundation of Louisville.

We are the happy beneficiaries of this outpouring of assistance and encouragement. It is certain that there will be errors in fact and emphasis; for these, we stand alone and accept full responsibility.

Introduction

Louisville, from its founding at the Falls of the Ohio River in 1778, has been a place between its environs and circumstances. The city quickly became an industrial center in a state that to this day retains strong agrarian sensibilities. Geographically and—even more important—culturally, Louisville is between North and South, between East and West. It is awkward at times determining just where Louisvillians place their allegiances, yet this quality of being "between" makes the city a place apart, unique in many ways.

The residents of Louisville understand that the city's distance and differentiation from other urban areas of America is not easily grasped, which might explain the relatively few publications on the city's history and evolution. We began this guide with the hope of filling in some portion of that gap, focusing on what we believe to be a rich yet overlooked architectural history. Closer examination of the fabric of the city has not only reaffirmed our ideas, but also enlarged them. The breadth of noteworthy architecture stretches across all of Louisville's history, from its founding to the present day. There are tens of thousands of buildings in Louisville, and we have written on just over 250 of them. How did we determine this selection as representative of the city's built history? Just as important, what does this mean about buildings that have not been included?

We chose to work with existing buildings and places. There is nevertheless a very significant building history in Louisville that is all too easily ignored: structures of an earlier age that were replaced for an accepted idea of progress; worthwhile, even exceptional, buildings and neighborhoods that were not maintained and came down. This is fertile ground for future scholarship.

As to the first question: the closer we looked at Louisville, the more remarkable its buildings and designed places became to us. This assessment applies not only to those buildings that are examples of the great stylistic periods in American architecture (of which

Louisville has more than its fair share), but also to two other groups of buildings that are sometimes overlooked in guides like this: urban vernacular structures and those of the contemporary and modern world. Both of these categories are also in need of new research. The breadth of industrial building types still standing from the nineteenth century is remarkable. And Louisville's mid-century modern architects, though largely uncelebrated in their lifetime, were as talented a group as those of any American city of that time. Here, too, there is a great deal of room for significant scholarship, and we hope that this guide will be a resource for those who choose to pursue it.

The process of selecting buildings began by examining each building in person. We used a number of printed resources in compiling a list and depended even more on the suggestions of a large number of people. From that point, we developed these criteria for including a building or place:

> ¶ It has made a significant contribution to the history of Louisville's architectural development.
> ¶ It is a rare example of its type or style.
> ¶ It has architectural integrity: it has not changed to the point that it no longer represents the architect's intentions.
> ¶ An important architect designed it.
> ¶ It has historical significance for the city.
> ¶ And, finally, we liked it.

We have organized our selection of buildings by neighborhood.

Dennis Domer is the lead researcher and writer on Louisville buildings and landscapes from 1787 to 1900, and his essay gives an overview of the pioneer period through the dynamic changes in Louisville's architecture in the last half of the nineteenth century.

Gregory A. Luhan is the lead author of the guide and provides new scholarship on buildings from 1900 to 1970 and several in the contemporary section. His essay reviews the work of those Louisville architects who were largely unknown outside the city, and who were often inspired by the signature architects of the first half of the twentieth century: Frank Lloyd Wright, Eero Saarinen, Mies van der Röhe, and Le Corbusier.

David Mohney focuses on works from 1970 to the present, and surveys Louisville's contemporary architecture, the planning efforts taken on by the city, and the climate in which architects practice today.

These three historical divisions are in many respects arbitrary, but, given the task, it made sense for us to divide our work. Nevertheless, the reality of the built landscape in Louisville does not divide so easily. In most neighborhoods and certainly downtown, there is a mix of the old and the new, and the buildings present their own order to the passerby. The guide helps the reader understand how buildings from different times come together, making a complex urban landscape. We also asked Edie Bingham, Susan M. Rademacher, and Grady Clay to write essays about historic preservation, the Olmsted legacy, and urban design, respectively, to provide the reader with a deeper understanding of Louisville's architectural history.

Throughout much of the twentieth century, the story of Louisville's building history has been told quietly. We are happy to note that this situation has changed substantially in the last generation. Three major publications have addressed both the history and resources of the city of Louisville, and we acknowledge them first and foremost among the many sources consulted in the preparation of this guide. They are *Two Hundred Years at the Falls of the Ohio: A History of Louisville and Jefferson County* (1987) by George Yater, and *The Encyclopedia of Louisville* (2001), with more than 500 entries, and *The Encyclopedia of Kentucky* (1992), both masterfully edited by John Kleber. These volumes were the foundation of much of our research and knowledge of the city. Theodore Brown's *Introduction to Louisville's Architecture* (1960) and Leslie Kees and Donna Neary's *Historic Jefferson County* (1992) were most helpful. Additional information came through the work of Samuel Thomas, Tom Owen, Grady Clay, and Clay Lancaster.

The audience for this book varies from the neophyte to the expert. Whatever the knowledge of our readers, we hope that they will always make a careful and methodical survey of the structure and landscape, and for that reason, we often point out the details we don't want them to miss. We hope that the overall balance of description and analysis provided here helps the reader get the picture, big and small, and that Louisville's rich architectural heritage enlivens their experience.

Cavehill Cemetery, Satterwhite Memorial Temple, 1928

Building and Rebuilding Louisville, 1787–1900: Antebellum Entrepôt to Industrial City

Dennis Domer

The Falls of the Ohio River proved to be an advantageous location for a river city like Louisville, which became a busy entrepôt and manufacturing center during the first fifty years of the nineteenth century.[1] For most pioneers, the 981-mile Ohio was the fastest, easiest, and by far safest route west, even though it was full of sand bars, snags, and treacherous holes that accomplished flatboat, keelboat, and steamboat pilots negotiated with skill and luck until they came to the Falls, where they had to stop, disembark, and portage. To facilitate passage, city builders surveyed five towns near the Falls: Louisville, Shippingport, Portland, Clarksville, and Jeffersonville. By the 1820s, it had become clear that Louisville had the best location and would prevail in the struggle for supremacy.[2]

Louisville, a town of jumbled log cabins and about 350 people in 1800, provided these pioneers the slightest of services as they passed, but things had changed dramatically in Louisville by 1824, when travelers could make a more pleasant stop in a small city of about 5,000 people. Three streets, parallel to the river and about eleven blocks long, created a downtown business center that bristled with buildings of wood and brick, produced commercially as early as 1815 by six brickyards in Smoketown, which used hired and slave African Americans from this neighborhood just east of downtown.[3]

From this federal and early Greek revival period to about 1815, only a small, scattered number of primarily brick or stone central-hall, side entry–hall, and one-room structures survive, and most of them are represented in this guide. The upper-class house Locust Grove was built in the 1790s as an imposing brick plantation house with an array of brick and log outbuildings.[4] The original Oxmoor, also a plantation house, is an early frame structure that retains an 1829 brick addition, many of its service buildings, and some of its slave quarters as well.[5] Farmington, built around 1815 for a plantation, has some of the characteristics that Thomas Jefferson favored in his domestic architecture but probably was drawn up by an itinerant gentleman architect who may have copied one of Jefferson's plans. Davis Tavern, Eight Mile House, Zachary Taylor's house, and the Joseph Abell House survived as vernacular buildings because they are masonry structures and have been maintained. They resemble hundreds of more temporary vernacular buildings that have perished. More typical of the working-class dwelling is the Farnsley-Kaufman House, which retains its original log-cabin section, built in 1811, within a larger, accretive structure.

All of these buildings served the agrarian economy that surrounded Louisville, but the forces of urbanism, spawned by river traffic, reinforced the city's center. The Louisville and Portland Canal, opened in 1830 on the Kentucky side of the river to facilitate the transfer around the Falls, gave momentum to the city, as did the Bourbon Stock Yards, established on the east side of town in 1834. James Dakin's Bank of Louisville (1835), carried out by Gideon Shryock, and Shryock's own Jefferson County Courthouse, which he and others hoped would be Kentucky's Capitol, strengthened the downtown commercial district.[6] A large influx of Germans and Irish settled in the neighborhoods east and west of downtown (including Portland, Butchertown, Germantown, and Phoenix Hill) from the 1830s to the 1850s and raised Louisville's population to 61,213 by 1860, not including the approximately 2,000 slaves who lived in the neighborhoods of Smoketown, California, and Little Africa.[7] By 1860, eight African American churches ministered to an enslaved people. The shotgun house continues to be one of the predominant house types in all of these neighborhoods.

Both African Americans and whites built shotguns because they fit on long, thin city lots, were easy to construct, and accommodated almost any nearby urban structure, including warehouses, foundries, and factories. A thriving center of retail stores, professional offices, banks, churches, hotels, wholesale houses, and whiskey concerns created a very wealthy class of people who lived on the south side of town, in splendid residences on Chestnut and Broadway Streets. These residences had become more lavish by the late 1850s and moved farther south, on roads such as the Western

Louisville Medical Center, 1857

Turnpike (today's Broadway), where Horatio Dalton Newcomb, who got rich in the 1830s by wholesaling whiskey, molasses, sugar, and coffee, built a fine Italianate stone mansion in 1859, designed by Henry Whitestone. Like much of Whitestone's work, it has been destroyed.[8]

Little of the lively antebellum city survives, though once robust and confident. By the 1840s, many of the late-eighteenth-century and early-nineteenth-century buildings faced certain destruction, because they were wearing out, had become too small, were obsolete technically or aesthetically, or were simply in the way of new urban realities. The thirty-six brick makers in Louisville were selling tens of millions of bricks by the 1850s, to keep up with builders' demands.[9] After the Civil War, the old locational advantages of the River and Falls combined with the catalytic effects of the railroads to create a powerful postwar economy, in which industry thrived on a cheap rail system that connected a growing network of regional markets. New waves of Irish and Germans and African American freedmen poured in to take a wide range of industrial jobs, fill the old residential neighborhoods, and settle new ones such as Limerick, near the massive rail yards. From the 1870s to the 1890s, bursts of new building near the center of town, east of downtown, and in residential neighborhoods south of downtown closely followed the harsh economic cycles of boom, bust, and recovery; but investments and profits continued to rise, especially at industrial plants in New Albany, just across the Ohio River. In 1860, there were 436

Ridgeway, 1816–1818

manufacturers in Louisville. This number rose to 651 in 1870 and to more than one thousand in 1880.[10] The benefactors of these industries invested heavily in Louisville's development into the early twentieth century.

Despite the relentless cycles of late-nineteenth- and twentieth-century building in Louisville, which tended to replace rather than restore, it has been impossible so far to erase entirely the antebellum period. From that time there remain at least nine government and religious structures, including Brown Memorial Christian Methodist Episcopal Church, the Cathedral of the Assumption, St. Martin of Tours, the U.S. Marine Hospital by Robert Mills, the Louisville Waterworks, the U.S. Customs House and Post Office by Ammi B. Young, the Jefferson County Courthouse by Gideon Shryock, the Bank of Louisville by James Dakin, Christ Church Cathedral and Parish House by W. H. Redin, and Seelbach's European Hotel by Henry Whitestone. Cave Hill Cemetery, the Hadley Pottery warehouse, along with about a dozen brick or stone central-hall houses and some of their related outbuildings, have also survived. Striking examples of extant domestic architecture include Ridgeway, Nunnlea, Selema Hall, and the Theodore Brown House.

It took a steady stream of sophisticated architects, engineers, landscape architects, carpenters, masons, and technicians to make the Victorian city that replaced the antebellum city. Henry Whitestone, Mason Maury, Charles D. Meyer, W. H. Redin, Charles Julian Clarke, Arthur Loomis, the McDonald Brothers,

West Main Street

D. X. Murphy, John Andrewartha, William James Dodd, Arthur Cobb, and Frederick Law Olmsted introduced the most advanced building and landscape competencies from the larger building culture of the U.S.—especially Philadelphia, New York, Boston, and Chicago—and Europe. They bridged the Ohio three times; manufactured copious amounts of brick, cast iron, wrought iron, and terra-cotta building parts for their own and many other cities; finished a water pumping and purifying system; introduced new and faster communication systems, electricity, indoor plumbing, elevators, interurban transportation, and parks and parkways; and laid down all-weather streets. Wealth of know-how and ambition built Old Louisville, a large middle- to upper-class neighborhood near where the University of Louisville eventually moved in 1925, filled with a variety of Victorian architectural excesses. Outlying neighborhoods and towns, such as Anchorage, the Highlands, Crescent Hill, Clifton, Beechmont, Buechel, and in 1901 St. Matthews, connected a growing number of white-collar suburbanites, via the interurban rail system, to the industrial, transportation, and manufacturing center. The old residential areas of these parts of Louisville still display a wide variety of late-nineteenth and early-twentieth-century architectural styles.[11] Berrytown and Griffytown were founded during this period as segregated communities collected in rural settings, usually in close proximity to white neighbors who hired African Americans as servants, gardeners, and farm workers. Louisville had good railroad connections for them. Continual influxes of people, seemingly unending profits, and surges of new building had by 1900 made Louisville a regional urban metropolis with a population of more than 200,000.[12]

The ardent work of many preservation-minded activists saved enough of this post–Civil War legacy from urban renewal and progress in the 1960s and 1970s to provide a small sample of the architecture from the Victorian period. Three main Olmsted Parks (Cherokee, Shawnee, and Iroquois) and six connecting parkways, three smaller parks, and another dozen parks designed by F. L. Olmsted Jr. and John Olmsted together present the most extensive Olmsted urban landscape in the U.S. Old Louisville, including its alleys, has a well-maintained variety of Victorian-era architecture, designed by local architects and built by local artisans who lived in the mixed industrial working-class neighborhoods of Germantown, Butchertown, Phoenix Hill, and Limerick. St. James Court and Belgravia Court are ideal examples of late-nineteenth-century upper-middle-class suburban residential design. The second-generation immigrants also built many churches of excellent craft, including the First English Lutheran Church, the First Unitarian Church, Quinn Chapel, Calvary Episcopal Church, Church of the Advent, St. Joseph's Catholic Church, St. Louis Bertrand Church, and St. Peter's German Evangelical Church. Main Street and other downtown streets still have many buildings from this period; of note are the German Insurance Bank and Insurance Company, the Levy Brothers Building, Louisville City Hall, Louisville Bank and Trust, the Hart Block, Carter Brothers Wholesale and Dry Goods (now the Louisville Science Center), the Trade Mart Building, Union Station, and the Vaughn Building.

Churchill Downs, designed in 1875 by Joseph Baldez of D. X. Murphy & Brothers, has been changed and enlarged considerably since its humble beginnings and now accommodates more than 160,000 persons on Derby Day. The current renovation includes a new clubhouse, luxury suites, Millionaire's Row and Skye Terrace, a new press box, elevators, escalators, restrooms, kitchen, delivery and storage facilities, waging areas, dining and entertainment areas, and premium indoor and outdoor box seating. The significance of the place, more than of the building, gives Churchill Downs its National Landmark status.[13]

All of these buildings create only a small sample of the historically significant architecture, not to mention the vast number of extant vernacular dwellings and businesses that filled up the dozens of existing and new neighborhoods in the 1880s and 1890s. Crescent Hill, the Highlands, Clifton, Beechmont, Anchorage, and Pewee Valley grew up as stops on the rail lines and present a picturesque landscape of residential architecture, streetscapes, landscapes, and rail right-of-ways from the late nineteenth century.

NOTES

1. For a concise history of Louisville, see George H. Yater, "Louisville: A Historical Overview," in *The Encyclopedia of Louisville*, ed. John E. Kleber, xv–xxxi (Lexington, Ky.: University Press of Kentucky, 2001). For a longer version of the city's story, see George H. Yater, *Two Hundred Years at the Falls of the Ohio: A History of Louisville and Jefferson County* (Louisville, Ky.: The Heritage Corporation of Louisville and Jefferson County, 1979). An excellent collection of maps, drawings, engravings, and photography of the city can be found in Samuel W. Thomas, ed., *Views of Louisville Since 1766* (Louisville, Ky.: EchoBooks, 1971).

2. See Kleber, *Encyclopedia of Louisville*, 204–5, 442–44, 716–17, 814–15.

3. Ibid., 830–31.

4. For a detailed study of Louisville's most renowned pioneer building, see Samuel W. Thomas, *History in Houses: Locust Grove near Louisville, Kentucky* (Louisville: Data Courier Journal, 1967).

5. Thomas has also written a thorough study of one of Kentucky's most important plantations in his book *Oxmoor: The Bullitt Family Estate near Louisville, Kentucky, Since 1787* (Louisville, Ky.: Oxmoor Cemetery Co., 2003).

6. For the most authoritative work on antebellum buildings in Louisville, see Clay Lancaster, *Antebellum Architecture of Kentucky* (Lexington, Ky.: University Press of Kentucky, 1991). However, the *Metropolitan Preservation Plan* of 1973 provides a broader selection of old buildings than Lancaster.

7. For substantial articles on all of these early historic neighborhoods, see Kleber, *Encyclopedia of Louisville*. Kleber also provides rough maps of the neighborhoods that are sometimes difficult to differentiate in the field. For a scholarly analysis of African American life in Louisville, see George C. Wright, *Life Behind a Veil: Blacks in Louisville, Kentucky, 1865–1930* (Baton Rouge, La.: Louisiana State University Press, 1985).

8. Urban renewal destroyed many of Whitestone's buildings and numerous other early Louisville landmarks in spite of anti-scrape preservation efforts. Theodore Brown was particularly vocal about the negative consequences of urban renewal, which he outlined in "Introduction to Louisville Architecture,"

Courier-Journal, December 7, 1960.

9. For a history of the brick industry, see Kleber, *Encyclopedia of Louisville,* 121–22.

10. A shorter, data-filled reference for Louisville's industries can be found in John E. Kleber, ed., *The Kentucky Encyclopedia* (Lexington, Ky.: University Press of Kentucky, 1992), 574–78. Kleber's *Encyclopedia of Louisville* also provides an extensive essay on iron foundries, one of Louisville's most important nineteenth-century industries.

11. Louisville's late-nineteenth-century neighborhoods have received considerable scholarly attention; see Theodore Brown and Margaret M. Bridwell, *Old Louisville* (Louisville, Ky.: University of Louisville, 1961). See also Samuel W. Thomas and William Morgan, *Old Louisville: The Victorian Era* (Louisville, Ky.: The Courier-Journal, The Louisville Times, 1975), which added many dimensions to that period of the city's suburban development and architecture. Thomas has also published books on other neighborhoods, including Crescent Hill and St. Matthews.

12. All population citations and most dates are taken from Kleber's *Encyclopedia of Louisville.*

13. The history of Churchill Downs' architecture and landscape is very complex. Samuel W. Thomas lays out the intricacies in *Churchill Downs: A Documentary History of America's Most Legendary Race Track* (Louisville, Ky.: Kentucky Derby Museum, 1995).

Louisville Modernism

Gregory A. Luhan

Louisville lies at the western limits of the Outer Bluegrass geographically and between the Midwest and South culturally. Its architectural
riches include cast-iron architecture, warehouse buildings, and several examples of modernism. Architecture in Louisville has generally followed the stylistic tendencies of architecture in America, and
some of Louisville's buildings rank among the nation's finest.

The expanding economy after the Civil War gave rise to a
significant upper class, which aligned itself with the architectural
directions of the country, most notably the emerging Renaissance
revival, the Beaux Arts neoclassicism of Richard Morris Hunt and
McKim, Mead, and White, the Romanesque manner of Henry
Hobson Richardson, and the Chicago School of William Le Baron
Jenney, Adler and Sullivan, and Burnham and Root. Louisville's
participation in the uniquely American architectural tradition that
grew out of the Richardsonian era produced sound and imaginative
architecture during the late nineteenth century.

While Louisville has never been a center of architectural innovation, it has nevertheless possessed both the clients and the
architects to produce buildings of quality and distinction. The
success of Louisville's architectural image provoked Kentucky
State Representative Albert S. Willis to state in 1884: "Not only
does architecture inspire patriotism, cultivate taste and advance
civilization, but it may and often does exercise a conservative influence upon society. In the shifting impetuousness of life of this new
and rapidly expanding country, our architecture should be a conservative element...that which is old."[1] The essence of this conservative
gesture remains throughout the modern period.

Prior to 1930, architectural training in Kentucky consisted of
apprenticeship with the firms that produced much of Louisville's

architecture, such as Henry Whitestone, D. X. Murphy, William J. Dodd, Mason Maury, Kenneth McDonald, James J. Gaffney, Brinton B. Davis, Hermann Wischmeyer, Charles Julian Clarke, and Arthur Loomis. These architects tended to practice within the state, although there were notable exceptions: William J. Dodd and his partner, Mason Maury, represented Kentucky at the 1893 World's Columbian Exposition in Chicago (Dodd would later continue his practice in Los Angeles); in 1922, Kenneth McDonald and William S. Arrasmith both participated in the international competition for a new administration building for the Chicago Tribune (McDonald would later

William S. Arrasmith, Chicago Tribune Tower competition entry, 1922

partner with Dodd before practicing in San Francisco); and Arrasmith, as Greyhound's architect, designed several art deco–inspired bus depots across the U.S., the most notable being the Greyhound Bus Terminal in Washington, D.C. (1939–1940).

The Commonwealth of Kentucky did not have a school of architecture until the 1960s, so the young architects of this generation augmented their knowledge of local heritage with techniques and aesthetics learned outside the state.[2] Louisville's apprentice architects studied at the University of Pennsylvania, Cranbrook Academy, University of Michigan, Massachusetts Institute of Technology, University of Illinois, University of Cincinnati, Harvard University, Yale University, Clemson, and Georgia Tech, spanning the range of design idioms from Beaux Arts to Bauhaus. It is precisely this amalgam of local culture and European style that gives the modernist architecture of Kentucky a unique identity. Young architects returned to Louisville with passion, idealism, and a renewed sense of purpose.

Apart from style, there were many streams of modernism at work in Louisville. Architects in the late 1800s and early 1900s often oscil-

Triaero, 1940

lated from styles that were unornamented and ahistorical to plans that were functional. For example, Henry Whitestone, the precursor firm to D. X. Murphy and later Luckett & Farley, produced several stripped-down, classical, and functionally planned buildings. William S. Arrasmith and J. Meyrick Colley produced art deco commercial buildings that continued a sympathetic dialogue within the context of Beaux Arts structures designed by firms such as McDonald and Dodd and Joseph and Joseph. E. T. Hutchings and Preston Bradshaw produced hotel and office buildings in the colonial revival style, and Kentucky natives James Gamble Rogers and Arthur Loomis planned the campus of Southern Baptist Theological Seminary in the same style but with different materials. From these streams emerged a handful of important signature architects influenced by the organicism of Wright and Aalto, the rationalism of Saarinen, the functionalism of Mies van der Rohe, and the purist individualism of Le Corbusier. These regional architects fostered innovation and individuality by spawning collaborations between architect, engineer, and the building industry.

In early 1937, one of the most devastating floods in American history inundated the Ohio River valley. Louisville was the hardest hit of all Kentucky cities: more than sixty percent of Louisville—nearly thirty-five square miles—was underwater. Many people relocated to the highlands, which initiated a renewed relationship between the built environment and the landscape.

The first evidence of truly modernist architecture to appear in this natural landscape was a residence designed in 1938 by Louisville architect Samuel Calvin Molloy. Maurice L. Miller ap-

Gilores House, 1957

proached Molloy to design a house that would be the most "modern" in this section of the country. A 1939 Louisville *Courier-Journal* article, titled "But People Do Live in Glass Houses," advocated a widespread introduction of the modern architectural language and style.

Two years later, Irma Bartman hired architect Bruce Goff to design a weekend house that would serve as a studio for her son, Kenneth, who was studying at the Chicago Institute of Fine Arts, where Goff was teaching. The Irma Bartman Residence (also known as Triaero) is located in Fern Creek. Goff used a glass structural system that was inspired by Wright and Mies van der Rohe. The impact of Wright, Goff's former teacher, is evident in the triangular plan with its central utility core, extensive use of glass, and spreading roof, which soars beyond the walls and over reflecting pools at two corners. The original design used exterior walls with floor-to-ceiling glass to express the integral relationship between nature and the enclosure.

The Wright-inspired Gilores House (1957), designed by Norman Sweet and Arnold Judd Sr., brings the landscape into the core of the house. The house pivots around a central courtyard and has a see-through fireplace with windows that visually extend the interior across the two-acre site. Later houses by Edd R. Gregg, Quintin Biagi Sr., A. Bailey Ryan, Robert A. Nolan, Victor Civkin, Jasper D. Ward, and John H. Bickel III of Design Environment Group Architects (DEGA) also integrate the natural context with the built enclosure.

The high standard of Louisville's modern architecture ranks with other leading cities in the U.S. Yet, with very few exceptions, its impact was not felt outside the region. The influence of Wright, Breuer, Le Corbusier, William Lescaze, Louis Kahn, Mies, and Saarinen is clearly evident in many of the area's modernist buildings. The Rauch Memorial Planetarium (1957–1962, razed in 1998) designed by Louis & Henry on the University of Louisville campus directly reflected Saarinen's Kresge Chapel (1953–57) on the MIT campus.

Local industry has been an important influence for innovations in design. The local brick and concrete industry sponsored design competitions for innovations in material use, and the impact of Reynolds Metals (located in Louisville at the time) and the aluminum industry on modern architecture throughout the region and beyond cannot be understated. One need only look to the 800 Apartment Building (1963), designed by William S. Arrasmith in association with Loewenberg & Loewenberg of Chicago, or the Liberty National Bank and Trust Company (1956–1960, now Bank One) designed by Wagner and Potts in association with the Brazilian architect Wenceslao Sarmiento, to see two of the first examples of aluminum curtain-wall construction in Kentucky. Through the 1950s and 1960s, Reynolds also sponsored annual design competitions for innovations in the housing industry. Entrants included a wide variety of architects from all over the nation.

However, the prevalence of neoclassicism and the overall nostalgia for the past resulted in the reluctance to wholly embrace the modern aesthetic and ultimately led to the emergence of a hybrid style referred to by local architects as "sandpaper Georgian." It was this hesitation that slowed the development of modern architecture in Louisville, which unfolded over the course of the four decades following World War II, later than in some other American cities. But the later work was unique in its pace of innovation and the set of circumstances that made it, especially during the fifties and sixties, a time of architectural variety in terms of form, material, and scale.

The 1950s and 1960s saw a marked expansion of the city in projects ranging from individual buildings to urban design. The 1950s was a landmark decade in the city's growth; construction boomed all around the city. For example, one hundred new subdivisions were started in 1956 alone. New schools were built to accommodate this rapid growth, adding as many as 2,500 additional students per year. The Board of Education hired the firm Hartstern, Louis & Henry to research design and construction methods that could be used as a prototype for these schools, and between 1950 and 1965 the firm designed at least one new school per year. Between 1950 and 1970, the firms of Louis & Henry, Norman Sweet, Nolan & Nolan, Arrasmith and Judd, Jasper D. Ward, and John Bickel emerged as the leaders of the modern movement in Louisville. These six firms designed the majority of Louisville's new schools and houses, and, with the reinvestment in downtown and the suburban expansion, most of the city's churches, temples, hospitals, housing projects, office buildings, and civic buildings.

In the 1960s, many American cities, including Louisville, adopted urban renewal as a tool to revitalize or "suburbanize" the inner city. When Wright visited Louisville in 1948, he commented on the city's historic fabric: "Louisville's architecture represents the quality of the Old South. We should not build this type of building any more"—referencing Gideon Shryock's Jefferson County Courthouse (1835–1860)—"but we should keep those that we have left."[3] Twenty-five years later, local developer Al J. Schneider stated, "Excessive historic preservation in Louisville is stifling development, and chasing new building to the suburbs and even to other cities." He continued, "We are going to have to push to work or we'll be back where we were 35 to 45 years ago."[4] As urban renewal began to run its generally destructive course through the downtown, Grady Clay and local architects John Cullinane (fresh from studying with visionary architect Paolo Soleri in Arizona) and John Bickel formed the Citizens Metropolitan Planning Council (CMPC) to provide the general public with critical insight into the design processes that shape the built environment and with a voice in that process.

At the urging of Clay, then editor of *Landscape Architecture* magazine and an advisory member of the local AIA, the City of Louisville sponsored a national open design competition for the Village West Urban Renewal site.[5] The winning entry came from John H. Bickel's office, and Louisville received a Citation for Excellence in Community Architecture. The award was significant because it placed the large-scale urban-renewal project in Louisville on par with projects like Philadelphia's Society Hill and Salt Lake City's Downtown Second Century Project.

Through the late seventies and mid eighties, architects had to consider a range of political, social, cultural, and economic issues. Despite the presence of architecturally optimistic ideas for modern living, the collective reaction in Louisville was often indifferent and skeptical. Clients for modern residential projects found that banks would not give loans simply because the houses did not look like the traditional Kentucky home.[6] Often these architects had to mask their innovations by designing a contextual front facade, while inside they explored spatial continuity and formal complexity.

The contribution of these Louisville modern architects has long been overlooked in the history of Kentucky architecture. Rarely are the names and works of this group of architects acknowledged in the press. The examples of Louisville modern architecture built from 1940 to 1980 only begin to convey the creative insight and passion of their architects. These architects did not write; they taught by example. Their buildings are the best representations of their ideals and work.

NOTES

1. Samuel W. Thomas, *Louisville Since the Twenties* (Louisville, Ky.: Courier-Journal and the Louisville Times, 1978).

2. An essay written by Stratton O. Hammon for the *Filson Club Quarterly* in 1968 states that the College of Arts and Sciences at the University of Louisville offered a college-level degree in architecture from 1913 to 1926 that aligned with the Society of Beaux Arts in New York (later the Beaux-Arts Institute of Design). Professors William Glossop (architecture), Solomon Turnheim (structures), and Bennett Brigman (mechanical drawing and engineering) taught architectural design. This course of study ended in 1926. The College of Architecture at the University of Kentucky (Lexington) emerged from the College of Engineering over a sixty-five-year period. Since 1895, courses taught in architecture focused on drafting and general architecture. In 1925, the first separate course added specifically for architecture became a required course in engineering, followed in 1935 with the introduction of a bachelor of science in civil engineering (with an architecture option). In 1959, the College of Engineering established a Department of Architecture as a five-year program. In 1960, with Charles P. Graves as the head of the department, Louisville architects J. Quintin Biagi Sr. and Jasper D. Ward, with Lexington architects Donald Wallace, Ernst Johnson, and Roy Burberry began teaching students. In 1964, the department was elevated to a School of Architecture with Graves as the dean, and in 1966 it assumed the title College of Architecture.

3. Marion Porter, "Noble Old Courthouse Gets Wright Approval," *Courier-Journal*, May 29, 1948.

4. Joan Riehm, "Schneider Urges a Push for New Urban Projects," *Courier-Journal*, April 13, 1973.

5. Grady Clay, interview by author, Louisville, Ky., February 7, 2002.

6. Mary-Louise and Patrick Gorman, interview by author, Louisville, Ky., April 5, 2002

Louisville, aerial view, c. 1960s

Contemporary Louisville:
Redefining a Place in the Wider World

David Mohney

The last two decades have witnessed a sea change in Louisville and how it thinks of itself. Many of these changes were perceived to be negative at first glance. At the very least, they were treacherous: the nature of local business has shifted from manufacturing to services, a wealth of family businesses that were mainstays of the local economy have been sold to nonresident owners, and downtown has lost ground to burgeoning suburbanization. As civic leader Michael Harreld, president of PNC Bank/Louisville, noted in a talk at the Filson Club in 1998, the way the city had operated since the Civil War was gone, and there were substantial questions about what and, perhaps more important, who would take its place.

At the same time, there was a recognition that these changes were not by definition negative. An economy based on services instead of manufacturing offered the potential of a higher quality of life, from better education to a better environment. City government, historically unwilling to address long-term planning issues, sought out a much more active role, based on a dynamic public-private partnership, in looking to Louisville's future and who would lead the city there. Relentless suburbanization finally brought about "merger," or the consolidation of city and county government.

These dynamic trends affected the design professions as well. Local architects struggled with the impulse among some business leaders to bring outsiders, nationally or even internationally recognized for their design abilities, to work on significant Louisville projects. In many regards, this defensiveness was earned: as Gregory A. Luhan argues, there was a substantial level of achievement in the work

Plan, 1969

of the architects practicing in Louisville in the middle of the century, although it was largely overlooked, especially at a national level.

Yet there were benefits from the arrival of these distinguished outside architects. Certainly Michael Graves's Humana Building is among his best works; Graves found the proximity of the Ohio River and all that it meant to Louisville's development, especially along Main Street, fertile ground for his assimilation of history into architectural form. The international attention given to that project served Louisville well, but the Humana Building had other benefits. Humana's own architect, Jim Walters, was able to move from the position of the in-house architect who coordinated Graves's efforts for Humana to a distinguished practitioner on his own. Walters's company, Bravura, has carried out some of the liveliest downtown buildings in recent years, from the Louisville Ballet to elements of the Waterfront Park.

Other senior professionals have also fared well. Louis & Henry, Godsey Associates, K. Norman Berry, Potter & Cox, QK4 (the former Presnell Group), and heirs of the William Arrasmith's firm have all found opportunities for collaboration that have benefited their practices and led to the diversification of their services. Individuals from these firms have been recognized nationally by the professional associations, and this has reflected well on the nature of the work culture in the city.

The newly dynamic intervention of the city in long-term planning was a welcome development as well. The advent of the Louisville

Development Authority (LDA) in Mayor Jerry Abramson's first term and the LDA's adoption of a plan to revitalize downtown were major steps. The LDA's plan was based on principles of enhancing public life, not zoning uses; this facilitated much new private development in areas targeted by the plan, specifically West Main Street, the Medical Center, and Park DuValle. Indeed, the plan was so successful that it had to be updated just a decade after it was adopted. All of the goals had been met.

To guide the plan, the LDA brought in nationally recognized architects and urban designers, such as Ray Gindroz, Alex Krieger, and the firm EDAW. But the work processes of these firms were open to local professionals and local residents alike through a design charrette; they were encouraged to participate and thus stretch their capacity for accomplishment into new territories.

A number of significant successes were achieved in this process: the West Main Street redevelopment was recognized nationally, and Park DuValle is a national model for the urban redevelopment of disadvantaged residential neighborhoods. Another project, which is presently underway but promises to be a profound success, is the redevelopment of the Ohio River waterfront. A public-private partnership facilitated this work, which has been led by landscape architect George Hargreaves of San Francisco. A vibrant waterfront of mercantile and transportation services was crucial to Louisville's economic health in the nineteenth century; now it is perceived to be crucial to its economic health in a vastly different manner, by demonstrating the kind of public amenities that lead to a higher quality of life for the city's residents.

Even if some of the major commercial and institutional commissions were awarded to out-of-town architects, there were areas where the locals had a distinct advantage and used it to great effect. Louisville benefited greatly from the presence of a number of contractors with great skill in working with concrete construction. Concrete was a material of choice, since it is less costly than steel, especially when there was competition among builders for a contract. The trades honed their skills, and the level of articulation and detail that is evident in the locally designed concrete buildings is one of the hidden successes of Louisville architecture in this period. Look at Louis & Henry's addition to the Free Public Library or at Jasper D. Ward's variations on a concrete theme in his parking garages on Sixth Street or at Seventh and Magazine; these are signifi-

Addition to Louisville Main Library (Louis & Henry), 1967–69

cant accomplishments in material and form, advancing the caliber of architecture in the city.

The architectural and planning successes of the last decades have primarily benefited downtown Louisville and the areas immediately around it. In contrast, the perimeter of the city has suffered, as anonymous suburban developments have covered former agricultural land, now stretching beyond the border of Jefferson County into Oldham and Bullitt Counties. Louisville has a marvelous tradition of suburban housing, largely from the first generation of suburbs: neighborhoods in Crescent Hill, Lakeside, St. Matthews, and other former municipalities should be models for these new developments, but they are not. One of the biggest missed opportunities of recent years was the attempt to bring a new urbanist development called Norton Commons to the former WAVE-TV farm on the Jefferson-Oldham County border. In 1996, Andres Duany led a massive charrette, with hundreds of local residents, professionals, and others participating; the hope was that Norton Commons would serve as a model for other developments at the perimeter of the city. But approvals for the project were delayed for years, and by the time the project finally started, the standard suburban model had swept past the Norton Commons site like a wave.

Although the professional design community in Kentucky is centered in Louisville, the professional education programs are not. The only architecture program in Kentucky is based in Lexington, at the University of Kentucky. Recognizing that this was a deficiency

Plan, 1990

for all concerned, the College of Architecture initiated an outreach center on Third Street in Louisville in 2000, in collaboration with the University of Louisville's Urban Planning program. Students and faculty work with the LDA to develop strategies and models for future urban design-opportunities in the city. At the very least, this effort has provided a welcome bridge between the professional program and the professional community. The effort has been recognized by the business community: Brown-Forman Corporation endowed a visiting professorship at the design center for leading architects to work on Louisville issues with members of the local community. Michael Rotondi, from RoTo Architects in Los Angeles, accepted the first appointment to this endowment and has been an active participant in discussions about Louisville's future with a wide variety of residents.

Finally, it is worth noting that the professional architecture program in Kentucky is just forty years old. Paraphrasing Louis Sullivan, "Architecture is an old person's profession," and the first graduates are only now reaching the point where their firms have grown as much as they could make them. A number of younger firms—some but not all with connections to the professional programs—are achieving distinction at either a regional or national level: Voelker-Winn, Michael Koch, Mark Isaacs, Michael Barry, and David Biagi are among them.

Construction of Interstate 64 tunnel, c. 1970

Notes on Preservation History in Louisville

Edith Bingham

In early 1964, there a was lively debate about plans to bring the
new Interstate-64 into Louisville through a corner of Olmsted's
Cherokee Park. Positions pro and con were flying from the community and local press.

At the same time, another issue of community concern was
Constantinos Doxiades's ambitious design for a large belvedere that
would overlook the Falls of the Ohio River, a unique, spectacular
site between Pittsburgh and New Orleans. Three blocks of nineteenth-century Main Street were demolished for this grand plan,
meant to bring the city "back to the river." The plan included a
three-story office building (to be designed by Mies van der Rohe),
a tall tower, a hotel, and underground parking. Louisvillians were
torn between participating in progress and losing the treasure of
its boom-period past. Gone were the Columbia Building, and the
Board of Trade, and soon the entire Tyler block would be lost to
the Louisville Convention Center, which would be completed in
November 1977.

In the early 1960s, urban-renewal policies permitted the
demolition of riverfront land and core downtown areas, freeing up
entire blocks for interstates and mostly one-story commercial buildings. This activity succeeded in removing a major portion of the
dense residential area along Walnut Street, where African American
culture and small businesses had flourished, as well as other down-
at-the-heels businesses and residential pockets. Although there were
voices lamenting the loss of so much urban fabric, the overriding
banner for progress was as simple as "Old is bad. New is good."
Federal loans for homes, schools, businesses, and highways made
way for the post–World War II generation's growth.

With the onset of large-scale urban demolition in 1962, a small group of citizens had formed the Citizens Metropolitan Planning Council (CMPC). It was an early voice to alert and educate the public about its urban history and built environment. CMPC held free public brown-bag lunches, with nationally known speakers such as Carl Feiss and Frank Gilbert, to inform the citizens of nationally successful projects to restore and reuse older buildings and preserve the importance of the downtown center. Grady Clay's contacts and private supporters kept these excellent forums in the public eye from 1962 to 1970.

By 1966, the National Preservation Act established the National Register of Historic Places, and in the same year the Kentucky Heritage Council was established, with Ida Lee Willis as its first executive director. Such national and state actions drew public attention to the loss of historic sites and neighborhoods. Locally, it mobilized citizens and the City of Louisville and Jefferson County to enact landmark ordinances to protect buildings, neighborhoods, and open spaces. The city passed its Landmark Ordinance in 1973, Jefferson County in 1978–79.

In the early 1960s, however, Eli Brown had begun buying and restoring Victorian houses in St. James and Belgravia courts, Farmington had been acquired and restored, and the Commonwealth and Jefferson County had jointly purchased Locust Grove. Soon after, Jefferson County Judge Marlow Cook purchased the Belle of Louisville, which became a symbol for the city.

Broad preservation efforts got underway in the late 1960s and early 1970s. Local landmarks eligible for the National Register were identified. Leaders such as Helen Abell, Mae Salyers of Old Louisville, and Clyde Crews set examples for others to follow. Mayor Harvey Sloane and his wife, Kathy, Jim Segrest of Butchertown, Aldermen Allan Steinberg, and Sharon Wilbert championed downtown and neighborhood revitalization.

This "new" idea of preservation developed slowly but offered opportunities that complemented those of the proponents of fast economic growth. Indeed, there were business leaders and developers, such as the George Underhill family, who saw the potential of rehabilitating and keeping older buildings. They offered destinations for tourism, convention business, and downtown living as well as pride in a river-town history, and the public realm of Downtown, the Courthouse, City Hall, and the Library. Police and public safety

Actors Theatre, 1835–1837

needed to work together to provide a safe environment for downtown and nearby neighborhoods.

Barry Bingham Sr., a local publisher, saw the opportunities to develop a progressive city in concert with thoughtful preservation. In 1972, he and other community leaders founded Preservation Alliance, and in 1973 the organization set up offices at 721 West Main Street, a warehouse district, deserted except for the very recent location of Stairways, the Junior League headquarters, on the street's 600 block.

Preservation Alliance was an umbrella group that brought together diverse city and county voices, energies, and partnerships. In just a few years, it helped transform Old Louisville, the largest Victorian neighborhood listed on the National Register. Many neighborhoods were strengthened by the federal and local tax incentives that residents used to restore houses and rekindle pride in local history. Still thriving are popular festivals such as the St. James Art Fair, Portland Homecoming, Butchertown Oktoberfest, and the Cherokee Triangle Fair. These attract regional visitors and raise funds for ongoing improvements.

Preservation Alliance provided staff, design assistance, a reference library, and a gift shop/bookstore. Most important, Preservation Alliance and neighborhood members testified at hearings about proposed development projects that would adversely affect historic structures or areas. Soon preservationists began to get concerned about gentrification and the "red lining" practiced by lending institutions. These forces undermined the efforts of Preservation Alliance and the Louisville Community Design Center, which provided neighborhoods with advice for historically appropriate repairs and infill development.

Among the earliest projects to give preservation a high and successful profile were:

¶ the 1837 Bank of Louisville Building, rehabilitated for the Actors Theatre lobby and new theater, designed by Harry Weese and Associates

¶ the 1977 Carter Dry Goods conversion into the Louisville Science Center, for which Louis & Henry received a national AIA Adaptive Reuse Award

¶ The 1980 conversion of the original Seelbach Hotel into a popular restaurant and office space, restored by Potter & Cox.

Continuing work to restore the Main Street facades has saved many nineteenth-century structures, designed by architects such as Henry Whitestone, Joseph and Joseph, and MacDonald & Dodd. The area has attracted a number of museums; and Main Street, Louisville's first Landmark District, has become an exhibit itself. Norman Berry Associates spurred a number of these West Main restorations and infill projects. Since the 1970s, industrial and warehouse buildings around the city have been converted: the Louisville Water Tower is now an art center designed by Joseph Oppermann; Billy Goat Strut was restored by Potter & Cox into offices and residences; and Brown-Forman Corporation hired Harry Weese & Associates to rehabilitate whiskey warehouses into exciting multipurpose spaces.

These and other outstanding examples greeted visitors who came for the 1982 National Trust Annual Preservation Conference. Tours of the city, neighborhoods, the five Olmsted parks, Cave Hill Cemetery, and the Ohio River and its early riverbank settlements sent conference attendees home marveling at the collection of nineteenth-century cast-iron-facade buildings on Main Street. The city's identity was not slavishly modernized, and the downtown was preserved in its tight grid, embracing the renovated Brown and Seelbach Hotels and a new Hyatt with a revolving rooftop restaurant.

While the 1970s and 1980s saw great efforts in organized preservation, there were conflicts. Of major note is the development

Will Sales Building, 1876

of the Galleria. Beginning in 1971, there was a proposal to build a four-block downtown development with residential, commercial, retail, and office components. Over the next six years, the developer, Oxford Properties, downsized the project for a variety of reasons, including the unavailability of key land parcels, opposition to wide-scale demolition, and rising interest rates. By 1978, the hope was to create the Galleria, anchored by two tall, standard-design office towers by Skidmore Owings and Merrill. Demolition was requested for all the buildings on both sides of the 400 block of Fourth Avenue. Preservationists persuaded the developers that the facade of the Chicago-style Kaufman-Straus department store could be included in the Galleria portion, but the Atherton and Will Sales buildings stood on the intended footprints of the office towers. As interest rates soared to fifteen percent, the developer and business community threw out an ultimatum to the preservationists and others opposed to the demolitions. Either the project would be a go or the preservationists would be blamed for halting progress and depriving the city of its last hope for economic revival.

Despite Department of Interior hearings, a temporary court injunction, and findings that the structures were sound, the Atherton and Will Sales buildings were both demolished. In 1981 the $70 million Galleria was completed. Twenty years later, as retail sales lagged and leases went unrenewed, the Galleria was studied for renewal. With the help of Cordish Company of Baltimore, city government decided in 2001 to convert the Galleria into an entertainment and restaurant center, which would accommodate convention visitors in nearby hotels.

The demolition of the Will Sales Building was a battle lost by the preservationists. It bitterly divided the community. Businesses and donors who supported Preservation Alliance's operating funds pulled away, and the Alliance's doors closed. However, the value and assets of older buildings were newly appreciated, and such structures were less likely to be doomed to demolition.

Belknap Hardware Building, 1923

In the last twenty years, Main Street, west from First to Ninth and east to Clay, has seen extraordinary restoration reuses and new development. The location of the Presbyterian National Headquarters in the massive Belknap Hardware Building created new offices and the need for a garage (all by Bravura), and the redevelopment of buildings around Brook to Second on Main includes the Medical Campus, the Waterfront Park, eMain, the Slugger Museum, Louisville Ballet, Kentucky Opera, and Slugger Field. All have been participants in the economic revival. The renovation of most nineteenth-century buildings has produced innovative and contemporary interiors. These factors have moved much of Louisville's commercial, business, and cultural activity closer to the Ohio River, which was the intent of the Doxiades plan some forty years ago.

Architects, developers, and entrepreneurs have taken older buildings in other downtown locations and achieved excellent creative synergy. Examples such as Glassworks, in the 1910 Snead Manufacturing Building, have glass blowing, art galleries, offices, and condominiums. Robert A.M. Stern's design influence revived the huge Bernheim Building on West Main into corporate, public, and restaurant spaces for Brown-Forman Corporation. The old YMCA building at Third and Broadway, renovated in the 1960s by Bill Receveur, has recently been rehabilitated into mixed use for St. Francis High School office space and residential units. Holly

Wiedemann of AU Associates (Lexington), who has led several award-winning adaptive-reuse projects in Kentucky, developed this current renovation. Saving the landmark Male High School and providing Central High School with a long-needed stadium were sister projects, resolved by hard community work, local investors, and the efforts of the Louisville Historical League. New buildings are filling spaces, and the demand for downtown housing is generating mixed-use and housing proposals that will strengthen the heart of downtown. Evidence of this effort to repair, reuse, and renew also exists in most neighborhoods in and near Downtown.

Outlying areas in the county have also restored historical sites and neighborhoods, such as Farmington, Locust Grove, Oxmoor, and Anchorage. Louisville's growth to the south was stimulated by the airport, General Electric Appliance Park, and other major employers, such as United Parcel Service. Better planning, more careful use of built and natural resources, job creation through new and rehab construction, revised lending policies, preservation of city and neighborhood schools, and better policing for residential safety have all partnered with preservation goals to make Louisville a better place to live and work. With the planning of new bridges across the Ohio, preservation and land-conservation issues are hotly debated again. The pressure for housing close to Downtown has revived neighborhood groups that use their voices to guide development that affects their local area and traditions.

In nearly forty years, Main Street has become the next-best thing to the Ohio River. Cafés serve lunch and drinks, a Mies van der Rohe building shares the Belvedere with the striking Kentucky Center for Performing Arts (Caudill Rowlett Scott, 1983), and Main Street is the focus of the preservation renaissance in the Louisville metro area.

NOTE

Undergirding almost 50 years of Louisville's preservation efforts were books, articles, research, and oversight by the following individuals: Grady Clay, Samuel W. Thomas's publications and books from 1966 to the present, George Yater, Walter Creese, Justus Bier, John Rogers's 1955 *Courier-Journal* series on Louisville neighborhoods, Theodore Brown and Margaret Bridwell's 1960s publications on Louisville and Old Louisville, Walter Langsham, Chuck Parrish, Jasper D. Ward, Doug Nunn, John Cullinane, Don Ridings, Bob Daugherty, Bob Vogelsang, William Morgan, Ron Gascogne, Carl Kramer,

Natalie Andrews, Penny Jones, Doug Stern, Clyde Crews, Marty Hedgepeth, Kenny Karem, Wendy Nicholas, Joanne Weeter, Mary Jean Kinsman, Richard Jett, Steve Wiser, and Ann Hassett, Louisville Landmarks director 1974–1994.

A Living Legacy: Louisville's Olmsted Landscapes

Susan M. Rademacher

The history and growth of Louisville can be marked and measured by its interconnected system of parks and parkways, which form an armature for the city. This system is the last of only five ever created by Frederick Law Olmsted Sr., the "father of American landscape architecture," and stands today as one of the best-preserved of Olmsted's works. It reflects his mature vision and his greatest achievement in purely scenic park design. For Louisvillians, these parks are touchstones and points of reference, oft referred to as Louisville's "emerald necklace," inexorably tied to personal and neighborhood identity.

Parks were promoted for Louisville as early as 1799, when George Rogers Clark recommended leaving every third block as open space. But no parks were created until 1880, when Mayor John G. Baxter acquired the first city park, Baxter Square (later designed by Olmsted). Colonel Andrew Cowan, a prominent Main Street leather merchant and great admirer of Frederick Law Olmsted's Jackson Park in Chicago, led the Salmagundi organization, an all-male social and literary club, in proposing the development of three large suburban parks in 1887 to spur economic and population growth for Louisville. The "Salmagundi movement" led to the establishment of the Parks Commission in 1890 by act of the Kentucky legislature. That same year, Mayor Charles Jacob purchased Burnt Knob (now Iroquois Park). The following year, Frederick Law Olmsted Sr., the designer of the U.S. Capitol grounds, New York's Central Park, and Biltmore Estate, was recruited to plan the system.

In his 1891 prospectus to the Parks Commission, Olmsted proposed that the designs for the first three parks—Shawnee, Cherokee, and Iroquois—capture the region's three distinct native landscapes.

Cherokee Park

Shawnee's broad Ohio River terraces, Cherokee's rolling Beargrass Creek valley, and Iroquois's rugged slopes of old-growth forest were planned to complement one another as the essential components of one great urban park. Totaling 1,200 acres, the parks were designed to offer a complete range of experiences as defined by Olmsted, from civic gatherings and social interactions to organized athletics and personal recreation. The parks' west, south, and east locations anchor the distinctive regions of the city, and the parkways connect people throughout the city to these parks. Shawnee Park is outfitted for a variety of activities that bring people together, including a formal flower garden, a bandstand, and a great lawn for sporting events. Cherokee Park, considered Olmsted's most scenic work, focuses on the landscape experience of traversing from stream valley to ridgeline. Iroquois Park provides Olmsted's recommended "scenic reservation"—a wilderness experience that was popularly referred to as "our Yellowstone"—its dramatic views rewarding those who attain the summit.

These parks achieve the hallmarks of Olmsted's social vision. As the source of healthful inspiration—through mental, physical, and social recreation—these design landscapes provide an antidote to the stresses of modern city life. The parks also provide democratic spaces, wherein people can come together on common ground to create a stronger community. These landscapes also exhibit all the

classic physical elements of an Olmsted park: graceful topography and alignments, ease and accessibility, balance of uses, expression of native character and materials, sanitation and drainage, separation of traffic modes, and subjugation of built elements to nature.

Nearly fifteen miles of Olmsted-designed parkways connect people throughout the city to these parks. While the parkways were developed incrementally and inconsistently, they nevertheless achieved Olmsted's idea of unifying the parks and making them accessible while providing the benefit of a linear park within easy walking distance of many neighborhoods. In the first three decades of the twentieth century, John Charles Olmsted and the Olmsted firm developed thirteen more parks throughout Louisville, ranging from Reform Era neighborhood parks with a Beaux Arts vocabulary to parks designed for African Americans after the passage of a seg-regation law in 1922.

The Olmsteds' work in Louisville was not limited to parks nor to the public. Archival records at Fairsted, the National Park Service Historic Site that was home and office to the Olmsted firm, list 188 project numbers. While not all dealings resulted in built projects or even in plans, due to the firm's "costly" fees, its local work ranged far and wide, high and low: Bernheim Forest, the town plan for Anchorage, the Louisville Free Public Library, University of Louisville, Brown-Forman Corporation, Barrett Middle School,

Iroquois Park

and numerous private estates and subdivisions, such as Indian Hills, Cherokee Gardens, and Alta Vista. Many other development projects were clearly modeled after the Olmsted firm's exemplary works.

After a period of decline that began with World War II, the Olmsted parks and parkways received renewed attention in the latter decades of the twentieth century. In the 1960s, the imposition of Interstate-64 through the eastern boundary lands of Cherokee Park and Seneca Park (the last to be designed by the Olmsted firm) stimulated citizen action to preserve the parks. Although small portions of each park were lost to the interstate project, activists were successful in obtaining a limestone-faced tunnel to preserve Cochran Hill, along with the nation's first and only overpass bridge designed to carry a bridle trail. A second crisis hit in 1974, when a tornado destroyed eighty percent of Cherokee Park's hardwood trees, an event that galvanized new support for restoring the parks. Public concern rose through the 1980s in response to the deterioration of the Olmsted parks, and the Louisville Friends of Olmsted Parks was founded with the support of the Parks Department.

The Friends conducted an inventory of archival resources for Louisville's Olmsted Parks and assessed ground conditions. As a result, they were able to work with Mayor Jerry E. Abramson to establish the Louisville Olmsted Parks Conservancy in 1989. A private, nonprofit partner dedicated to renewing the Olmsted parks

system, the Conservancy provided planning and design expertise, raised funds, and involved the community through volunteer programs and projects.

When master planning began in 1991, the parks were in a state of great disrepair: infrastructure had collapsed, natural systems were threatened, and the community was disconnected from its parks. Recognizing that the parks' value had eroded, the Conservancy determined not only to arrest that process and preserve the parks, but to invigorate them as well. The master plan addressed a central question: how to introduce new and evolving uses without destroying the Olmsted legacy. Officially adopted by the city in 1994, the *Master Plan for Renewing Louisville's Olmsted Parks and Parkways* called for an investment of more than $55 million over twenty to thirty years. The plan is notable for its interdisciplinary approach to restoring both the cultural and ecological landscape upon a foundation of historic research, public participation, and maintenance and management evaluation.

With joint Conservancy and city funding, the first projects to carry out the recommendations of the *Master Plan* were opened to the public in 1996 and include active sports facilities, woodland and savannah restoration, wetland creation, multi-use recreational paths, reconstruction of bridle and hiking trails, and reinstatement of place names within each park. Three projects were implemented to illustrate key themes of the plan in core areas of each flagship park. The Shawnee Park project relocated baseball fields from the park's most significant historic space, the Great Lawn, to a new sports complex on annexed property adjacent to the historic park. Current work in Shawnee focuses on restoring the Ohio River vistas. Baringer Hill was the focus in Cherokee Park, involving a rehabilitation of the tornado-damaged vista and woodlands; reconstruction of an Overlook Shelter, paths, pedestrian bridges, and Baringer Spring's historic dry-laid stone walls; and relocation of parking, a playground, and restrooms. The Iroquois Park project restored a native "knob top" savannah and created wetlands to address storm-water problems and improve wildlife habitat. Olmsted's original path alignments were reinstated, and a new design standard for rustic architecture was established. Subsequent projects have included reconstructing an extensive bridle-trail system, installing prototype signs, and rehabilitating a WPA-era amphitheater.

All the Olmsted parks will receive master plans over the next several years, to guide future improvements. New master plans have been completed for Chickasaw Park and Shelby Park, and planning is underway for Algonquin Park. The Conservancy and Metro Parks have produced new design standards for the parkways, using planning and development tools to implement them and demonstrating the standards at several renovated locations along the parkway system. Community connections have been strengthened as park use has increased and people work together through the Conservancy's volunteer program, called Park Champions, which restores natural areas to ecological health. The overarching goal is to recapture Olmsted's original design intent as closely as possible, so that people can see and feel for themselves what an Olmsted space is all about.

The Olmsted parks are a magnificent work of art that must be restored, preserved, and enhanced in order to continue their enormous contribution to the quality of life in Louisville. They are an incomparable gift from a remarkable civic partnership that a century ago championed planning, raised substantial money, and summoned the goodwill and resources of the community at large. The Olmsted parks and parkways were just the beginning. Today Louisville has 122 parks, totaling 12,000 acres, needing to acquire thousands more. Like their Olmstedian predecessors, these new parks must seek the optimum balance of natural systems, historic values, use, and management. The Conservancy is working to ensure that the

Olmsted system is the inspiration for parks of the future. It is help-ing Metro Parks to expand upon these superb landscapes, never forgetting Frederick Law Olmsted's urging—not so long ago—to "adopt an ideal" and let it guide all future planning and actions.

Louisville, aerial view, 1950

The Urban Context as Battleground

Grady Clay

These observations are based on my recollections of 1940, when a handful of elderly male architects, remnants of the Beaux Arts tradition, still dominated noonday conversation at the big center table of the Arts Club atop the old Hotel Watterson in downtown Louisville. Not yet, nor for years to come, would younger architects surge upward to take over the conversation and practice.

When I was a young newspaper reporter, this was my Louisville. This was my share of bricks and grime and sooty air (if I may borrow from Stephen Vincent Benét's *John Brown's Body*).

In those days, my daily runs on South Third Street northward to the *Courier-Journal* (then crammed into the old Post Office building on Liberty Street) exposed me to a cross section of a city struggling out of the shadow of a *Harper's* magazine article that lambasted Louisville as the "great American museum piece."

Louisville's population had just passed a quarter million, not much different from that of Atlanta, whence I had recently migrated. (There is yet to be written a book contrasting Atlanta's economic growth into a million-plus regional capital with Louisville's more modest expansion, chiefly by annexation.)

It would be easy—but not too far off the mark—to say that for Louisville World War II changed all that sloth of the thirties. The wartime economy brought new industry to town, 25,000 troops to nearby Fort Knox, military glider landings to Bowman Field, and a giant military powder plant, with thousands of jobs, to Charlestown, Indiana, "just up the road a piece."

Beyond all this, the war-time and postwar construction booms imported not only pneumatic tools, the forklift, and critical-path method to local construction, but also stimulated a home-builders' lobby and a Citizens Metropolitan Planning Council (CMPC),

Louisville, figure ground diagram, 1900

which brought newcomer voters and old-family Junior Leaguers into local land-use politics.

Planning and zoning policy migrated into local debates. Housing moved into everyday conversation—a wartime shortage having been alleviated by the hurried building of apartments and by mass production of bungalows in ranch house guise, making their appearance by the hundreds along Dixie and other radial highways.

On one memorable postwar Sunday, two New Jersey home builders sold more than 400 houses in one Dixie Highway subdivision called "Valley Village," with no down payment and monthly payments of less than fifty dollars. In the spring of 1958, New York builders moved in to build houses on the project's remaining 350-plus lots. Meanwhile, another out-of-state firm bought 135 lots in the Klondike Acres subdivision. Word was out that the Louisville market was hot.

A similar event was expected to occur in the sixties when Hamilton Crawford, a production house builder from Baton Rouge, Louisiana, bought the 240-acre Hendon farm near Bowman Field, at what was then the edge of town. Crawford, however, was ahead of the market for contemporary design—low-pitched roofs wide overhanging eaves, enclosed patios—and sold few houses before selling his remaining lots to other builders. Yet his venture paved the way for neighboring landowners to sell out for more subdivisions.

In the postwar boom, labor was scarce and expensive. It was at that time that women had speeded up their long migration into the local work force, a transition that had begun during World War II.

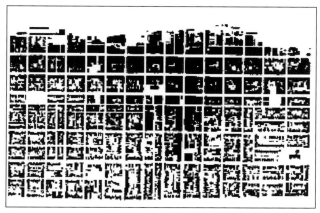

Louisville, figure ground diagram, 1990

Then came a distant bombshell from London. In the 1960s, Gordon Cullen, an eloquent, contentious editor of the British magazine *Architectural Review,* published a book titled *Townscape.* Cullen maintained that the modern city was a wasteland that needed to be saved by joining its separate bits and pieces into a new unity, to be achieved by urban designers, under the banner of the term *townscape.*

The key question Cullen asked of any new construction was *Does it fit?* And the context into which it was supposed to fit was—surprise!—a familiar, if not historical, array of unified structures whose roots were in the Middle Ages. He was especially contemptuous of those intrusive new structures, wholly out of context with the traditional scene, called new brutalism.

In those early years, I found myself attracted to what came to be known as the Townscape School. I visited Gordon Cullen in London and made much of his message (which verged on being a formula) in the pages of *Fortune* magazine and in *Landscape Architecture* when I became its editor, as well as in the *Courier-Journal,* where I had a lesser role.

Time has diminished the influence of the Townscape School on this side of the Atlantic. In the competition for attention from the revivified American Institute of Architects, there arose a clamor for "great works of architecture," which were usually centerpieces for urban-renewal projects. These, for the most part, were freestanding structures, often on spectacular sites in dramatic places, preferably isolated and, above all, photogenic. Whatever context may have sur-

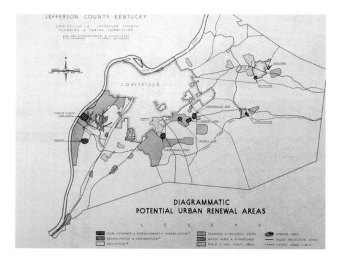

Louisville, urban-renewal plan, 1952

rounded these "great works" was to be overshadowed, if not out-shouted, by these assertive newcomers, often playing roles in some corporate image-making campaign. The rise of corporate power made its mark on hundreds of showcase locations across the land.

I trust this is not an unfair appraisal of the situation in the sixties and seventies, when I ventured forth as a part-time journalist to survey the broad field of urban design. Since then, a host of influences has barged onto the scene to insist that new construction at least go through the motions of fitting into its context, usually urban. Many downtown plans, backed by design-review boards, have narrowed the path toward project completion for architects and developers. This is apparent in downtown Louisville, Old Louisville, and the Cherokee Triangle.

Other influences were the oft-contentious urban-renewal plans for Louisville and other cities, whereby the condemnation of land to conform to the plan proved unpopular.

A major influence has been language itself, which has become an intermediary between works of architecture and the media-absorbing public. In this process, a new crop of publications has fragmented the market; several traditional architectural maga-zines—the old *AIA Journal* among them—have ceased publication.

Meanwhile, many architects have joined citizen activists to lambast "schlock development" and to insist on better design.

During all this time, water—especially its scarcity, notably in the West—has become a concern of citizens and the plans of many developers. Louisville's waterfront on the Ohio River was the subject of a dramatic plan by Constantinos Doxiades, the Greek theorist planner. It was much modified to become the extensive Louisville waterfront development we see today. Beyond the old city edge, natural-waterfront lots began getting top-dollar price tags, and scores of new subdivisions in Jefferson County were laid out around man-made ponds and lakes. Hydraulic engineers became members of many a developmental team.

Today most American cities have new plans, revised zoning codes, and commissions. Many have set up design-review boards, some with extraordinary powers and others with little more than trivial hand wringers.

Since passage of the Housing Act of 1954, urban-renewal plans have offered design-conscious citizens—as well as professional designers—public hearings at which to plead their case for better design or to attack what they perceive to be a bad fit for a particular location. The phrase *out of context*—once a staple of literary criticism—became part of the vocabulary of urban-design critics and was employed by neighbors who objected to a proposed commercial project next door.

Urban renewal and other federal efforts, growing out of the New Deal slum-clearance programs, had a wide impact on the Louisville housing scene, with its recent renovation of a housing project of the thirties into the prize-winning Park DuValle development. Though much contested by traditional real-estate groups, renewal has left impressive improvements on the townscape. It has also taken a high social toll, dividing neighborhoods and causing serious business losses.

So, in a long and roundabout process, "context" has acquired new significance for an increasingly urban public—in Louisville and elsewhere—a public that has become more suspicious of power as manipulated by political parties, by large public agencies, and by corporations. I would not be surprised if the symbols of that power—showy national headquarters and regional showplaces—should come under increasing attack in a not-too-distant future for being out of context with their neighbors.

A Note About the Descriptions

Landmark Designations:
NRHP   National Register of Historic Places
NHL   National Historic Landmark
LL   Local Landmark
LPD   Local Preservation District
None   No Designation (as of publishing)

Buildings contained in *The Louisville Guide* have four primary designations that refer to the nature of their historic status—National Register of Historic Places (NRHP), National Historic Landmark (NHL), Local Landmark (LL), and Local Preservation District (LPD). Structures that do not currently meet the age requirements for historic designation or have yet to be surveyed and characterized by the criteria listed below have no listing.

Criteria Definitions:
The National Register of Historic Places (NRHP) is administered by the US Department of the Interior – National Park Service. This program, initiated under the National Historic Preservation Act of 1966, seeks to coordinate public and private efforts to identify and protect historic and archeological resources and evaluate them according to a set of uniform standards. Properties listed in the register include districts, sites, buildings, structures, and objects that are significant in American History, architecture, engineering, archeology, and culture.

The National Historic Landmarks (NHL) designation includes structures that possess exceptional qualities which illustrate or interpret the heritage of the United States. There are currently 2,500 landmarks nationwide.

The Local Landmark (LL) category designates buildings that have distinguishing architectural, cultural, and regional historic value. The Local Preservation District (LPD) expands this category to include districts and sites within the community that have significant concentrations of buildings that meet those same criteria.

BUILDING DESCRIPTIONS

Map 1: Buildings 1–12

1. CARNEGIE LIBRARIES- LOUISVILLE MAIN LIBRARY

301 York Street, Central Business District
George Tachau and Lewis F. Pilcher, Olmsted Brothers (Boston)
Landmark designation: NRHP, 1980
1906–1908

Nine Carnegie-endowed libraries were built in Louisville between 1906 and 1914. Located in or near the urban core, all nine buildings reflect the prevalent architectural styles of the time, ranging from classical revival to Beaux Arts to Renaissance revival. Typically, the buildings are the focal points of the neighborhoods in which they are located. The Western Colored Branch, one of the first public libraries in the nation constructed for African Americans, along with the Eastern Colored Branch, earned Louisville the distinction of being one of the few cities in the south with two free public libraries built for African Americans. Under the leadership of Thomas F. Blue, a prominent African American librarian, these libraries served as the training ground for African American librarians from across the country, many of whom lacked access to proper professional training. Prominent Louisville architects designed all of the city's Carnegie libraries with the exception of the main library for, which a New York architecture firm with strong ties to Louisville provided the designs.

The Louisville Free Public Library, described as the jewel of the city's library system, was the result of a national design competition in 1906, which included prominent national firms such as Albert Randolph (New York), McKim, Mead, and White (Boston), F. M. Andrews (Dayton), Mairain, Russell, and Gardiner (St. Louis), and Tachau and Pilcher (New York) and local ones such as Clark & Loomis, D. X. Murphy, Henry Wolters, and J. B. Hutchings.

With funding from the Carnegie Foundation, Louisville architect George Tachau collaborated with Lewis F. Pilcher to design the Main Branch building. It is an outstanding example of Beaux Arts classicism. The second of nine Carnegie libraries in Jefferson County (but the first to begin construction), the library adapts classical motifs in particular through the clustered and fluted Ionic columns and ornamental friezes. The project is well crafted with mosaics, paintings, a stained-glass barrel vault, and white marble floors and trim on the interior. The entrance is constructed of a set of large bronze doors at the center of the columned portico on the south facade.

In contrast to the original library, a modern addition, designed by the Louisville architecture firm Louis & Henry in 1969, is devoid of classical ornamentation and detail. While the project defers to the old structure in terms of proportion and rhythm, it bares a striking resemblance to the brutalist Boston City Hall (1963–68) by Kallman, McKinnell, and Knowles. The dentils in both the Louisville Main Library and the Boston City Hall projects serve as external shading devices. A plaza that surrounds the library addition on three sides is reached by gently graduated stairways and ramps from both Third and Fourth Streets, which also lead to the main entry, located along the north facade of the plaza. The original Louis & Henry master plan called for a formal entrance through a garden on the north side of the building stretching to Broadway. To make room for the garden, the main building of the Weissinger-Gaulbert Apartments (1903) was razed in 1963. However, the formal garden never materialized, and the space remains an asphalt-covered parking lot.

The Highland Branch (1000 Cherokee Road) was the first of the Carnegie libraries completed in Louisville and one of the first branches erected south of the Ohio River. Built in 1908 and designed by Hutchings & Hawes, it is the only Carnegie-endowed library located in a wealthy residential enclave. L-shaped in plan, it deviates from the typical rectangular footprint used for the other Louisville libraries.

The Crescent Hill Branch (2762 Frankfort Avenue), built in 1908, was designed by the prominent Louisville architecture firm Thomas and Bohne, a practice founded in 1894 as the successor to Drach and Thomas, Architects.

The Parkland Branch (2743 Virginia Avenue) was designed by Brinton B. Davis and built in 1908. It is the first library built in a western streetcar suburb.

The Western Colored Branch (604 South Tenth Street) was constructed under the direction of Thomas Blue. The Beaux Arts building, built in 1908 and designed by Louisville architects McDonald and Dodd, consists of Roman brick and elaborate stone trim and detailing capped by a low, tiled hipped roof. The front facade has five bays and a central entrance.

The Shelby Park Branch (600 East Oak Street), built in 1911, sits in the center of an Olmsted Brothers–designed park and is one of two Carnegie-endowed libraries to be faced entirely of stone (the other being the Main Branch). The Louisville firm Loomis and Hartman designed the library in the second Renaissance revival style, a style popularized by firms such as McKim, Mead, and White. It is a relatively small structure yet it exudes a monumental character with strong proportions, restrained elegance, and simplicity of form. The building's location served the Shelby Park and Germantown neighborhoods.

The Jefferson Branch (1718 West Jefferson Street), which is located in a city cemetery, is the seventh Carnegie-endowed library in Louisville and one of two Carnegie libraries dedicated in 1913 (built in 1912), along with the Portland Branch. The prominent Louisville architecture firm D. X. Murphy & Brothers designed the building in the Beaux Arts style. A *Courier-Journal* article on February 29, 1912, characterized the building as "one of the most attractive buildings of its type in the city." The library served the Russell neighborhood for more than sixty years before closing in December 1975. The building now serves as office space for a local architecture firm.

Louisville architect Valentine Peers Collins designed the Portland Branch (3305 Northwestern Parkway) in the Beaux Arts style. The library, built in 1913, has a distinctive curved wall at its corner and, like most of the Carnegies libraries, sits a half story above street level.

The Eastern Colored Branch (801 South Hancock Street) was designed by Louisville architect Fred T. Erhart, known for his dynamic ecclesiastical projects, such as St. Therese Roman Catholic Church and the original St. Francis of Assisi Church. Built in 1914, it was the last of the Carnegie-endowed libraries in Louisville.

2. BROWN-FORMAN CORPORATION
(Old Forrester Warehouse)
850 Dixie Highway, California
Architect unknown, renovation by Harry Weese
Landmark designation: NRHP, 1978
Date unknown

Brown-Forman Corporation has long and substantial ties to Louisville, where the company was founded in 1870. It continues to base its administrative offices, part of its distillery operations, and some warehousing in the city. Its campus is located in the California neighborhood, an area where a diverse set of industries were once based, including tobacco production and manufacturing.

With the expansion of the company in the 1970s, a decision was reached to renovate an existing bourbon warehouse into administrative offices. Chicago architect Harry Weese was hired. Weese left the exterior of the building largely intact, except for a massive skylight system he installed in the roof. Inside, he removed substantial sections of the floor areas to create an eight-story atrium, lit primarily by the skylight. The tight spacing of the columns of the warehouse—so necessary for the dense storage of aging whiskey barrels—was opened up by the atrium. New glass-faced offices were built on the remaining floors, with planters throughout, creating a breathtaking interior landscape. Note the building's water tower, which is in the shape of an Old Forrester bourbon bottle.

3. ST. PATRICK'S APARTMENTS
(St. Patrick's Parochial School)
1524 West Market Street, Russell
D. X. Murphy
1916

St. Patrick's Church was built in 1862. Two years later, Martin Spalding, Archbishop of Baltimore, asked the Xaverians to open schools in Kentucky and several other states. The original school was housed in a building behind the church. In 1916, Louisville architect D. X. Murphy designed a new school building for St. Patrick's Church (now the St. Patrick's Apartments) in the Beaux Arts style. The two-story brick and stone structure sits on a raised basement and has a red-tile hipped roof that extends over the eaves of the building. The primary facade, along West Market Street, sits a half story above the street. Entrance is through three symmetrically placed double doors, above which is a wide stone band upon with the name "St. Patrick's School" spelled out in copper letters. In 2002, the Brown-Forman Corporation renovated the building into loft apartments.

4. ST. PETER'S GERMAN EVANGELICAL CHURCH

(Deutsche Evangelische St. Peters Kirche)

1231 West Jefferson Street, Russell

Clarke & Loomis

Landmark designation: NRHP, 1980

1894–1895

This church of Indiana limestone and brick, designed by Clarke and Loomis, demonstrates outstanding tooled masonry work, but, ironically, the 1894 cornerstone marked the beginning of the end of this ethnic urban church and its cohesive culture. In that year, the church abandoned its German liturgy and adopted English, setting into motion the forces of cultural disintegration that accelerated after World War II with out-migration, in-migration, the death of the founding generations, and the contemporary residents' lack of interest. This beacon on Jefferson Street, without a minister, now attracts only a tiny group of mostly senior citizens. Its finely laid front facade presents an asymmetrical mix of stylistic elements and associations, including three pointed arches and windows, an ogee arch entrance, a central pediment, a bell tower with pinnacles and a hexagonal spire, a shortened stair tower, and front doors flanked by polygonal minarets. Double-shouldered buttresses divide the side elevations into seven bays of stained-glass windows, alternating with trefoil and quatrefoil heads. Cross gables in the roof once brought light to a large stained-glass window in the flat-arched ceiling, which filtered it into the nave. The nave is divided into three parts by two aisles, and the raised chancel supports a choir, organ, and pulpit. The plain white walls contrast with the colorful windows, the dark wood floor, the pews, carved lectern, baptistery, chairs, murals, and the casework of the Prant and Pilcher organ (considered one of the finest unaltered three-manual instruments in the U.S.). Entering the church, one passes an alms plate *Für die Armen* ("For the poor").

5. FIRE DEPARTMENT HEADQUARTERS AND FIRE PREVENTION BUREAU

1135 West Jefferson Street, Russell
Brinton B. Davis
Landmark designation: NRHP, 1981
1936–1937

The Fire Department Headquarters has a symmetrical limestone facade and six sections, with the four center bays defining the fire-truck garage. The far-left bay provides private access to the living quarters above, while the right bay provides entrance to the administrative area. The entire building has a simple, elegant, and detailed parapet that has colorful blue and peach-colored terra-cotta inlays. A medallion inscribed with "City of Louisville" caps the center bay, depicting the downtown office buildings, framed by two modes of transportation–train (land) and ship (water). A woman carrying a harvest basket and pennant inscribed "Progress" dominants the center of the logo.

A 1967 addition, designed by Louisville architects Tafel and Schickli (built by Henry A. Steilberg), attaches to the eastern portion of the original structure. The clean-lined modern addition mimics the terra-cotta parapet detailing with concrete panels (compared to the limestone panels on the original structure) and uses a red brick veneer on a structural steel frame. The addition continues the proportional massing of Davis's building and extends the garage by one bay.

6. VILLAGE WEST

Area bounded by Ninth Street, Eleventh Street, West Broadway, and Muhammad Ali Boulevard, Russell

McCulloch and Bickel, Design Environment Group Architects (DEGA), Cox and Crawle

1966–1972

The Village West Housing project is a residential and mixed-use development that resulted from an open national design competition sponsored by the City Urban Renewal Agency and juried by architects and planners including Ralph Rapson of Minneapolis and George Qualls of Philadelphia. Donald L. Williams, who led a group from McCulloch and Bickel, won the competition.

The architects presented a contemporary scheme for urban housing. The DEGA plan inserted four-story terraced apartments at the edges of the 34-acre competition site. Separating pedestrians from automobiles, pathways lead to the school and to shopping without interference. In keeping with the historic context of Louisville, all buildings have masonry walls.

Phase I of the project (1966–70) provided 263 central-court-yard apartments and was awarded a citation for Excellence in Community Architecture by the AIA in 1966. Phase II (1968–71) included an additional 250 apartments. Phase III (1970–72) consisted of another 102 units, an elementary school, and broad, tree-lined walkways that link to a shopping center and a central plaza and playground, the focal point of the complex. Coleridge-Taylor Elementary School (now Coleridge-Taylor Montessori) was the first in Louisville to present the new educational concept of an open classroom. This project reflected educational planning of the time, including a circular amphitheater around which the classrooms open.

In 1991, the U.S. Department of Housing and Urban Development (HUD) began managing Village West. With increased security, the neighborhood improved. In 1996, with support from the University of Louisville's Sustainable Urban Neighborhoods (SUN) program, Village West was saved from demolition. With over $33 million in new investment, the property has been renovated and restored.

7. YMCA BUILDING—CHESTNUT STREET FAMILY BRANCH
(Knights of Pythias Temple)
930 West Chestnut Street, Central Business District
Henry Wolters
Landmark designation: NRHP, 1978
1914–1915

The Knights of Pythias Temple was built as the state headquarters of the African American Knights of Pythias Lodge, an organization that has long been associated with the African American community in Louisville. The building was a multiuse facility with a drugstore, movie theater, and restaurant located on the ground floor. A portion of the building contained hotel rooms and apartments. Lodge meeting rooms were on the second floor. After World War II, the building was the home of the Davis Trade School for African Americans. In 1953, the YMCA purchased and renovated the building (moving in 1977 to 920 Chestnut Street, a building designed by Louis & Henry). A 1978 renovation of the original structure provided a teen center and ballroom on the sixth floor. The building continues to serve the African American community.

8. QUINN CHAPEL AFRICAN METHODIST
EPISCOPAL (AME) CHURCH
(Chestnut Street Baptist Church)
912 West Chestnut Street, Russell
Henry Wolters
Landmark designation: NRHP, 1980
1884

Recently boarded up and abandoned for a new church at Nineteenth Street and Muhammad Ali Boulevard, this landmark church with a

limestone foundation and exceptional brick details is the fifth location of Louisville's oldest African American congregation. It is the
site of many historic gatherings and protests, attended by some of
America's leading civil rights advocates, including the Reverends
Martin Luther King Jr. and Jesse Jackson. This structure is distinctive in its eclectic presentation of many architectural components,
as well as in how it reflects an approach to design taken by many
architects of the period in the attempt to find an American style.
The front facade presents a high central nave with a diapered pediment at the apex, a large pointed window divided into a rose window and four smaller, pointed stained-glass parts; an entablature
with dentils; and four rectangular windows. An arcade of segmented, pointed arches, held by crocketed capitals and unusual stacked
columns, has diapered pendentives between the arches. The arcade
forms an entry loggia, reached from the churchyard by six stone
steps, that leads to the three main doors of the church. A heavy,
white stringcourse stretches across the front from one tower to the
other. The two towers, neither of which is finished, are divided into
three parts and have entrances with pointed arches, but otherwise
they are quite different. The left tower has stepped-back corners in
its middle section, capped by a heavy cornice that yields to a hexagonal but adumbrated bell section with divided, pointed windows
and hood moldings. The other tower is square, has double corner
buttresses, a large ocular window, and a false arcade of pointed windows in the third section. Double-shouldered buttresses divide the
five bays of the brick sidewalls with tall pointed-arch windows. A
brick educational wing projects from the rear of the nave.

9. BROADWAY TEMPLE AME CHURCH
662 South Thirteenth Street, Russell
Samuel M. Plato
Landmark designation: NRHP, 1980
1915

The Broadway Temple AME Church is a community landmark and presents a significant example of the early work of Louisville's first African American architect, Samuel M. Plato. A native of Alabama, Plato began the study of architecture by taking correspondence courses at Simmons University (Municipal College). He was the first African American architect to receive a federal commission to design U.S. Post Offices, of which he designed more than forty. In 1924, Plato designed Steward Hall, a boys dormitory and classroom, on the Simmons campus.

The Broadway Temple AME Church has a variety of roof forms and an imaginative combination of elements, without having a specific alliance to one particular architectural style. The church is a two-story brick structure that rises above street level on a painted limestone base. The Broadway facade has a portico that protrudes from the building. Two Ionic capitals, which frame a central entry into the chancel of the church, support this portico. Above the entry, a grouping of three stained-glass windows is set into a stone surround. The Thirteenth Street facade echoes many of these details. However, at the roofline, a pronounced cornice runs beneath a low parapet wall.

A two-story north annex was added to the original structure in 1926. While not specifically attributed to Plato, the material selection and language of Plato have been maintained. A three-story tower connects to the original building.

10. AUTO WAREHOUSE USED CARS
(Whiteside Bakery)
1400 West Broadway, Russell
Arthur Loomis
Landmark designation: NRHP, 1979
1908

The former Whiteside Bakery building is a unique commercial structure for Louisville and is one of only a few examples of the mission style in the city. Loomis's use of this style represents a radical departure from his other notable structures, including the Gothic St. Paul's Evangelical Church (1906), the Romanesque revival Shelby Park Library (1911), the Chicago School Kentucky Electric (HSA Broadband Building) (1912), and the neoclassical J. B. Speed Museum (1927). The building's massing and strong horizontal reading create a commanding presence on the Broadway site.

The adjacency of the site to the Pennsylvania Railroad, the increased facility of delivering bulk raw materials, and the convenience of not having to rehandle materials all affected the design of the building. When it was completed, the building was hailed as the largest and most sophisticated bakery in the U.S. The original owner, Isaac Whitestone, died one year after the building was completed.

General Baking Company purchased the building in 1928 and completely remodeled, re-equipped, and modernized the facility in 1929. Dixie Baking Company purchased the building in 1966; it then changed hands again in 1973. The building is currently occupied by a used-car business.

11. LOUISVILLE & NASHVILLE (L & N) RAILROAD OFFICE BUILDING

908 West Broadway, California
W. H. Courtenay, J. C. Haley
Landmark designation: NRHP, 1983
1902–1907

The Louisville & Nashville Railroad Office Building replaced the old L&N offices on Second and Main Streets. The Beaux Arts building is attributed to L&N chief architect, W. H. Courtenay. It was begun in 1902, but labor disputes delayed its completion until 1907.

An eight-bay addition to the west duplicates the detailing of the original building. This addition, referred to as "the annex," dates from 1930, and its design is attributed to J. C. Haley, the chief architect of L&N at the time. The unified structure is one of the finest and largest existing Beaux Arts commercial buildings in Louisville.

The location of the building, adjacent to the Romanesque revival Union Station (1880), designed by F. W. Mobray, is of several significant block-long structures on Broadway, including the Courier-Journal building and the U.S. Post Office. The facade composition addresses three primary scales: the pedestrian, the adjacent Union Station, and the size and prominence of the L & N Railroad Company at the time. The lower stories consist of rusticated ashlar stonework, with a series of pilasters topped by capitals. The windows between the pilasters are grouped in threes, a pattern that continues throughout the structure. Modillions and dentils continue across the facade, while quoins at the building's corners accent the lower level. The middle section, floors four through ten, has a red brick finish, framed by ashlar pilasters, and relates to the full massing of Union Station. A one-and-a-half-story attic containing the company signage sits above an extended cornice, giving it a permanent place in Louisville's skyline.

12. TRANSIT AUTHORITY OF RIVER CITY
(Union Station)
1000 West Broadway, Shawnee
F. W. Mobray
Landmark designation: NRHP, 1975; LL
1881–1891

The third L & N Railroad Station in Louisville, Union Station, was designed by the company's architect, F. W. Mobray, and built by local craftsmen at the height of H. H. Richardson's influence on architecture in the U.S. Like much of Richardsonian Romanesque architecture, this gigantic edifice of brick, faced with limestone, is eclectic in detail, uses a variety of architectural elements, and is a reflection of numerous European precedents. The monochromatic Kentucky and Indiana limestone calms the busyness of the facade, which is tied together with a double stringcourse between the mezzanine and second floor and white, single stringcourses on the upper levels. The tower that rests on each corner of the main gable and the large turret on the south elevation give the station a soaring vertical dimension, which balances the overall horizontality of the building. Passengers entered the station under an iron and glass porch and crossed a spectacular central concourse under a high barrel-vaulted ceiling, large rose windows twenty feet in diameter at each end, and a stained-glass skylight that replaced the dome that was destroyed by a fire in 1905. Original wooden benches for waiting passengers remain. The concourse floor is made of ceramic tile and has an abstract quatrefoil design. Muscular iron columns with mixed capitals and engaged pilasters with scrolled braces hold the circling gallery on the mezzanine level and its organic wrought-iron railing. An arcaded wall, composed of engaged pilasters and arches that encompass doors and windows, gives the long sides of the mezzanine a powerful architectural rhythm.

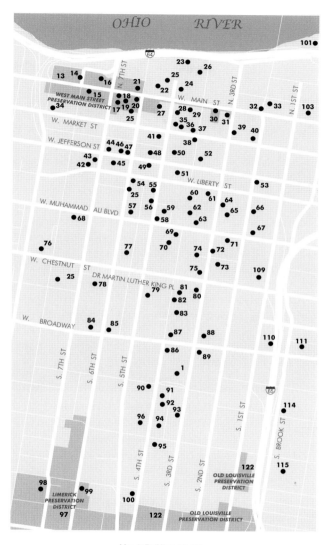

Map 2: Buildings 13–115,
including West Main Street and Limerick Districts

13. WEST MAIN STREET HISTORIC COMMERCIAL DISTRICT

Main Street, Central Business District

Landmark designation: NRHP, 1974, expanded in 1980; LPD

1787–Present

The Falls of the Ohio River created this ancient north/south high-way's only natural break in its course from Pittsburgh to New Orleans. Travelers disembarked, loaded and unloaded cargo at the northern end of the rapids (now Louisville), and repeated this task below the rapids at Portland (consolidated with Louisville in 1838). First hundreds and then thousands of people joined the vigorous settlement and trade activities westward following the Revolutionary War. This bustling traffic stimulated the growth of Louisville's Main Street, which ran parallel to and one block away from the river's edge. Soon warehouses replaced cabins and one-story buildings, and passengers headed for Main Street hotels, such as the spectacular Greek revival Louisville Hotel (1834), which was razed in 1949 for a parking lot, and the Galt House (1835), which burned in 1865. The demolished Bank of the U.S. (1832) and the extant Bank of Louisville (1837) provided capital and financial services to merchants, adventurers, wholesale traders, and an increasing number of retailers who built stores such as the demolished National Seed Company (1850). Main Street's activities stimulated business and the residential growth of the city, south, west, and eastward, establishing the early urban amenities of roads, small parks, beer gardens, and residential areas, which slowly eased farther south and in later years included mansions on Broadway. Succeeding waves of transportation improvements, such as steamboats in the 1820s and the railroads in the 1850s, produced a new generation of buildings.

Louisville was also a city of foundries and machine shops, spilling off Main Street onto Market Street. These foundries supplied local and regional customers with cast-iron commercial fronts and many hardware parts for industrial enterprises through catalog sales and railroad shipments. Kentucky's neutral position during the Civil War helped spur economic recovery and produced its boom period of building and cultural life during the final quarter of the nineteenth century, when most of the Historic District's cast iron–facade buildings were built.

As Edith Bingham notes in her essay on historic preservation in Louisville, Main Street buildings during the twentieth century eventually fell into disuse. In the 1960s and 1970s, all addresses on the north side of West Main's 200, 300, 400, and 500 blocks were razed, because they were regarded as architecturally and functionally obsolete, and replaced with modern structures. Despite Main Street's and Downtown's loss of commercial importance to nearby malls and strip malls in the burgeoning suburbs, preservationists, architects, developers, and politicians by 1972 had begun to turn around the fortunes of Louisville's most important thoroughfare, reviving the city's connection to the Ohio River.

Shortly after assuming his first term as mayor of Louisville in 1982, Jerry Abramson created the Louisville Development Authority (LDA). A partnership between the public and private sectors, the LDA acted to coordinate various governmental agencies in pursuing development goals on behalf of the city. The LDA carried out a master plan in 1990 to determine its goals for redevelopment, and West Main Street emerged as a priority. The central portion of Main Street, from Second to Sixth Streets, had fared well in the 1980s. The renovation of the Bank of Louisville into Actors Theatre and the building of both the Kentucky Center for the Arts and the Humana Building brought additional vitality to those blocks. The LDA worked to extend that redevelopment energy further west. Working with the Washington D.C.–based landscape-architecture firm EDAW, the development authority concentrated on enriching the public realm. The streetscape was dramatically improved by amenities such as bicycle racks designed by local artisans. New museums, such as the Louisville Slugger Museum, located on West Main, and those already there—the Museum of Natural History and Science and the Kentucky Gallery of Arts and Crafts—upgraded their facilities (and changed their names to the Louisville Science Center and the Kentucky Museum of Art + Design, respectively). Plans are underway to establish a major military-arms museum at the corner of Ninth and West Main Streets.

Private investment has followed the public program established by the LDA. Robert A. M. Stern has renovated and added an atrium to the Bernheim Building at 626 West Main; New York architect Deborah Berke is presently working on a boutique hotel on the 700 block; and Louisville architect K. Norman Berry has completed a new office building at 614 West Main that skillfully fits into its context.

14. FORT NELSON BUILDING
801 West Main Street, Central Business District
Architect unknown
Landmark designation: NRHP, 1974
1880s

This is a typical nineteenth-century brick commercial block that has only 25 feet of commercial frontage on Main Street but rises four stories and has a raking roof that runs more than 100 feet back, providing commodious, inexpensive, and easily maintained space for retail sales and warehousing. The interior space is designed to be adaptable to many business needs, and the exterior facade could have been any architectural style. In this case, the Romanesque revival brick facade is faced with limestone and has a tall, rusticated base and high arches above the doors that lead into the main retail area. The second-floor retail space has two broad arches with worked voussoirs, held by squat columns and foliated capitals. The third and fourth floors, indicated respectively by three small arches and four even smaller arches, repeat the materials and architectural details begun on the second. A barbican with a conical roof, built into the corner of the third and fourth floors, anchors the building's roots in a medieval past, draws attention to the business, and serves as a reference point for travelers and pedestrians along Main Street. A cannon in bas relief fills the pediment.

15. HART BLOCK

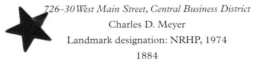

726–30 West Main Street, Central Business District
Charles D. Meyer
Landmark designation: NRHP, 1974
1884

By the 1880s, Main Street was a busy commercial center for hotels, warehouses, retail stores, and businesses that catered first to the vigorous trade brought by Ohio River traffic and later by an extensive railroad system that connected Louisville to cities and small towns in all directions, especially Chicago. The mass production of cast-iron building facades and interior structural systems, first developed in New York City by James Bogardus for the Lang Stores (1849) and the Harpers Brothers' Building (1854), eventually aided the quick development of main streets across the U.S. Almost any facade imaginable could be manufactured cheaply in relatively small parts, which were shipped by rail and assembled on site. Louisville had the advantage of being a city of foundries that manufactured its own cast-iron buildings and shipped cast-iron architectural parts to clients in cities throughout the Midwest. The five-story Hart Block, a hardware store designed by Charles D. Meyer into three vertical sections and manufactured by the local Merz Architectural Iron Works Company, presents a dazzling stacked facade of columns, pilasters, double colonnettes, stringcourses, square and rounded window arches, brackets, dentils, anthemia, rosettes, fluting, egg and dart details, and a heavy cornice. The thin but strong external structure, bolted together, makes possible an elevation of more glass than iron, allowing light deep into the open floors.

16. KENTUCKY MUSEUM OF ART + DESIGN
715 West Main Street, Central Business District
Architect unknown
Landmark designation: NRHP, 1974
Date unknown

Part of the cast-iron district along West Main Street, this building has been thoughtfully renovated by Annie Chu and Rick Gooding so that an abstract interior space complements the nineteenth-century facade. The Museum of Art + Design (formerly the Kentucky

Gallery of Arts and Crafts) has been a vital part of Louisville's artistic and cultural scene for two decades from its location in the 600 block of West Main Street. The decision of the museum's board to move a block west allowed for a substantial increase in both gallery and administrative space. The architects were able to open up the interior volume through the use of a large stair that orients itself to the gallery volumes around it. Local artisans were engaged to provide key elements of the building; notable among these are Craig Kaviar of Kaviar Forge (the wrought-iron door handles) and Kenneth von Roenn (the decorative glass installations in the lobby).

17. BROWN-FORMAN CORPORATION
(St. Charles Hotel)
634 West Main Street, Central Business District
Architect unknown
1830–1850

This modest brick, vernacular structure is the epitome of the two-part commercial block that over time presents a variety of facades as it responds to the changing needs of the owner and the evolving built environment. This building, the oldest survivor on West Main Street, has been a hotel, drugstore, bar, and antique shop and is now an office complex. The interior has a universal space that is just as adaptive to change as the facade. In this case, the facade, with its plain windows, jack arches, stone sills, and small rectangular lights at the frieze level, has remained relatively unchanged. The diagonal corner door and pillar is part of a larger cast-iron window-frame set that must have been added after the Civil War. The current owner, the Brown-Forman Corporation, has been one of Kentucky's leading bourbon distillers since the 1870s and also owns the Labrot & Graham Woodford Reserve distillery, a National Historic Landmark in Woodford County. In 1999, Brown-Forman preserved the exterior and renovated the interior. Since that time, a new infill building, designed by Robert A.M. Stern, has been constructed immediately to its left to utilize the space between the building and the L-shaped Bernheim warehouse (1872).

18. BERNHEIM BUILDING
626 West Main Street, Central Business District
Architect unknown, renovation by Robert A.M. Stern
Landmark designation: NRHP, 1974
Date unknown

Brown-Foreman purchased the empty Bernheim Building at 626 West Main Street in 2000 and hired noted New York architect Robert A.M. Stern to renovate the structure and add an adjacent atrium to it. Stern complemented the Richardsonian Romanesque style of the original structure with a more restrained classical composition for the addition. The atrium interior is a grand double-height volume, which opens onto a multifunctional space on the ground floor. Used for exhibitions, lectures, and special events, the two spaces complement each other nicely. One wall of the Bernheim gallery is composed of interlocking barrel staves, scavenged from the company's distillery operations; it serves as an exhibition surface for the company's significant art collection. Upper floors provide offices for the divisions of Brown-Forman's staff.

19. 614 WEST MAIN STREET
614 West Main Street, Central Business District
K. Norman Berry
2001

K. Norman Berry's office is a descendant of one of the first major architectural firms in Kentucky, that of Leo Oberwarth and his son, Julian, in Frankfort, which dates from the early twentieth century. Appropriately for a firm with such a rich history, Berry's office has specialized in a number of significant historic restorations and renovations, including the old Jefferson County jail and the Highland Branch of the Louisville Free Public Library.

Berry's office has been located on West Main Street since it moved from Frankfort in 1971; as pioneers in this location, they have been closely involved with a number of renovations on West Main Street. One is adjacent to its property, the Doe Anderson Building, which Berry renovated in the early 1990s. The owners of that building commissioned the construction at 614 West Main as a new office building; the floors at 614 align with those in Doe Anderson, so that expansion from one building to the other could take place on each floor. Despite the fact that 614 West Main is new construction, its architecture clearly reflects the historic context in which it is built. Berry varied the masonry materials to define the different colors and textures, much like the building's neighbors. The building is much wider than those around it, but the vertical elements of the building are emphasized, not the horizontal, which accentuates Berry's sensitivity to the nineteenth-century ideal of verticality found in neighboring buildings.

20. CHAMBER OF COMMERCE
(Seelbach's European Hotel)
600 West Main Street, Central Business District
Isaiah Rogers and Henry Whitestone
Landmark designation: NRHP, 1974
1856–1857

Louisville's economic vitality brought many architects to the city, and some stayed on to make important contributions to Louisville's architectural history. Having trained as an architect in Ireland, Henry Whitestone (1819–93), one of Louisville's most important early architects, owing to the superior quality of his design aesthetic, immigrated to the U.S. in 1852. In 1853, he came to Louisville after joining America's foremost hotel architect from Boston and New York, Isaiah Rogers, and together they designed a store and probably a hotel in 1856–57 that later would become Seelbach's European Hotel (1879). Rogers also worked in Cincinnati and Columbus and went on, from 1862 to 1867, to supervise the construction of the U.S. Capitol Dome with Ammi Young. Whitestone stayed in Louisville to design many mansions, especially Bashford Manor and the Ford and Newcomb houses, two hotels (including the second Galt House) and a number of commercial buildings along Main Street, such as the Board of Trade Building and the extant L & N Railroad Offices at Second and Main. In spite of spirited efforts by preservationists, throughout the 1960s and 1970s, many of Whitestone's buildings were razed. Seelbach's European Hotel is a good example of his commercial palace architecture, often called Renaissance revival (after Italian palazzi), which eventually came to be known as Italianate. The American commercial and domestic style, with roots in Tuscan, Romanesque, Gothic, and Rundbogenstil architecture, came to predominate nineteenth-century commercial centers such as Louisville. The hotel's floors, with repeating round-headed windows along Main Street and paired rounded windows along Sixth Street, are stacked into a two-part vertical front that had an interior court, now a closed atrium.

21. MUHAMMAD ALI CENTER
1 Muhammad Ali Plaza, Central Business District
Beyer Blinder Belle (New York), Lee H. Skolnick Architecture &
Design Partnership (New York), Bravura, EDAW (Alexandria, Virginia)
2002–2005

The Muhammad Ali Center is a dynamic 93,000-square-foot, six-story building, designed to honor the spirit and values of Muhammad Ali and to continue his humanitarian efforts to promote respect, hope, and understanding throughout the world. Located in Ali's hometown of Louisville, on a prominent downtown site overlooking the Ohio River, the Ali Center extends the city's waterfront development west of Sixth Street, dramatically adding to the city's skyline.

The architectural design is a collaboration between Beyer Blinder Belle, Lee H. Skolnick Architecture & Design Partnership (New York), and Bravura Corporation of Louisville. The exhibition is designed thematically according to six core values of Ali's life: respect, confidence, conviction, dedication, spirituality, and giving. Formations Inc. (Portland, Oregon) was responsible for the visitor experience, including the exhibition design and fabrication.

The building massing separates into three intrinsically linked components: a solid masonry base, an opaque "wrapper," and a floating butterfly roof. The masonry base grounds the building and ties it in scale and material to the adjacent urban context of the city of Louisville. The rectangular wrapper around the exterior of the building distinguishes the Ali Center from its surroundings as Muhammad Ali distinguished himself during his career. This wrapper, designed by the New York–based graphic design firm 2x4, consists of fixed, pixel-like, one-foot-by-two-foot ceramic tiles that form a continuous forty-foot-tall montage of photographic images of Ali's life.

The roof appears to float above the main structure, and its double-winged shape, which extends outward to the river, brings to mind Ali's famous dictum, "Float like a butterfly. Sting like a bee," and speaks to the inspiration of Ali's life and work. Above the entrance to the main lobby, a torch-like cylinder, representing the torch Ali used to light the flame at the 1996 Olympics, provides a beacon for the city and a constant reference point for orientation both inside and outside the building.

Organized from the inside out, the diverse programming of the project makes the building more than just a boxing museum. Rather it becomes an active center for learning that links its contents with the surrounding context and community. In addition to the exhibit areas, the center offers classrooms and spaces for educational pro-grams, distance-learning facilities, a public auditorium and archives, and a double-height, glass-enclosed 6,700-square-foot multifunc-tional meeting space with sweeping views of the Ohio River and the public plaza area.

The narrative of Ali's life seamlessly extends from the building into the urban plaza, designed by EDAW of Alexandria, Virginia, in association with Athena Tacha of Washington, D.C. and Architectural Glass Art of Louisville. The center's multilevel landscaped plaza provides an exciting and inspirational new downtown centerpiece. Its various levels include formal gardens, sculptural seating, and a unique celebratory fountain of architectural glass, offering a peace-ful retreat from the surrounding urban fabric, as well as a vibrant public space.

The Ali Center's new international headquarters is scheduled to open in November 2005.

22. KENTUCKY CENTER FOR THE ARTS
501 West Main Street, Central Business District
Caudill Rowlett Scott (Houston), Design and Construction
Department of Humana Corporation
1983

Louisville has maintained a strong civic commitment to the arts throughout much of the last half century. It is one of only a handful of American cities with an orchestra, ballet, opera, and recognized regional theater company, remarkable given the size of its population. That level of civic support led the city, county, and state to join private benefactors to support arts organizations, forming a unique partnership to build the Kentucky Center for the Arts. The site on West Main Street is prominent: it was a vital component of the West Main Street redevelopment and is sited across the street from Michael Graves's Humana Building, also under construction in this period.

Houston architectural firm Caudill Rowlett Scott prepared the initial designs for the center; later changes were facilitated by the Humana Corporation's in-house architects (Wendell Cherry, Humana's chief operating officer at the time, was designated to manage the project). The geometric design is a noteworthy example of late-modern architecture, emphasized by the building's proximity to one of the first major American postmodern buildings, Humana. An angled, raised forecourt leads to the entrance of the building. Regular volumes delineate the two theaters within: Whitney Hall, which seats

2,400 people, and the 626-seat Bomhard Theater. The facades are a sleek combination of linear glass curtain walls and taut brick. Behind the center, the Belvedere was extended to provide more public areas overlooking the Ohio River. Major sculptures by Alexander Calder, Jean Dubuffet, Louise Nevelson, and John Chamberlain, among others, enhance both interior and exterior spaces.

23. RIVERFRONT PLAZA

Main Street between Third and Sixth Streets, Central Business District
Constantinos Doxiades, Lawrence A. Melillo, Jasper D. Ward
1973

Discussion about an enhanced waterfront area in downtown Louisville dates from the Bartholomew Plan (1932), but the Depression and World War II delayed any hope of implementation for several decades. In 1960, Reynolds Metals Company, then based in Louisville, engaged Constantinos Doxiades, a leading urban planner at the time, to design a park, skyscrapers, apartments, and a marina on a four-block stretch of Main Street leading down to the Ohio River. The project stalled a few years later due to the siting of the Riverside Expressway (now I-64). A revised plan was prepared in 1966 by two Louisville architects, Lawrence Melillo and Jasper Ward, working with Doxiades. Seven bumpy years later, due to issues of financing and approval, the Belvedere was dedicated in April 1973. The LDA carried out a substantial renovation in 1998, largely to make the plaza more accessible from Main Street.

The project is a raised park and plaza over both I-64 and a large parking garage. The park is enclosed by Schneider's Galt House to the east and by Mies van der Röhe's American Life Building and Caudill Rowlett Scott's Kentucky Center for the Arts to the south. The Muhammad Ali Center, presently under construction, will anchor the western edge of the plaza. Views of the river and falls from the Belvedere are spectacular. Note the bronze statue of General George Rogers Clark that ends the walkway from Main Street; the sculptor was Felix de Weldon, designer of the Iwo Jima Memorial

24. AMERICAN LIFE BUILDING
3 Riverfront Plaza, Central Business District
Mies van der Rohe
1973

Building on the efforts to redevelop West Main Street in the late 1960s and early 1970s, the American Life and Accident Insurance Company hired Mies van der Rohe to design its headquarters on the Belvedere Plaza. Mies, the émigré German architect known for his

modernist steel-and-glass skyscrapers, such as the Seagram Building in New York City, took on the project. Unfortunately, it would be his last; he carried the project through the preliminary design phase before his death in 1969, and it was completed by his firm.

The American Life Building demonstrates Mies's signature design virtues: his commitment to authenticity in materials and to refined systems of proportion. As an office building, it is actually small: just four floors and a penthouse, on a raised lobby as a podium. The lobby is nearly transparent, with expanses of glass that allow views from Main Street through to the Belvedere. Two elevator cores flank a central axial space from the entrance. The building (except the penthouse) is square in plan, set back from Main Street through the use of a small, raised court. The penthouse is set back from the front and rear elevations; a small roof terrace at the rear takes advantage of views over the Ohio River. Cor-ten steel, which uses the natural oxidation of its surface as a finish, is the primary building material (it was the only project for which Mies used this material). During construction, a dispute with the contractor over the specifications for the steel—the panels as they were installed were too thin and warped—was ultimately resolved by the flip of a coin; the client, Dinwiddie Lampton, decided that that would be more expedient for all concerned than taking the matter to court, keeping the project on schedule. Unfortunately for Lampton, he lost the coin flip.

25. PARKING GARAGES
Multiple locations, Central Business District
Jasper D. Ward
1968–1989

Jasper D. Ward's inventiveness is amply demonstrated in the parking-garage commissions he executed throughout downtown Louisville in the 1970s and 1980s. Working in concrete, Ward emphasized geometric qualities in the public areas of the garages to give them a sense of place and life. On Magazine Street, he separates the elevator and stair components into individual blocks, turns them on an angle to the garage and street, and gives them enough fenestration to make them appear to be a building, not just an add-on to a garage. For the Sixth Street Parking Garage (120 South Sixth Street, 1985–87, in association with Luckett & Farley), he used different geometric elements to achieve the same result: interlocking piano curves around the stairs and elevator and glazed public areas within the curves make them building elements. His facility with concrete is also evident here. Part of his rationale for using concrete, especially in the historic portions of downtown, was not to trivialize the preservation efforts in the area (which were so often focused on older brick structures) but to carry on a sympathetic dialogue with the surrounding context. Architects, at least, noticed the qualities Ward brought to these projects: he received several design awards from professional associations.

The Louisville Gardens Parking Garage (Sixth Street to Armory Street at Cedar Street, 1989) replaced a two-story maintenance garage behind the Old Jefferson County Jail. The garage steps back at the top two floors along Sixth Street to create a volumetric parity with the historic jail structure. The location of a small gas-metering and -distribution building along Armory Street prevented a continuous facade. As a result, Ward designed the garage around the existing building.

Ward also designed two other garages. The Federal Garage (711 Magazine Street, 1968–70), pictured here, is set back from the street, allowing a swath of grass to separate the facility from the sidewalk. Ward takes advantage of this setback to insert two stair towers—one at the corner (freestanding and cantilevered) and another at the entry (solid and enclosed). The Riverfront Plaza Belvedere Parking Garage (One Riverfront Plaza) was built in 1973 in association with Lawrence Melillo.

Riverfront Plaza Belvedere Parking Garage: Seventh Annual Award for Excellence, first-place winner, Federal Highway Administration, 1974

26. GALT HOUSE AND GALT HOUSE EAST
140 North Fourth Street, Central Business District
Thomas Nolan, Al J. Schneider
1972

The plan for the Riverfront Plaza and Belvedere focused new attention on the prospects for redevelopment along Main Street. One of the first developers to act on this was Al J. Schneider, who came from a family of Louisville builders. Once the plaza and parking garage were underway, Schneider hired Louisville architect Thomas Nolan to design a hotel at the eastern edge of the plaza, using the name of two historic hotels from nearby sites. The Galt House was finished in 1972, nearly a year earlier than the Belvedere. In 1985, another building was completed, the Galt House East; a raised and enclosed walkway across Fourth Street connects the two buildings.

Schneider was a developer who cultivated a public persona, and the Galt House, symbolizes his sensibilities. The buildings have elements that resonate with vernacular river culture, ranging from eclectic to the edge of kitsch, rather than with the crisp modern, architectural detailing of other notable projects of the same period. Yet, on an urban scale, Schneider's investment in a major riverfront property just as access to the river was being compromised by the construction of I-64 should not be underestimated. The Galt House anchored a key section of Main Street and facilitated additional redevelopment.

27. HUMANA BUILDING
500 West Main Street, Central Business District
Michael Graves (Princeton, New Jersey)
1984

Michael Graves's design for the Humana Corporation's headquarters confirmed the architect's place as a leader of postmodernism as that movement emerged in the early 1980s. Graves's use of traditional urban precedents in the composition of the building's form and his adaptation of details from classical architecture are distinguishing features.

Humana organized an invited competition for its corporate headquarters, fully intending to showcase the company's civic commitment to the arts and Louisville, as well as its public emergence among health-care corporations. The other competitors included Helmut Jahn, Cesar Pelli, Norman Foster, and Ulrich Franzen.

Graves's design was selected in large part because of its sensitivity to the historical qualities of downtown Louisville.

A six-story component along the edge of West Main Street respects the scale and fenestration pattern of the buildings around it. The tower is set back from the street edge to preserve the scale. The building also acknowledges the importance of the Ohio River to Louisville with a large open-air terrace on the twenty-fifth floor, cantilevering away from the mass of the tower and over Main Street, providing spectacular views of the river. That space and the arcade along West Main Street, with a curving waterfall that flanks the entry to the building, are notable architectural amenities.

28. NATIONAL CITY TOWER
(First National Tower)
101 South Fifth Street, Central Business District
Harrison and Abramowitz (New York)
1972

In mid-twentieth-century America, there was a sense that modern architecture could represent a broad-based, even universal style. This monolithic forty-story office building represents perhaps the purest modern architecture in Louisville. It was the tallest building in Louisville until 1992, when the Aegon Tower by Philip Johnson and John Burgee was completed. The prismatic quality of the tower and clean fenestration pattern of the facade idealize the building in terms of its style but decontextualize it as well: it has little to do with Louisville. The Humana Building, a decade later, is an interesting foil in this regard, since it succeeds in relating to the context of Main Street and the Ohio River.

29. STOCK YARDS TRUST COMPANY
(Louisville Trust Bank Building)
200 South Fifth Street, Central Business District
Mason Maury, William J. Dodd
Landmark designation: NRHP, 1977; LL
1889

This bank is similar (although much smaller in scale) to Adler and Sullivan's famous Auditorium Building (1886–90) in Chicago. The influence of Chicago School buildings and architects was significant throughout the middle of the U.S. because Chicago was the heart of the region's post–Civil War economic and cultural networks, which connected cities and towns through an elaborate rail, mail, and telegraph system. The transfer of goods and services between Chicago and Louisville is remarkable. Mason Maury and William J. Dodd worked in Chicago and brought back the most recent architectural fashions to Louisville. Maury designed Kentucky's building for the Columbian Exposition (1893), and Dodd studied under William Le Baron Jenney and S. S. Beman, both notable nineteenth-century Chicago architects. Maury and Dodd were heavily influenced by Richardson's pivotal monochromatic Marshall Field Wholesale Store and Warehouse (1885–87), also an important architectural source for Adler and Sullivan.

The base of this bank is a line of polished granite columns, piers, crocketed capitals, and large Romanesque arches (formerly leading to entrances) that hold an entablature and a heavy limestone stringcourse. The six floors above are composed of rough, striated limestone blocks with rows of squared-off windows, interrupted by arched windows on the second and fifth floors. The facade has richly detailed spandrels, arches, entablatures, clustered columns, capitals, and cornices. The turret-like flag tower operates as a weak vertical compositional element. Much, but not all, of the historic interior has been lost. The historic plaster walls have been replaced, although the wainscoting remains, the cast iron stair and marble steps are still intact, and the floral capitals of the interior columns have been preserved. Extensive original woodwork and panels with neoclassical details on the ground floor and interior marble stairs and arches invest the building with a polished materiality appropriate to a bank. The plan of the building is a doughnut, similar in plan to many Chicago School buildings, that provides light and air to all of the offices. This atrium is closed with a skylight, to provide a bright interior space protected from the weather. A marble stair, with a Sullivanesque capital, a cast-iron balustrade, and an oak handrail, winds seven stories to the top floor. Some floors retain their marble floors and walls, and some floors still have their nineteenth-century double-loaded hall arrangement with oak doors, floral doorknobs, etched-glass windows, and transoms. There are many polished-brass doors, elevator doors, and windows with etched glass throughout the building.

30. ACTORS THEATRE
(Bank of Louisville)
320 Main Street, Central Business District
James Dakin, John Rogers, Gideon Shryock
Landmark designation: NHL, 1974; NRHP, 1974, 1980
1835–1837

In 1834, James Dakin, a New Orleans architect who earlier had worked for the firm of Town and Davis in New York, designed this Greek revival bank in the form of a Delphic treasury. Dakin visited Louisville with his drawings, and John Rogers undertook the construction. After he died in 1835, the bank hired the Kentucky architect Gideon Shryock to supervise the completion of the building. Constructed of brick, limestone, and iron, this one-part commercial block has an elevated base and four steps that lead to a *distyle in antis* portico with two gigantic, fluted Ionic columns, framed by two battered end pilasters and a full entablature, crowned with an iron cornice of palmetto, taenia, and antefixes. On the interior, two sets of fluted columns with Corinthian capitals provide entrance screens for a six-bay banking room, flanked by engaged pilasters that carry an elliptical dome, a skylight, and an entablature with dentils. Dakin's drawings were published as plates in Minard Lefever's *The Beauties of Modern Architecture* (1835).

This building remained a bank under several names until 1930 and was vacant until 1937, when the Louisville Credit Men's Association purchased it. Since 1972, Actors Theatre of Louisville has owned the building, renovated it, and located the theater proper

behind the bank building that Harry Weese designed. The new theater, named the Pamela Brown Auditorium, opened in 1972. Brown
was lost in a balloon accident over the Atlantic, and her brother,
John Y. Brown, honored her with a lead gift for the new space.

31. VAUGHN BUILDING
(Income Life Insurance Building)
300 West Main Street, Central Business District
McDonald Brothers
Landmark designation: NRHP, 1979
1890

The influence of H. H. Richardson and the commercial architecture
of the Chicago School is apparent in the Vaughn building, originally
designed as an L-shaped steel-frame bank structure with a six-floor
atrium and faced with monochromatic limestone of large dimensions. The McDonald Brothers created two lively facades, composed vertically with seven bays on the long side and three bays on
the short side. Horizontally, the building is divided into a two-part
rusticated base, with a heavy water table over the basement and a
molded stringcourse capping the piano nobile. Two floors compose
the second section, which is divided by a carved stone stringcourse
at the third floor and a dentiled secondary cornice ending the fourth
floor. The third floor of the east facade has four sets of five clustered columns surrounded by a ribbon of foliated stonework. As

is often the case, the facade indicates nothing about the interior spaces behind it. A third section of three floors displays muscular, engaged pilasters and Sullivanesque capitals, which carry an arcade of soaring stone arches. An entablature, dentils, a cornice, a corner minaret, and a diapered parapet (with carved finials that also work as brackets) form a composite crown for the top section. A historic atrium and most of the historic interior have been lost in a progression of renovations. The foyer, however, offers an array of polychromatic marble, facing the walls, floors, and stairs. The Louisville Orchestra occupies the basement and piano nobile.

32. GEORGE ROGERS CLARK MEMORIAL BRIDGE APPROACHES
(Louisville Municipal Bridge Approaches and Pylons)
Second Street and Main Street, Central Business District
Paul Cret (Philadelphia), Ralph Modjeski and Frank M. Masters,
American Bridge Company (Pittsburgh)
Landmark designation: NRHP, 1984
1928–1929

A pair of limestone bridge pylons designed by internationally known architect Paul Cret flanks the entrance to the George Rogers Clark Memorial Bridge, which connects Louisville with Jeffersonville, Indiana. Paul Cret trained at the Ecole des Beaux Arts and is best known for his civic architecture, including the Detroit Institute of the Arts and the Folger Shakespeare Library, and for his students, among them Louis Kahn and George Howe. In 1928, he received the commission to design the approaches to the Municipal Bridge in Louisville.

The Philadelphia engineering firm Ralph Modjeski and Frank M. Masters designed the four-lane automobile bridge; and the American Bridge Company, of Pittsburgh, was responsible for its construction. The simple form of the pylons exemplifies Cret's design aesthetic and his understanding of surface. The design of the pylons has both Beaux Arts and art deco characteristics, a rare combination in Louisville. The pylon surface contains engraved lettering, marking the entrance to Kentucky. The front of the pylons has a fluted column on a smooth base. Halfway up the column, a band with a bas relief depicts two "friends," a pioneer and a statesman, shaking hands, reflecting Kentucky's motto, "United we stand, divided we fall," which was adopted the same year the bridge pylons were designed. The top has an American bald eagle, a national symbol, carved on its surface. The pylon tapers at the top, where an art deco lantern sits. Renamed in 1949, the bridge is now called the George Rogers Clark Memorial Bridge.

33. TRADE MART BUILDING
(Louisville and Nashville Railroad Office)
131 West Main Street, Central Business District
Henry Whitestone
Landmark designation: NRHP, 1973
1875–1877

Henry Whitestone, one of Louisville's leading architects, apprenticed in Ireland before immigrating to the U.S. in 1852. He came to Louisville as a partner of Isaiah Rogers and later designed the second Galt House (1869). Much of Whitestone's work, known for its chaste Renaissance revival expression, has been destroyed. The Trade Mart Building was built for the L & N Railroad staff and has architectural roots in the tripartite, rectangular Renaissance palazzi. Three stories accommodated offices for all of the shareholders of the railroad. Corinthian capitals and columns separate rectangular windows on each side of the central door, also bracketed by Corinthian columns standing on plinths, and carry a plain entablature and dentiled cornice, topped by a balustrade and balcony, creating an emphatic stringcourse between the first and second floors. The central bay on the second and third floors supports a double window with rounded pediments, indicating where the vertical circulation occurs on the interior. The cast-iron stair rises to the third floor from the central hall on the first, which has a polychromatic tile floor. Quoins articulate the corners that terminate in a cornice composed of an entablature, dentils, and modillions, which bracket the flat overhang of the roof. The footprint of this building is an L shape, providing a stream of light into the offices through the tall windows that march across the facade.

34. GLASSWORKS
(Snead Manufacturing Building)
817 West Market Street, Central Business District
D. X. Murphy & Brothers
Landmark designation: NRHP, 1978
1909–1910

The Snead Manufacturing Building (now called the Glassworks) is located on the site of the former Market Street Architectural Iron Foundry. Samuel P. Snead, the son of a prominent Louisville merchant, purchased the foundry in 1849. The Snead and Company Iron Works was one of the most noted manufacturers of iron buildings and ornamental iron fronts in the country. Its products are visible on many Louisville buildings along West Main Street and on several manhole covers throughout the Central Business District. The company also manufactured metal book stacks for the Library of Congress and the Vatican Library in Rome, as well as the columns and ornamental ironwork for Louis Sullivan's Auditorium Building in Chicago. Following a devastating fire that destroyed the iron plant in 1898, the Snead Company hired leading Louisville architect D. X. Murphy in 1909 to design a "first-class fireproof power building" on the site of the original ironworks. The eight-story, rectangular, reinforced-concrete structure has a central, three-bay, pedimented facade and terra-cotta brick noggins. It is an excellent example of early-twentieth-century design, devoid of decorative details and elegant in its simplicity.

A group of investors, led by William Weyland (architect), Kenneth von Roenn (architectural art-glass designer), and Edward Allgeier (real-estate appraiser) purchased the building in 2000 and began an extensive rehabilitation project. The Glassworks utilizes the free plan of the former industrial building for multiple purposes, including loft apartments, classrooms, offices, and galleries.

Tours are available: $6.50 (adult), $5.50 (seniors), $3.50 (students). Open Monday–Saturday, 10 AM to 4 PM. For a private tour, contact Kenneth von Roenn (502-992-3266).

35. MARSHALL BUILDING (left)
(Almstedt Brothers Building)
425 West Market Street, Central Business District
Joseph and Joseph
Landmark designation: NRHP, 1982
1931

The Almstedt Brothers Building is a work of prominent Louisville architects Joseph and Joseph, whose other notable project is the Republic Building (1913) on Muhammad Ali Boulevard. Now called the Marshall Building, it is a three-story limestone structure in the Beaux Arts style. It is attached to the Louisville Trust Company, which was designed by Nevin, Morgan, and Kolbrook in 1928–29. Built in 1931 on the site of a former café, the building has housed investment-brokerage firms since 1931. Despite its small size, the details and proportions of the design exude a monumental stature with a two-story arched entryway, framed by fluted pilasters and a dentiled entablature.

36. NATIONAL CITY BANK—
LEONARD V. HEBRON BUILDING (right)
(Louisville Trust Company)
421 West Market Street, Central Business District
Nevin, Morgan, and Kolbrook
1928–1929

The Louisville Trust Company Building, built on the site of the former Morris Plan Bank, is a four-story limestone structure. Designed by Nevin, Morgan, and Kolbrook, the architects of the Pendennis Club (1922–28), the building represents a unique amalgamation of traditional French motifs and streamlined art moderne detailing. The primary facade is broken into three bays, with the central bay punctuated by a three-story limestone archway and entrance. The right bay contains bas relief seals of the U.S. and Louisville. The left bay contains the bas relief seals of the U.S. and Kentucky.

The original vestibule was magnificent, with decorated walls of St. Genevieve marble bordered in black-and-gold marble from Egypt, black Belgian-marble strips, and travertine flooring. Large sliding bronze gates separate the lobby from the main room. The main banking room is decorated with Italian Renaissance details and has richly colored ceilings, oversize square columns, and beams.

The Louisville Trust Company occupied this building until 1931, when the Lincoln Bank and Trust Company took over. A 1960 merger with First National Bank made the building part of the First National Bank's properties. Today it serves as a community center.

37. VINCENZO'S RESTAURANT
(Louisville Home Federal Building)
150 South Fourth Street, Central Business District
D. X. Murphy & Brothers, Grossman Chapman Kingsley
Landmark designation: NRHP, 1984
1914

Built on the site of the former German Bank Building is a two-story
Beaux Arts limestone building, arranged with an abundance of clas-
sical details and motifs. In comparison to the Old Jefferson County
Jail (1902–05), one can see the range of architectural styles that
D. X. Murphy was able to utilize. The original footprint included
the Market Street facade and the pedimented portico, supported
by four fluted Ionic columns, that defines the Fifth Street entry.
In 1918, the name was changed to the Louisville National Bank.
In 1924, a northern addition was built that replicated the detailing
and proportions of the Market Street facade along Fifth Street. The
property was later sold to the Federal Reserve Bank and Louisville
Home Federal Savings and Loan Association.

In 1983, Humana purchased the building. A subsequent renovation by Louisville architects Grossman Chapman Kingsley converted the building into a conference and fitness center for Humana
and updated the banking space to accommodate Vincenzo's, one of
Louisville's finest restaurants.

38. PROVIDIAN CENTER/CAPITOL HOLDINGS CENTER

(Aegon Tower)

400 West Market Street, Central Business District
John Burgee and Philip Johnson (New York)
1993

The tallest building in Louisville, this 35-story structure was one of the final projects of the 25-year partnership of Philip Johnson and John Burgee. Aegon Tower demonstrates the firm's sophistication in tall-building design: the base, shaft, and cap are clearly delineated and honor the American skyscraper as it developed in the early twentieth century. The dome is a particularly strong feature of the design; along with the Humana Building, it defines the Louisville skyline. At the same time, the design's relative anonymity is a shortcoming: one could as easily imagine this tower in Houston as in Louisville.

39. OLD SPAGHETTI FACTORY
(Levy Brothers Building)
235 West Market Street, Central Business District
Clarke & Loomis
Landmark designation: NRHP, 1978
1893

Charles Julian Clarke and his main draftsman, Arthur Loomis (who joined Clarke's firm in the 1880s), became partners in 1891. By that time, Clarke was one of Louisville's leading architects, and, as a member of the Western Association of Architects, he was very familiar with H. H. Richardson's architecture. Clarke and his younger partner, who came to Louisville from Massachusetts in the 1880s, made good use of Richardsonian Romanesque in this five-story commercial building at the prominent location of Third and Market Streets, which their clients, the Levy Brothers, had purchased for their clothing store. The reddish-yellow brick construction, with red terra-cotta details that articulate the arches, windows, stringcourses, cornice, and tower, made for a stylish building that attracted the attention of men and boys who sought fashionable attire. The corner tower pulls together the two exuberant facades, the floors of which are indicated by a variety of window sizes, forms, and treatments, including loggias, which create lively fronts on both streets. On the interior, the pressed metal, coffered ceilings, mixed capitals, and hardwood floors have survived many uses since the Levy Brothers closed their doors in 1979. The apartments on the upper floors retain the original paneling with cornices, elaborate cast-iron stair balustrades, and light fixtures. This was one of the first electrified buildings in Louisville. The structure has housed the Old Spaghetti Factory on the first and second floors for the last seventeen years and was renovated in 1984 for the restaurant on the first floor and businesses and apartments above. Strings of lights decorate the building year-round. When one has been drinking too much, the boozer is sometimes said to be "lit up like Levy's."

40. GERMAN INSURANCE BANK
207–209 West Market Street, Central Business District
Charles D. Meyer, Godsey Associates Architects
Landmark designation: NRHP, 1985
1887–1900

This German American bank was established for the first wave of German immigrants, mostly Protestant and Republican, who came to antebellum Louisville. After the Civil War, more Germans, this time working-class Catholics, streamed into Louisville, requiring the erection of a new bank in 1887. Charles D. Meyer, a German-born architect of the community, designed an ebullient, eclectic building of Indiana limestone for this conservative banking insti-tution. He used clashing architectural elements, contrasting treatments, conflicting scales, and a thoroughly detailed wall on a front elevation that, when added up, exuded solidity, dependability, and culture. The manifold facade was also part of the advertisement, making the bank building stand out among competing, neighboring institutions and, owing to its complex mix of inventive details and architectural orders, is somewhat akin to the much more radical work of Frank Furness, who was working at the time in equally conservative Quaker Philadelphia. The Second Empire Baroque clock tower and the Furnessian southern facade remain intact after destructive exterior and interior renovations in 1992. The bank changed its name after World War I to the Liberty National Bank and Trust Company, a name dropped in a buyout during the 1990s. Historic photos of the building are on view in the foyer as well as a beautiful Rookwood-pottery drinking fountain and sculpture by Enid Yandell, a Louisville native who won a gold medal for design at the Columbian World Exposition in Chicago in 1893. She designed numerous statues and fountains in the city, including the Daniel Boone statue and Hogan Fountain in Cherokee Park.

41. LOUISVILLE TRUST BANK BUILDING
400 West Main Street, Central Business District
Nolan & Nolan, Inc.; Al J. Schneider
1972

The redevelopment of Louisville's riverfront area, first proposed by
the Bartholomew Plan of 1930, began in earnest in the 1960s with
Doxiades's designs for the Belvedere. This plan called for a four-
block area to be rebuilt with commercial skyscrapers, apartment
buildings, a marina, and a park. Like many major civic development
efforts, there were numerous advances and setbacks. One unan-
ticipated consequence of the redevelopment effort in general, and
of Reynolds Metals Company's decision to withdraw its financial
backing in 1967 in particular, was the commitment of Louisville's

major banking institutions to complete the project. That decision had additional implications, primarily in leading a number of individual banks to build new offices downtown. These projects brought contemporary architecture to Louisville.

The Louisville Trust Bank took full advantage of the riverfront redevelopment, taking a prime site overlooking the Belvedere and the Ohio River. Two simple rectangular forms combine in this building—a twenty-story tower and a four-story base—creating an awkward relationship between the two. The tower is pushed back on the base to take advantage of the river views; but this moves the vertical circulation to the back of the site, making it a long walk for visitors arriving from Main Street. Al J. Schneider, who developed and built the structure, was involved in a number of the projects that made up the waterfront redevelopment, including the Galt House.

42. JEFFERSON COUNTY JUDICIAL CENTER
700 West Jefferson Street, Central Business District
Louis & Henry
1999

In the last decade, Louisville has seen the emergence of a significant art-glass industry, led by architect/artist Kenneth von Roenn. Von Roenn's designs have become substantial components of a number of important buildings, including the fountain at the Louisville Water Company. At the same time that Louis & Henry designed the Water Company, they were working on the Jefferson County Judicial Center, a major expansion of Arrasmith, Judd & Rapp's Justice Complex of 1974.

Throughout much of their history, Louis & Henry's work has exemplified a willingness to refine the local facility with concrete construction; but this building, like the Water Company headquarters, turns its explorations to glass curtain-wall construction. A ten-story curving curtain wall acts as a major element of the building, contrasting nicely with a monumental Corinthian pavilion, seven stories in height, at the entry.

43. LOUISVILLE POLICE DEPARTMENT HEADQUARTERS
633 Jefferson Street, Central Business District
Arrasmith and Tyler, Al J. Schneider
1954

Modernist William S. Arrasmith is known for his streamlined moderne Greyhound bus terminals throughout the U.S. The police headquarters is one large mass, divided vertically into two volumes. The lower one-and-a-half story is sheathed in polished, pink, Texas-granite panels, while the upper two-story volume is unpolished green-and-white Vermont marble. The facades have steel horizontal ribbon windows that divide the primary facade into three bays. The original main entrance was at the ground level on Seventh Street. In the early 1970s, that entry was closed, and access to the building is now made via a concrete ramp near the corner of Jefferson Street. The two-story main lobby is largely original. The floors are green terrazzo, and the walls are polished pink granite panels that extend from the floor to the ceiling. The staircases have polished stainless-steel handrails. An enclosed concrete bridge, added in the late 1970s, attaches the police headquarters to the Hall of Justice across Jefferson Street.

44. LOUISVILLE METRO OFFICE BUILDING
(Fire Station No. 2/Sinking Fund Building)
617 West Jefferson Street, Central Business District
McDonald Brothers
Landmark designation: NRHP, 1980; LL
1891

Composed of red sandstone and English bond brick, this asymmetrical Richardsonian Romanesque fire station is one of the city's several adaptively reused old stations. The handsome red facade is divided vertically into three parts by projecting minarets with rounded pinnacles and floral Sullivanesque bases, a five-story drying tower, which once supported a domed belfry, and two three-story pedimented sections of equal size. Relief sculptures in the two-diapered pediments depict on the left, Benjamin Bache, who was an early fire chief, and on the right, Emile Barbour, who was a bookkeeper. Horizontally, the facade is composed of five parts. A heavy, rusticated, sandstone first floor is tied together by three broad arches for fire-truck entrances and a dentiled string-course. The pendentives, formed by the voussoirs of the arches, contain

relief sculptures of a fireman's hat, an axe, and a horn surrounded by a curled fire hose and nozzle. A second floor made of brick,
which was used for offices, meeting rooms, and sleeping rooms, is
articulated by segmental arch windows, separated by engaged columns and sandstone window heads and sills. A third-floor dormitory is indicated by rectangular windows with sandstone heads and
sills, a fourth floor with four small arched windows, and a fifth floor
with a single window, false pediment. An arcade lookout tops off the
tower. The historic interior has been obliterated by renovation, but
inside on display is a historic photo depicting the fire station, fire
engines, and firemen.

45. JEFFERSON COUNTY HALLS OF JUSTICE
(Jefferson County Jail and Courts Complex)
600 West Jefferson Street, Central Business District
Arrasmith and Judd
1974

The Arrasmith, Judd & Rapp firm is one of Louisville's oldest
architectural firms, dating back to at least 1926, when William
Arrasmith joined Hermann Wischmeyer's firm (itself established in
1906). It has distinguished projects throughout the twentieth century and is most noted for more than one hundred Greyhound bus
terminals, built across the country in the 1930s and 1940s. The firm
has carried out significant institutional and municipal work and

in recent decades has been actively involved in the creation of the medical-center complex east of downtown.

The Jefferson County Jail and Courts Complex marries the geometric forms of modern architecture to the strengths of Louisville's construction industry. The concrete building is well crafted, utilizing a significant cantilever of the upper stories to emphasize its massing and to increase its presence on the street. It is connected by pedestrian walkways to new judicial facilities both south and west of it, anchoring a major municipal complex.

46. LOUISVILLE CITY HALL ANNEX
611 West Jefferson Street, Central Business District
C. A. Curtain
Landmark designation: NRHP, 1976
1905–1909

C. A. Curtain, a Louisville architect better known for his restrained ecclesiastical projects than for his civic work, designed this annex in 1905. His other local projects include the Columbia Building (now demolished), St. Charles Borremeo Church, Church of St. Brigid (1912), and the Priory for St. Louis Bertrand Church done in association with John Bacon Hutchings (1890, now demolished). This colossal three-story building is adjacent to City Hall and one of three buildings—with City Hall (1870–73) and the Sinking Fund Building (1891)—that make up the Louisville City Hall complex.

The composite Corinthian tetra-style portico supports a third-story attic. The entablature of this portico is heavily articulated and adorned with modillions and dentils. The mass of the entablature completely conceals the third floor along West Jefferson Street. The ground floor contains a grand marble hypostyle hall, decorated with carved-wood desks and counters and marble busts of Louisville politicians. John Diebold and Sons Stone Company completed the stonework.

47. LOUISVILLE CITY HALL
601 West Jefferson Street
John Andrewartha and C. S. Mergell, Henry Whitestone
Landmark designation: NRHP, 1976
1870–1873

This eclectic stone structure expressively represents the boisterous government and burgeoning bureaucracy that served a fast growing post–Civil War commercial, industrial, and agricultural center of diverse interests and people. Winners of an 1867 design competition that brought a prize of $500, John Andrewartha and C. S. Mergell finished working drawings for three stories and a basement in 1870 with C. L. Stancliff & Co. and I. M. St. John, the city engineer who supervised the construction at a cost of $464,778. The combination of a classical revival temple front with an Italian palazzo and a Second Empire clock tower (replaced in 1876 by Henry Whitestone's tower after a fire destroyed the original) yields an awkward design that is rich with varied architectural details. This building consolidated government offices efficiently and symbolized the people's values and identity through mixed but fashionable architectural expressions, relief sculpture, a clock on all four sides of the mansard tower, and the scale and mass of the building. A train powering through a wilderness (including palm trees, indicating Louisville's southern inclinations) in the tympanum of the pediment that crowns the high temple entrance represents industrial "Progress 1871." Sculpted heads of horses, mules, cattle, pigs, and sheep over the windows on the second floor acknowledge the agricultural meaning of the city and the Bourbon Stock Yards. Visitors can view original drawings in the main lobby (unfortunately, it has lost its vaulted three-story space through renovation). The interior has a number of original details, including a stair to the main entrance with cast-iron steps and glass plugs.

48. JEFFERSON COUNTY COURTHOUSE
527 West Jefferson Street, Central Business District
Gideon Shryock, Albert Fink
Landmark designation: NRHP, 1972; LL
1835–1860

Upon its completion in 1860, the *Louisville Daily Journal* called Shryock's imposing Greek revival structure (the fifth Jefferson County Courthouse) an "elephantine monstrosity." Yet when it was threatened with demolition in the late 1940s, Louisville citizens mounted a spirited campaign to save it. Even Frank Lloyd Wright argued for its preservation. Gideon Shryock, who designed the building in 1835, studied under William Strickland and is responsible for other Greek revival buildings in Kentucky, such as the second State Capitol in Frankfort and the old Morrison College at Transylvania University in Lexington. He gave the courthouse a Doric portico with six columns, porticos on the wings, and a cupola. A full entablature with unelaborated frieze and metopes and a regular sequence of engaged pilasters help tie the building together.

This design was never fully realized, and Shryock resigned in 1842. Albert Fink, a bridge engineer, completed the courthouse in 1860, reducing Shryock's columns to four and eliminating the wing porticos and cupola. The old Fiscal Court retains its repeating ranges of cast-iron walkways and stairs. Over the years, other changes were made: in the rotunda, the first stair was replaced with a double cast-iron one, and the main floor was altered to carry the statue of Henry Clay. The courthouse was completely renovated in the early 1980s.

49. PNC BANK PLAZA
(Citizens Fidelity Bank)
500 West Jefferson Street, Central Business District
Welton Becket and Associates (Los Angeles)
1971

Maurice D. S. Johnson, board chair of Citizens Fidelity Bank at the time its offices and bank were built, was a strong advocate for modern architecture. His service on the boards of numerous civic organizations facilitated the acceptance of this new style of architecture across Louisville. Unfortunately for the talented local practitioners, he was also an advocate for architects from other cities: Welton Becket was hired for the Citizens Fidelity Bank commission. The building is a serviceable example of mid-century modernism but suffers in comparison to its neighbor on West Jefferson, the Liberty National Bank and Trust. The facade of the tower is particularly anonymous with its gridded array of identical precast-concrete panels, which form the fenestration pattern. A social club on the top floor and visible access at street level are the only variation in the system.

50. KENTUCKY HOME LIFE BUILDING
(Inter-Southern Insurance Building)
239-247 South Fifth Street, Central Business District
Brinton B. Davis, D. X. Murphy
Landmark designation: NRHP, 1980
1912–1913

The 20-story limestone and buff-brick Inter-Southern Insurance Building was the tallest building in Louisville until 1955. The president of Inter-Southern, James Richard Duffin, took the lead in securing the construction as the home of the company and one of the largest and finest office structures in Louisville. Brinton B.

Davis's other significant projects include much of Western Kentucky University in Bowling Green, the Jefferson County Armory (now the Gardens of Louisville), and the First Church of Christ Scientist in downtown Louisville. D. X. Murphy designed a matching east-wing addition in 1922 that contained banking offices. Kentucky Home Life Company purchased the building in 1932.

The massiveness of the exterior and its decorative proportions do not hint at the scale and magnificence of the interior. Based on the Baths of Caracalla, superbly detailed Corinthian columns line the three-story volume of the banking room and support the vaulted coffered ceiling above.

51. BANK ONE
(Liberty National Bank and Trust Company)
416 West Jefferson Street, Central Business District
Wagner and Potts with Wenceslao Sarmiento (Brazil)
1956–1960

The Louisville architecture firm Wagner and Potts, in association with the Brazilian architect Wenceslao Sarmiento (who at the time was the chief designer for the Bank Building and Equipment Corporation of St. Louis), designed the Liberty National Bank and Trust Company's ultra modern headquarters in 1956. The six-story building, intended to enhance the street and bring visual distinction to the entire neighborhood, is set back thirty feet from Jefferson

Street and has an open grass courtyard. The primary facade is composed of panels of granite, glass, and brass hung from a metal framework and is considered the first example of curtain-wall construction in Louisville. This skin is divided into a rhythmic pattern of twenty-foot bays, broken down into four equal five-foot subdivisions. At each end of the curtain wall is a massive volume, which acts as a visual anchor for the curtain wall and heightens the dynamic expression of the transparent nature of the building envelope.

A dramatic free-floating stainless-steel staircase, resembling a stack of falling quarters (adapted from Michelangelo's Laurentian Library in Florence, Italy, 1559) was unfortunately removed during a 2002–03 renovation. The building is now owned and operated by the Bank One Corporation.

52. KENTUCKY INTERNATIONAL CONVENTION CENTER
(Commonwealth Convention Center)
211 Fourth Street, Central Business District
Luckett & Farley
1977

The initial version of the Commonwealth Convention Center was a major component of the effort to revitalize downtown Louisville in the 1970s. Located on Jefferson from Third to Fourth Streets (known as the Tyler block when the Tyler Building and many other businesses were a vital commercial core of the city), the center's design was greeted coolly by a citizen advisory board for its "fortress-like appearance." Alternatives were considered, but, in the interest of time, the decision was made to go ahead.

Twenty years later, when it was decided to expand the center, great care was taken by the designers to connect the building to the street through the extensive use of glass from the conference rooms lining the major convention space. However, the initial design of the expansion created a new controversy: it proposed to close Third Street between Market and Jefferson Streets, a vital and symbolic thoroughfare in the city. This time there was a much better conclusion: the center was raised a story to allow Third Street to pass underneath the connection from the new addition to the original building. The addition's strongest features are the double trusses, each 55 feet tall, which allow the roof to span the convention area without internal columns, and the terrazzo floor in the Third Street vestibule, patterned on the course of the Ohio River.

53. LOVE BOUTIQUE
(City Blueprint Company)
140 West Jefferson Street, Central Business District
Jasper D. Ward
1968–1969

The City Blueprint Building is a simple structure in the context of Louisville's architectural heritage, for it uses elementary forms to generate dynamic volumes and unified spaces. As with most of Jasper D. Ward's civic projects, he used a brutalist concrete structure to define the exterior envelope, which oscillates between form, texture, surface, and space.

By using various details such as ocular windows, an enlarged rain-gutter system, and a floating blue cube above the entry, Ward's solution becomes more than a place for making blueprints. It becomes a sign, not only an external introduction of the company logo to the consumer, but also an internal signifier of the two-story display space that looks out through round windows along the West Jefferson Street facade.

The details embedded in the concrete have rich surface textures and depict an interplay between the structure and the formwork used to create it. A second-story storage room runs along the south facade and is reached by an exterior ramp and an interior staircase. The interior of the building is developed as a series of interlocking spaces marked by their original function and is one open and continuous volume that reads as rooms with varying heights and passages.

The City Blueprint Company closed its business in 2003. The new owner kept the sign cube intact, and the new sign is faithful to the architect's intent for it. The building is now an adult book and movie store named the Love Boutique.

54. OLD JEFFERSON COUNTY JAIL
514 West Liberty Street, Central Business District
D. X. Murphy & Brothers
Landmark designation: NRHP, 1973
1902–1905

The jail is an outstanding example of American civic architecture and reflects the Chicago School style (the cornice of the cell block bears a strong resemblance to that of Burnham and Root's Monadnock Building, 1889–91) and is reminiscent of Egyptian prisons of the nineteenth century. It comprises two wings: one for cells and another for administration. Architecturally, they are differentiated by function and internal arrangements, yet they form a unified whole. Each wing exhibits a base (rusticated limestone), body (tapered rusticated limestone), and head (brick). The corbelled brick cornice and tall arched windows lighten the appearance and lend a vertical presence to the brick building mass.

Designed by D. X. Murphy & Brothers (a descendant firm of mid-nineteenth-century Louisville architect Henry Whitestone), the building reflects the era's trends in sanitation, security, and mechanics. The 240 cells had an innovative locking system that allowed guards the choice of opening only one cell or all cells on each tier. The building was a unique solution to corrections design, and at the time of its completion in 1905 it was widely considered the most modern correctional facility in the country.

Stratton O. Hammon and Wehr Construction Company were responsible for the 1947 renovation, and K. Norman Berry and

Associates, with the R & W Construction Company, renovated the structure in 1982–83. The old jail now houses the Jefferson County Court facilities, government offices, and the Jefferson County Law Library.

55. FEDERAL RESERVE BANK OF ST. LOUIS— LOUISVILLE BRANCH

410 South Fifth Street, Central Business District
Russell, Mullgardt, Schwarz, and Van Hoefen (St. Louis)
1958–1959

The Federal Reserve Bank of St. Louis has four locations in the U.S. Eighth District: its headquarters in St. Louis and branch offices in Little Rock, Memphis, and Louisville. The St. Louis–based firm Russell, Mullgardt, Schwarz, and Van Hoefen designed the Louisville branch. This St. Louis firm is known for its comprehensive redevelopment plan of the St. Louis Central City area.

The building is actually the reincarnation of the Federal Reserve Bank in Louisville: the Louisville Home Federal Building (Louisville National Bank) was designed by D. X. Murphy in 1914 on the site of the former German Bank Building along Fifth Street. Modern in style, the steel-framed building has three discrete masses and facades of reinforced concrete clad with buff-colored Bedford Indiana limestone. It sits on a polished black granite base, with plantings that introduce a pedestrian scale to the building. The main entry, along South Fifth Street, is at the intersection of the two volumes above. Square columns mark this entrance. The building's surfaces have fin walls attached to them that act as brise soliel sun-screens. This fenestration continues around the western side as well, but with fewer window openings.

The building operates around the clock. Interior spaces include cash and check-processing services, banking operations, office spaces, a cafeteria, fitness facilities, and below-ground parking. The interior lobby is simple yet elegant with its polished marble finishes and light yellow-orange terrazzo floors, which give a regal presence to the bank.

56. OLD HOUSE RESTAURANT
432 South Fifth Street, Central Business District
Rezon E. Butler
1829

This raised-brick, side entry hall townhouse with two stories and a basement is the oldest extant residence in downtown Louisville. The stair leads to a porch, and the segmental arch over the entrance with attenuated Doric columns on each side of the door indicates incipient Greek revival influences during the late federal period. The street facade presents a "two-thirds" Georgian elevation of English bond masonry, divided into three bays, articulated by rectangular windows with stone lintels and wood sills, and capped with a heavy wood cornice. Original cast-iron fence and stair railings, painted over and over, suggest the generations of people who have lived here.

The basement floor may have been used as a doctor's office in the 1830s; in 1868, Dr. J. F. Canine, a dentist, and his wife, Elizabeth, purchased the structure. He designed and produced dental instruments in the house, and two additional generations of Canine dentists lived here after the first Dr. Canine died. Dr. Canine was the first dentist in Louisville to replace the foot drill with a steam-driven drill and the first to use a bowl with running water. This may also have been the first steam-heated and electrified residence in Louisville. A steel frame holds in place a buckling side wall of this rambling urban house, which stretches far back into its narrow city lot. The building has been vacant several years.

57. GARDENS OF LOUISVILLE
(Jefferson County Armory)
525 West Muhammad Ali Boulevard, Central Business District
Brinton B. Davis
Landmark designation: NRHP, 1980
1905

The Jefferson County Armory was the first armory built in the state of Kentucky and was designed by the prominent Kentucky architect Brinton B. Davis. Caldwell and Drake Builders constructed the armory in 1905. Through 1946, the structure operated as a military-training hall and induction center until the Kentucky National Guard outgrew the facility and moved to the state fairgrounds. The building has served many functions, including a refugee shelter for the more than 6,000 people affected by the flood of

1937; an entertainment venue for Louis Armstrong, Frank Sinatra, Elvis Presley, and Igor Stravinsky; and the site of national conventions and political rallies for President Harry S Truman and Martin Luther King Jr.

The main facade is three stories high. The center of the building entrance has six two-story fluted Ionic columns supporting the building cornice and arched facade details. The original entry has been replaced with pinkish-brown granite and an illuminated marquee sign. The exterior is mostly original. The building has a rusticated limestone base, a running bond buff-brick veneer shaft, and a smooth ashlar cornice. The armory was extensively renovated in 1963 and renamed the Convention Center. In 1975, the name was changed to the Louisville Gardens to avoid confusion with the newly opened Commonwealth Convention Center (now the Kentucky International Convention Center). Following a $350,000 renovation in 1998, the name was changed to the Gardens of Louisville. It is currently managed by the Kentucky Center for the Arts and is used for public assemblies, large-scale exhibitions, concerts, conferences, and sporting events, including the Kentucky State Sweet Sixteen basketball tournament.

58. REPUBLIC OFFICE BUILDING
429 West Muhammad Ali Boulevard, Central Business District
Joseph and Joseph
Landmark designation: NRHP, 1982
1912–1916

The Republic Office Building is one of the first office buildings designed by the Louisville firm Joseph and Joseph. Like most of their projects, the Republic Building combines the different stylistic tendencies of the two brothers. Alfred S. Joseph Sr.'s preference for classical styles was a direct result of his training at the architecture offices of McDonald Brothers, McDonald and Sheblessy, and McDonald and Dodd, which he left in 1908 to start the Joseph and Joseph firm. Oscar Joseph, who received his formal training as a civil engineer at the University of Michigan, preferred the stylistic influences of the Italian and Spanish Renaissance. Dominating the composition of the building are classical revival characteristics, but there are strong elements of the Italian Renaissance, especially in the details.

The Republic Office Building is an eleven-story buff-brick and stone commercial building. Stone with green terra-cotta tile unifies the first, second, and third floors; buff brick makes up floors four through nine; and stone with ornate detailing composes floors ten and eleven. A black cornice with modillions and dentils tops the building.

59. CATHEDRAL OF THE ASSUMPTION
443 South Fifth Street, Central Business District
William Keely, spire restoration by Bickel Gibson
Landmark designation: NRHP, 1977; LL
1849–1852

This Gothic revival cathedral is the seat of the Archdiocese of Louisville, but it began in 1805 as a simple Roman Catholic parish church called the St. Louis Church. The parish built its second church, of brick and stucco, on this site in 1830. In 1841, that church was changed to a cathedral and was replaced in 1852 with the current soaring structure, which has a central nave and two side aisles leading to a one-bay chancel at the east end. Initially, the cathedral also had stuccoed brick walls and buttresses with stone trim that helped the interior octagonal piers form side aisles and held the pointed arched windows and the clerestory above. William Keely, a prominent ecclesiastical architect of Roman Catholic churches in the nineteenth century, designed the core church without a tower. Isaiah Rogers and Henry Whitestone designed the Wren-like octagonal clock tower and spire that forms the main entrance, the two side entrances, and the stepped narthex on the west front of the church. Behind and underneath the altar in the chancel is an undercroft with remains of two nineteenth-century bishops. Patrick Bannon designed and built the interior details and plasterwork. The church was remodeled in 1910 with a new altar and floor, and in 1912 the plain windows of the nave were replaced with stained glass. In 1969, another extensive renovation was undertaken, but, after a restoration study, the church was returned to its pre-1969 condition. Bickel Gibson restored the spire in 1988. This current condition includes a striking nave ceiling of cross vaults, bossed liernes, and stars on a blue background.

60. GALLERIA

South Fourth Street, at Muhammad Ali Boulevard, Central Business District
Skidmore Owings and Merrill (New York)
1982

The Galleria has been controversial throughout its history. An out-growth of the 1968 plan by Victor Gruen to redevelop downtown Louisville, the project took more than a decade to implement. Plans developed in 1975 by Skidmore Owings and Merrill were ultimate-ly carried out. In the style of a suburban development, the design called for two large office towers flanking Fourth Street and a mall of enclosed retail stores at the street and mezzanine levels. The proj-ect was controversial in part because it called for the demolition of two significant historic structures, the Will Sales Building and the Atherton Building. Additionally, it reinforced the closing of Fourth Street to vehicular traffic, which had been implemented in the late 1970s in an effort to replicate pedestrian malls in other cities. Even though a large, sloping glass roof was built over the street to enhance the pedestrian experience, retail activity continued to decline.

The Galleria may have had its best effect on areas around it. For example, the Seelbach Hotel was renovated after plans for the Galleria were implemented. But, after an initial surge of interest, the retail component foundered; the suburban mall works best in the suburbs, not when transplanted to downtown. Because Fourth Street (traditionally the center for commercial property in down-town Louisville) was closed to Broadway, the project also had a deleterious effect on retail activity along its length. Only in recent years has Fourth Street been partially reopened. In 2001, plans were announced to renovate the Galleria as an entertainment venue and to completely open Fourth Street to vehicular traffic again (although the sloping glass roof will remain).

61. LANDMARK BUILDING
(U.S. Customs House and Post Office)
304 West Liberty Street, Central Business District
Ammi B. Young
Landmark designation: NRHP, 1977
1851–1858

This is one variation of several customs houses and post offices that Ammi B. Young designed for sites throughout the U.S. as the first supervising architect in the U.S. Treasury Department. Typically, the supervising architect provided the design for local superintending architects, in this case Ellias E. Williams, to carry out in cooperation with the Treasury's Bureau of Construction and local builders and suppliers. Designed in the fashionable Italianate palazzo style with three main floors, a rusticated base, bracketed cornice and parapet, and rounded windows with drip moldings, this building's regular massing, chaste detailing, and finely cut Indiana-limestone walls helped reduce the cost of materials, because industrial methods for fabricating building parts could be taken better advantage of. The simplification of parts also lowered construction costs, an advantage that twentieth-century architects developed into an art

form. Like all federal buildings at that time, this structure was tech-
nologically advanced, standardized, and fireproofed. It had cast-
iron stairs and window frames, concrete floors, interior brick walls,
running water, water closets, and a hot-air furnace. The standard
floor plan provided a post office on the first floor, a courtroom
on the second, offices on the third, and storage in the basement.
Walter Haldeman, publisher of the *Courier-Journal* and *Louisville
Times,* bought the building in 1896 for storage and remodeled it
for the newspaper business in 1911–12. WHAS, the first Louisville
radio station, began broadcasting here in 1922. After a remodeling
in 1950, the Louisville Chamber of Commerce became the main
tenant of the office building, which was remodeled extensively on
the exterior in 1979 and 1999. Only the third-floor windows are
original. This landmark is among the few remaining pre–Civil War
buildings in Louisville.

62. KAUFMAN-STRAUS BUILDING
(L. S. Ayres Building)
427–37 South Fourth Street, Central Business District
Mason Maury
Landmark designation: NRHP, 1983
1902–1903

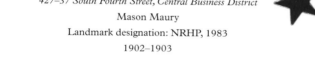

The L. S. Ayers Building is located on the site of the original Public Library. It was constructed by the library for both additional space and commercial rental units. According to architectural historian Theodore Brown, the six-story building (also known as the Kaufman-Straus Building) is "one of the best works of Louisville architect Mason Maury." Maury, a proponent of Chicago School architecture, designed the Kentucky Electric Building (1912) in the same style. This building consciously reflects characteristics of the Gage Building (1898–99) in Chicago, designed by Holabird & Roche, who hired Louis Sullivan to design the structure's decorative facade. The original facade of the Kaufman-Straus Building remains intact, although it was substantially rebuilt after the 1937 flood undermined it. The dominant characteristic of the facade is its verticality, which is emphasized by the four slender piers that follow the line of the steel structure behind the masonry and terra-cotta. To minimize the impression of a heavy mass, Maury carried the piers from the base to the cornice. As in the Gage Building, the top of each pier is decorated with terra-cotta floral ornamentation. Until recently, the building has been encased inside the Louisville Galleria. In 2003, the Galleria connection along Fourth Street was removed, once again exposing the building. Current designs will maintain the street level as commercial space, and the street will serve as a pedestrian thoroughfare.

63. STARKS BUILDING

455 South Fourth Street, Central Business District
D. H. Burnham & Company (Chicago)
Landmark designation: NRHP, 1985
1913

This Louisville landmark building, on the site of the former First Christian Church, is a fifteen-story commercial office building, located in the heart of the Central Business District. Louisville businessman John P. Starks purchased the church site in 1909 for $350,000 and in 1913 commissioned the prominent Chicago architectural firm D. H. Burnham & Company to design the building in association with the Louisville architectural firm McDonald and Dodd. The building's massing and form reflect the Chicago School tradition. It is an excellent example of turn-of-the-twentieth-century commercial architecture, with Beaux Arts details, cream-colored brick, and terra-cotta trim.

The plan, originally U-shaped, became a four-sided building with a central light well in 1926, when the Chicago architectural firm Graham, Anderson, Probst & White expanded the north and south wings eastward along Muhammad Ali Boulevard, taking over the site of the Macauley Theater, one of America's premier playhouses since 1873. In 1982, the Louisville firm Bickel Gibson spanned the interior courtyard with a dramatic Plexiglas-covered aluminum space frame. The Bickel Gibson project includes a ten-story velvet chandelier that suspends from the space frame and is viewed through a lower-level aperture. A marble promenade, which serves as an air-conditioned dining area during the day and as a banquet hall for receptions at night, completes the interior of the courtyard.

64. MORRISEY PARKING GARAGE
(Bosler's Fireproof Garage)
423 South Third Street, Central Business District
J. J. Gaffney
Landmark designation: NRHP, 1983
1919

Bosler's Fireproof Garage was one of the first parking structures in Louisville. Located in the heart of the Central Business District, it was heated and provided related services, such as cleaning and polishing. This Romanesque revival structure accentuates its utilitarian function. The massing of the facade provides architectural continuity with the buildings along Third Street and is symmetrical and divided into three bays. The central bay provides entry to the parking structure and is flanked at the first floor by two rectangular business storefronts, with three arched openings at the second floor. Several businesses, such as Goodrich Tires, Garage Equipment and Supply, a fruit market, bookstores, and a surgical supply store, have occupied the storefront. The structure has a basement, three levels of parking, and a spiral ramp that forms a cylindrical mass at the rear of the building.

65. SECOND DISTRICT POLICE SUBSTATION
(Louisville Water Company Building)
435 South Third Street, Central Business District
Theodore A. Leisen
1910

The Louisville Water Company Building is a three-story, buff-brick structure with a central one-story porch with double Ionic columns and capitals and flanking side stairs. The Water Company had been located on Third Street since 1882, and this building opened on December 19, 1910. At the time of its opening, it was one of the best-equipped and most spacious water company offices in the U.S. In 1914, a meter house and shop were erected on the adjoining lot. Theodore A. Leisen designed this addition in a similar architectural style to the original structure. In 1998, the Louisville Water Company moved into its new headquarters at 550 South Third Street. The building is currently the Second District Police Substation.

66. CHRIST CHURCH CATHEDRAL
421 South Second Street, Central Business District
Architect unknown, renovation by John Milner Associates
Landmark designation: NRHP, 1973
1824–1911

Attributed to two carpenters by the names of Graham and Ferguson, Christ Church was built as a rectangular, brick federal meeting house with a 56-foot interior span of wood and an entrance and bell tower. A western gallery was added in 1832, and John Stierwalt created the first additions to the east end in 1845–46. The church stayed in that form for only a decade, then began to evolve dramatically in response to outside religious and architectural influences. During his formative student years at the National Academy of Design in New York City, from 1843 to 1844, W. H. Redin learned the mandates for correct churches, laid down by the Pugins in England, through Richard Upjohn's Trinity Church (1839–46). Accordingly, in 1858, Redin made the chancel space ecclesiologically more correct by designing an apse over the altar in a crescendo of vaults with liernes held by foliated columns.

In 1870, after he had designed churches in Pewee Valley and Anchorage, Redin enlarged the chancel and replaced the original tower on the west side with a Norman Romanesque facade of Pewee Valley limestone, which has a pedimented entrance and narthex, framed by two asymmetrical towers. Only the smaller two-story left tower has been completed. The larger right tower is strengthened at the corners by double buttresses that end as minarets. In 1894, the church became a cathedral. It has a number of striking stained-glass windows, some of which were constructed by Tiffany Glass Company in New York. The cathedral has recently undertaken a renovation designed by John Milner Associates.

67. LOUISVILLE MAGAZINE
(Independence Life and Accident Insurance Company Building)
137 West Muhammad Ali Boulevard, Central Business District
Nevin & Morgan
1962

The Independence Life and Accident Insurance Company Building is constructed of reinforced concrete with limestone facing. The building sits back from the property line and on a plinth above the street to allow vegetation to exist at the pedestrian level, accentuating the building's appearance. The entrance to the office building is through three sets of glass doors, covered by a low concrete overhang that forms one of the building's three distinctive massings. The insurance company used the curtain-wall system to provide an image of stability. The design incorporates a variety of fixed and operable panels, which include bright-blue glazed-aluminum inserts at the spandrel conditions to mask the structure behind them. The third building mass is a cubic volume that sits behind the entry and curtain wall. The building is now the headquarters for *Louisville Magazine*.

68. GREYHOUND LINES
(Greyhound Bus Terminal)
720 West Muhammad Ali Boulevard, Central Business District
Harrison and Abramowitz (New York)
1970

The Greyhound Bus Terminal was one of the few built components on the site of a mostly unbuilt urban-renewal project west of downtown Louisville. The decline of the Central Business District began in the 1950s and forced reluctant city officials to take a much more active role in planning and development than they had in the past. A ten-block area east of downtown was successfully developed into a medical center, but a larger area of development, more than 300 acres, intended for local government buildings just west of down-town did not materialize. Instead, a few scattered office buildings and structures for housing were built.

A low modern building, the facility is largely taken up with a waiting room. Concrete construction, much in favor in Louisville during this period, was used. The design has slight resonances with the low, streamlined elements of the art moderne style associated with the glory days of bus travel, although its proportions seem more in keeping with an airline terminal. The architect was the New York firm Harrison and Abramowitz, known best for its work on the United Nations Building. Harrison and Abramowitz were also designing the First National Bank Building on Main Street in Louisville at the same time. It is ironic that the architect primarily responsible for the great modern bus stations across the country, William Arrasmith, practiced in Louisville. This project replaced Arrasmith's own Greyhound Bus Terminal of 1928, which was demolished in the 1970s.

69. SEELBACH-HILTON HOTEL
500 South Fourth Street, Central Business District
Frank Mills Andrews
Landmark designation: NRHP, 1975
1905

Frank Mills Andrews, the architect for the state capitols in Kentucky and Montana and known for his hotel designs in New York (the Hotel McAlpin) and Washington, D.C. (the George Washington and the Arlington Hotels), designed the "new" Seelbach Hotel at 500 South Fourth Street. This Beaux Arts structure replaced the Renaissance revival European Seelbach Hotel (1856–57) designed by Isaiah Rogers and Henry Whitestone at 600 West Main Street. Opening in 1905, it was one of the first buildings in Louisville to incorporate steel-frame construction, which had been developing in Chicago and New York since the late 1880s. In 1907, William

J. Dodd expanded the hotel by designing a wing on the southwest portion of the building.

The building is noted for its architecture and decor. The entrance lobby maintains many of the original materials, such as marble finishes from Vermont, Switzerland, and Italy, as well as mahogany-and-bronze paneling and accents. The chandelier that illuminates the lobby originally hung in the Phoenix Hotel in Lexington. In 1904, Arthur Thomas, one of the leading artists of his day, was commissioned to paint large murals, depicting scenes from Kentucky's history, in the hotel's lobby. An attempt in 1960 to "modernize" the lobby by lowering the ceilings covered the murals for almost 20 years, until a 1970s renovation uncovered them. Unfortunately, the owner at the time tried to remove one of the murals to sell it, and it was destroyed. A renovation in the 1980s by then owner Roger Davis meticulously cleaned and restored the murals. Since an original or photographic image of the destroyed mural did not exist, Davis commissioned a California artist to paint a mirror image of the remaining mural above the bell stand.

The hotel has three exemplary public rooms that merit seeing, the Rathskeller (on the lower floor), the Oakroom (on the mezzanine), and the Grand Ballroom (on the tenth floor). The Rathskeller (1907) is believed to be one of the last remaining large-scale spaces in the world made entirely of hand-decorated Rookwood pottery of Cincinnati. Intricately painted leather, detailing the signs of the zodiac, covers portions of the vaulted ceiling and bar area. The Oakroom, decorated in hand-carved American oak, was also part of the 1907 addition. The space originally served as a gentleman's billiard hall and card room and was a favorite hangout for gangsters such as Al Capone. The Grand Ballroom, immortalized by F. Scott Fitzgerald in *The Great Gatsby,* is the centerpiece of the hotel's architectural elegance and decor. A 1982 renovation restored the ballroom in the Beaux Arts style. An eighteenth-century mantelpiece salvaged from a private home in Pennsylvania, creates a focal point in the West Ballroom. A 1990 restoration installed an intricately designed carpet by the London-based Axminister Carpet Company.

70. MARMADUKE BUILDING
(Parr Building)
520 South Fourth Street, Central Business District
J. J. Gaffney
Landmark designation: NRHP, 1991
1885, 1916 (new facade)

The Marmaduke Building was built in 1885 for Daniel G. Parr, a local merchant. In 1904, Parr died and left the building to his daughter, Virginia Marmaduke Sail. Sail hired Louisville architect J. J. Gaffney in 1916 to redesign the building's storefront. Although the plan of the building is typical of commercial buildings of that time, in terms of its elevation the Marmaduke represents an intriguing amalgamation of classical revival and Chicago School styles.

The building, known for its uniquely engineered construction method, is adjacent to the Seelbach-Hilton Hotel. It is five stories and has brick-bearing exterior walls faced with stone, but an internal frame of structural steel at the second-floor level cantilevers six feet away from the primary structure and supports the remaining facade above. The storefront as seen today more closely represents the original facade design. The primary facade was reconstructed in 1991 to replace the 1947 design in order to better represent the 1916 commercial storefront with its deep entry recesses and large expanses of glass.

71. PENDENNIS CLUB

218 West Muhammad Ali Boulevard, Central Business District

Nevin, Wischmeyer & Morgan

1927–1928

Modeled after an English gentleman's club, the Pendennis Club was established in Louisville in 1881 and became one of the most widely recognized social clubs in Kentucky. Its first clubhouse was located at the former William B. Belknap mansion on Walnut Street (now Muhammad Ali Boulevard) between Third and Fourth Streets. In 1928, the Pendennis Club opted for Frederick Morgan's plan for a Georgian building at Second and Walnut streets, site of the old Caldwell mansion and the Cadle Memorial United Brethren Church.

The building is a three-story Georgian revival structure of brick and Indiana limestone. Set back from Muhammad Ali Boulevard, it sits upon a stone terrace outlined by a limestone balustrade. The building houses a library, several dining and meeting rooms, a men's athletic area (complete with a squash court), and a main ballroom, where Louisvillian Muhammad Ali fought several of his early amateur boxing matches. Henry Bain, creator of the now-famous Henry Bain meat sauce—a Kentucky Derby and year-round Louisville favorite—was an elevator operator who worked his way up to maitre d' of the club in the 1880s.

72. BARRINGTON PLACE APARTMENTS
(Trinity Towers)
537 South Third Street, Central Business District
Tafel and Schickli
1962

The Trinity Towers, along with the 800 Apartment Building (800 South Fourth Street), represent Louisville's experimentation in high-rise living in the 1960s. Sponsored by the Trinity Temple

Methodist Church, the tower uniquely incorporates both religious activities (on floors one and two) and residential units for elderly citizens (on floors three through seventeen). The vertical emphasis of the north and south walls leads the eye upward to the Chapel in the Sky, a rooftop sun deck and penthouse lobby.

The building was designed to lessen the negative effect of solar-radiated heat and glare. The result was a nearly enclosed and blank facade on the east and west sides of the building. A narrow vertical slit in the wall opens into the hallway on each floor, allowing light deep into the building interior.

73. HILLIARD LYONS BUILDING
(Louisville Recreational Building—Madrid Ballroom)
543 South Third Street, Central Business District
E. T. Hutchings
Landmark designation: NRHP, 1985
1929

The Louisville Recreational Building, containing the Madrid Ballroom, was considered "the place to dance" from the 1920s to the 1940s. The Madrid had a large dance floor and was decorated with golden walls and richly colored tapestries. As the Big Band era declined, the ballroom eventually closed when its lease expired, and in 1952 the building underwent a significant interior renovation. It was later purchased by the Hilliard Lyons Company and currently serves as its offices.

74. SPEED BUILDING

311–33 Guthrie Green, Central Business District
Hartman and Loomis
Landmark designation: NRHP, 1983
1913–1917

The Speed Building is a four-story structure clad in white terra-cotta tile. Hartman and Loomis's other commissions in Louisville include the Norton Company Building and the J. B. Speed Art Museum. Completed in 1917, the Speed Building combines new materials and classical motifs. Both the Guthrie Green and Fourth Street facades have lower-level storefront windows, which remain relatively unornamented. While similar in style and material, the Guthrie Green facade is composed of four distinct sections that vary in height and detail. It is one of the largest surviving structures in Louisville to use glazed brick and terra-cotta detailing exclusively.

75. LOUISVILLE WATER COMPANY HEADQUARTERS
550 South Third Street, Central Business District
Louis & Henry
1998

The Ohio River has bedeviled and benefited Louisville from the founding of the city. Floods have been a recurring obstacle, leading to the creation of major flood walls in lower-lying areas. On the positive side, in the mid-nineteenth century a waterworks was created, almost entirely owned by the city, and located on River Road at the foot of what is now Zorn Avenue; it has proved to be a substantial asset as the population has grown. The pumping station's tower remains in place as an emblem of that structure and its importance to Louisville.

The offices for the Water Company moved downtown early in the twentieth century; in 1998, they were moved a block to the present location, on the northwest corner of South Third and Chestnut Streets. The architects Louis & Henry honored the legacy of the river by incorporating design elements based on the Zorn Avenue tower and the flood wall. These elements protrude from a crisp glass curtain-wall facade, which curves back from South Third Street to create a public plaza. A gurgling fountain, accented with glass sculptures by Louisville architect and glass artisan Kenneth von Roenn, highlights the plaza.

76. BROWN MEMORIAL CHRISTIAN METHODIST EPISCOPAL (CME) CHURCH
(Center Street CME Church)
809 West Chestnut Street, Central Business District
Gideon Shryock
Landmark designation: NRHP, 1979
1864

Built in 1864, purchased by the Center Street CME Church in 1907, and renamed the Brown Memorial C.M.E. Church in 1954, this is the last work of Gideon Shryock (1802–80). A native Kentuckian, Shryock studied architecture under William Strickland, a pupil of Benjamin Henry Latrobe (designer of the U.S. Capitol), who worked with Thomas Jefferson on Monticello. As the city architect from 1835 to 1842, Shryock designed the Jefferson County Courthouse. Brown Memorial is a two-story rectangle with red brick walls, and its front elevation presents a complex but balanced mix of Greek and Romanesque revival details. The tall, brick gable end, composed of a white pediment with modillions typical of the Corinthian order, a plain entablature, and a pair of engaged pilasters on faced lime-stone plinths at the corners, is decidedly Greek revival. A projecting central plane, framed by tall Italianate windows, provides the sur-face for a modillioned pediment over the entrance with a support-ing entablature. Two engaged side pilasters with Corinthian-order capitals and limestone plinths frame the space; within, a scroll from the entablature attaches to a Italianate arch and hood molding with a tripartite stained-glass window in the tympanum over the modern front double door. The exterior side walls of alternating piers with corbelled capitals, plinths, and rounded windows with hood moldings are Italianate. A narthex provides a double stair to the large second-floor nave with a central aisle.

77. AT&T BUILDING
(South Central Bell Company Office Building)
521 West Chestnut Street, Central Business District
Marye, Vinour, Marye, and Armistead (Atlanta)
Landmark designation: NRHP, 1980
1930

The South Central Bell Company Office Building is one of Louisville's remaining intact art deco examples. Built on the site of the Casseday family mansion, the structure was designed by the Atlanta architectural firm Marye, Vinour, Marye, and Armistead, who had done similar structures for South Central Bell across the south. The building has five bays and concentrates its detailing at the first floor and at the roof parapets. It is composed of a granite base and has limestone entries that extend to the second floor. The remaining structure is composed of buff brick, a portion of which has ornamental chevron patterns.

The art deco lobby and foyer remain intact. The walls are sheathed in a golden-beige marble with terrazzo floors and a plastered ceiling. Original light fixtures remain.

78. ROMANO L. MAZZOLI FEDERAL BUILDING
600 Martin Luther King Jr. Place, Central Business District
Thomas J. Nolan & Sons, Hartstern, Louis & Henry
1968–1969

The Federal Office Building is a unique collaboration between four different Kentucky-based architecture and engineering firms. Congressman Frank W. Burke helped foster this joint venture to keep the project local. The architects were Thomas J. Nolan & Sons (Louisville) and Louis & Henry (Louisville); the engineers were

Fred J. Hartstern and Osman Senler (Louisville), and Watkins, Burrows, Mills, and Associates (Lexington).

Facing north, the Federal Building anchors the civic center. The building pulls back from the street to create a public plaza in front but has been characterized by noted architects Philip Johnson and Harry Weese as being out-of-scale with its surrounding context. A 1979 ten-story proposal for the Bell South Headquarters across Chestnut Street, designed by Keith Clements of Louis & Henry, addressed Johnson's and Weese's concern for scale by offering a comparable massing to that of the Federal Office Building. The Bell South Headquarters was eventually constructed as a six-story building.

The Federal Office Building has a reinforced concrete frame and poured-in-place concrete waffle-slab structure on a standard five-foot bay system, as determined by the General Services Administration (GSA). Larry Leis of Louis & Henry, the chief design architect, and Leslie Fream of Hartstern and Senler, the project engineer, utilized this grid system to establish bays of 25 feet on the north and south facades, within which precast concrete window bays were inserted. In keeping with Louisville's sophisticated concrete construction methods at the time, the building uses 3,346 precast units, designed by the precasters Dolt and Dew (the firm responsible for Norman Sweet's Catalyst and Chemicals Building, 1965). In contrast, the east and west facades are composed of four-by-eleven-foot limestone panels and are windowless, with the exception of the narrow nine-story window at either side. The building was renamed the Romano L. Mazzoli Federal Building in 1995, in recognition of the congressman's contributions to the federal government and to the city of Louisville (Congressman Mazzoli was in office from 1971 to 1995). In 2001, the Louisville architecture firm Godsey & Associates upgraded and modernized the facility.

79. RONALD-BRENNAN HOUSE
631 South Fifth Street, Central Business District
Architect unkown
Landmark designation: NRHP, 1975; LL
c. 1868

This is one of the few extant mid-Victorian brick mansions that were among the dozens built south of the commercial district in the 1850s and 1860s. The orderly Italianate facade has three stories, divided by limestone stringcourses; three bays, divided by different sizes and shapes of windows with varied hood moldings; and a side-entry bay with a delicate cast-iron porch, balustrade, and intricately carved doorway above. Limestone quoins give the corners expressive edges. The cornice of brackets, dentils, and wide overhang is capped with a flat roof. The main entrance, also with an elaborate mixed-Italianate surround, is recessed and leads to a side hall and stairs that wind to the third floor. The Victorian entry hall, with its reception mirrors and furniture, is original, and this is generally true of the furniture and appointments throughout the house, filled with the fashionable paraphernalia of Victorian days. Marble hearths, limestone hearths with carved sculpture, gas and electric dual chandeliers, glass chandeliers and fixtures, gas lights, Tiffany lamps, and ornate bay-window spaces combine to create one of the most preserved examples of a Victorian interior in Louisville. The doctor's office addition (1912) is an intact surgeon's office with waiting room, examination and operating room, and doctor's study with library, medicines, and instruments. The dining room has its original woodwork, doors, lead-glass windows, a stone hearth, and the original table, chairs, and sideboards. Upstairs, the bedrooms are in their original state, showing stained glass, hearths, beds, closets, chests, clothing, and photos of the famous Brennan family.

Now owned by Brennan House, it is open to visitors. Hourly tours are given Tuesday through Saturday, 1 P.M. to 4 P.M.

80. YWCA
(Elks Athletic Club)
604 South Third Street, Central Business District
Joseph and Joseph
Landmark designation: NRHP, 1979
1924

When the Elks Athletic Club opened in 1924, it had a large auditorium, ornate plaster moldings, marble staircases, a bowling alley, and an indoor swimming pool. The building, a strong example of the firm's work, incorporates classical details. Other significant Joseph and Joseph projects in Louisville include the Republic Office Building (1912–16) and the Kentucky Theater (1921). The upper floors—five through eight—served as sleeping quarters for club members, their guests, and the general public. The building contained all of the best obtainable modern conveniences of the time—telephone booths, a gymnasium, and grand ballroom.

The club was purchased in 1928 and adapted into a hotel, renamed the Henry Clay Hotel. In 1963, the Young Women's Christian Association (YWCA) purchased the building and relocated its facilities and programs there until it sold the property. The building closed in 1985, and, despite numerous failed attempts to revitalize the property, it sits vacant. Currently owned by the city, the concrete-framed building has a ballroom (capable of holding more than 1,000 people). Efforts to rehabilite could provide the area with apartments, a hotel, or a mixed-use development and offices.

81. HSA BROADBAND BUILDING
(Kentucky Electric Building)
619 South Fourth Street, Central Business District
attributed to Mason Maury or Clarke & Loomis, renovation by
Grossman Chapman Klarer
Landmark designation: NRHP, 1985
1912

The Kentucky Electric Building (now the HSA Broadband Building
and home to Louisville's three public radio stations) is a three-story
building, modest in scale but unique for Louisville in its integration
of cast-iron ornamentation with Chicago School detailing. It is one
of the last remaining buildings on Fourth Street's Theater Row.

The HSA Broadband Company (a provider of high-speed
Internet services) provided more than $500,000 for the building's
renovation. The lobby is named for former *Courier-Journal* president
Cyrus L. MacKinnon, whose widow, Helen, contributed $250,000.
Coupled with a major gift from the Kresge Foundation and more

than $500,000 from the radio stations' listeners, the building, which was nearly destroyed by fire in 1997, was elegantly renovated by the Louisville architecture firm Grossman Chapman Klarer, whose design emulates the emanation of sound waves. This motif continues onto the front facade. Undulating perforated metal panels, attached to the entrance canopy, float above the floor-to-ceiling storefront glass windows. These windows invite passersby to look deep into the main technical hub of the radio stations while listening to the music on the street. The total footprint accommodates a performance studio, studio, newsroom, music library, boardroom, and staff offices for the Public Radio Partnership, which moved into the historic facility in 2000.

82. LOUISVILLE PALACE THEATER
(Loew's and United Artists State Theater)
625 South Fourth Street, Central Business District
John Eberson
Landmark designation: NRHP, 1978
1928

The Loew's theater chain hired nationally known theater architect John Eberson to design an atmospheric theater in Louisville.
Eberson's earliest atmospheric experiments are found in his stage
design and painting work for the Johnston Realty and Construction
Company between 1901 and 1903. While his early commissions
are characterized as traditional, by the mid-1910s Eberson had
clearly forged a new direction. His first truly "atmospheric" theater,

the Houston Majestic, opened in 1923. The atmospheric theaters reflected Eberson's European heritage in their pervasive landscape and garden influences, especially found in the statuary and interior motifs.

The 1928 Loew's and United Artists State Theater (now called the Louisville Palace Theater) is no exception. Eberson designed the building in a dynamic Spanish Baroque style called churrigueresque. The primary role of the facade was to introduce the opulence that lay behind its baroque surfaces while masking its immense interior. This volume contains an elaborate vaulted lobby, decorated with busts of such notables as Beethoven and Eberson, and an auditorium with a ceiling that emulates a night sky with light fixtures that twinkle. The Palace has had four renovations: in 1953, a new wide screen was installed; in 1954, it was bought and renamed United Artists Theatre; in 1963, the balcony was blocked off, and a second-floor screen was installed and renamed the Penthouse. The original Wurlitzer Theater Pipe Organ was renovated in 1964 and sold in the 1980s to a restaurant near Atlanta, Georgia. The Louisville Palace Theater is still a venue for classic films, concerts, and performing arts.

83. KENTUCKY THEATER

649 South Fourth Street, Central Business District

Joseph and Joseph, Modern Amusement Company

1921

The Kentucky Theater is one of a number of elegant movie theaters that formed Movie Row on Fourth Street in downtown Louisville. Other notable theaters included the Majestic Theater by Joseph and Joseph (1908), the National Theater by Albert Kahn (1913), the Loew's State Theater—now the Louisville Palace—by John Eberson (1928). Originally there were at least eleven theaters that formed the movie district, but today only the Kentucky Theater and the Louisville Palace remain.

The Kentucky Theater has a concrete foundation and a main volume that is two stories in height. The exterior is composed of a variety of colorful textures and contrasts, with an orange-glazed brick marked with diamond patterns. The walls on the first-floor facade are clad in various materials, including Cararra marble. Glazed terra-cotta decorations emphasize the parapet of the South Fourth Street facade. A major renovation in 1940, overseen by Michael Switow, president of the Modern Amusement Company, increased the theater's seating by adding a balcony. However, the modernizing of the interior included the removal of most of the extravagant details of the original theater. The original lobby interior was adorned with marble imported from Italy and Greece, inlaid with Italian rosata and Caen stone. A stained-glass skylight that was lit from above covered the main auditorium. In 1951, the theater was redecorated and opened as a first-run movie house. In 1982, preservationists saved the theater's front facade and lobby, and the 1983 remodeling by Ward & Taylor created an auditorium.

84. GENE SNYDER U.S. COURTHOUSE AND CUSTOM HOUSE
(U.S. Post Office, Courthouse, and Custom House)
601 West Broadway, Central Business District
Treasury Department with James A. Wetmore
Landmark designation: NRHP, 1999
1930–1932

The original design in 1930 for the U.S. Post Office, Federal Courthouse, and Custom Building was a five-story building. However, from 1937 to 1939 an additional floor was inserted into the structure by lifting the roof an additional eleven feet, six inches, thus increasing the square footage. The U.S. Postal Service moved out in 1987, and the building was renamed the Gene Snyder U.S. Courthouse and Custom House, in honor of former Kentucky Representative Marion Gene Snyder (1963–65 and 1967–87).

The building is a block long, with a structural steel frame and concrete floor and roof slabs. The exterior walls are finished in limestone and faced with brick. The low-hip roof is made of copper. The entrances to the building are located above street level. Floors two and three are dominated by a three-story colonnade of fluted stone columns, which are three feet in diameter, with Corinthian capitals. A roof balustrade tops the modillion cornice. Spandrels between the second and third stories have various bas relief designs, including the American eagle and the Great Seal of the U.S.

Each of the two corner lobbies has coffered ceilings, fluted marble columns, inlaid Tennessee-marble floors, and brass grilles and elevator doors. Frank Weathers Long, of Berea, Kentucky, designed and painted ten murals that adorn the entrance lobbies and corridors. They represent the life and activities of the post office and were executed during the artists program of the Works Progress Administration (WPA) in 1937. They were painted on canvas and then glued onto the walls.

85. COURIER-JOURNAL AND LOUISVILLE TIMES BUILDING AND STANDARD GRAVURE

525 West Broadway, Central Business District

Joseph H. Kolbrook

1945–1948

The art deco–inspired Courier-Journal and Louisville Times Building combined three uniquely different programs—a newspaper, a rotogravure business, and a radio station. Lockwood-Greene Engineers of New York (known for their newspaper-headquarters buildings for the *New York Herald-Tribune*, the *New York Daily News*, the *Toronto Globe and Mail*, and the *Christian Science Monitor*) designed the building in collaboration with Louisville architect Joseph H. Kolbrook.

The solution is straightforward and functional, to the point that Philip Johnson characterized the building in a 1952 *Courier-Journal* article as "looking like a factory." The seven-story main building is a steel-framed structure with a Bedford-limestone skin and polished black granite base trimmed with aluminum. The functional characterstics of the structure are offset in the interior by the colorful lobby, with murals painted by renowned artist Henry Varnum Poor. The tripartite fresco panels depict the areas of Kentucky from the mountains in the east to the river towns and finally to the Bluegrass region. Each of the three panels exemplifies qualities of those places, including coal life, city life, and farm life. Four figures frame these panels—John James Audubon, Henry Clay, George Rogers Clark, and Daniel Boone. On the opposite side of the lobby hangs a large globe that rotates on its axis (the globe was placed upside down, so that all of the U.S. is visible). The wall behind the globe was originally painted to emulate the heavens with electrified twinkling stars. This wall has since been painted over, and there are currently plans to restore the original finish.

The building has three additions. In 1956, a three-story bindery was added. In 1959, Hartstern, Louis & Henry designed a four-story addition for the Standard Gravure Corporation to enlarge its publishing facilities. In 2002, Hart Freeland Roberts (Tennessee) designed a five-story addition that connects to the east facade of the original Courier-Journal Building. The addition opened in 2004 and sits on nearly four acres of land north of Broadway between Armory Place and Fifth Street, which doubles the newspaper's press-run capacity.

Tours of the Courier-Journal Building complex are available. Call 502-582-4545 for an appointment.

86. HEYBURN BUILDING

332 West Broadway, Central Business District
Graham, Anderson, Probst & White (Chicago)
Landmark designation: NRHP, 1979
1927–1928

The Heyburn Building is one of three commercial buildings in Louisville designed by the architectural firm Graham, Anderson, Probst & White (Chicago). The other two commissions, the Belknap Hardware Building (1929) on Main Street and the Starks Building (1926) on South Fourth Street, are similar in style to this classical revival office building. Built on the site of the former Avery mansion, the Heyburn Building is a steel-framed skyscraper, covered in buff brick and stone, with classical elements such as modillions and ornate detailing.

A major renovation in 2001 improved the structure, including the addition of a geothermal heating and cooling system, the replacement of the original windows, the restoration of the original marble in the lobbies, and a major cleaning of the building's exterior. In 2003, the owners hired Carol R. Johnson Associates of Boston to design the streetscape on Broadway and Fourth Street. Changes include different sidewalk paving at the building's entrances, additional traditional lampposts, uplighting on the building, and the installment of planters and outside seating.

87. CAMBERLEY-BROWN HOTEL, BROWN BUILDING, W. L. LYONS BROWN THEATRE
315–35 West Broadway, Central Business District
Preston J. Bradshaw
Landmark designation: NRHP, 1978
1923

Preston J. Bradshaw, an architect noted for his hotel designs throughout the Midwest (in particular, his Coronado Hotel in St. Louis has a similar use of materials and proportions), designed the Brown Hotel. The sixteen-story structure of matte-face brown brick with limestone and terra-cotta trim has a reinforced concrete structural frame with brick curtain walls. A roof garden was added in 1928. The interior has a colonial plan that was popular in the early twentieth century and a variety of architectural motifs: the lobby is colonial, the grill room is Elizabethan, and the dining room is French. The hot brown sandwich (white toast with sliced turkey, Mornay sauce, and Parmesan cheese, garnished with pimiento and bacon), famous in Kentucky, got its start at the Brown. The hotel was completely modernized in 1965, but by 1972 the building closed as a hotel and was sold to the Board of Education, which used it as an administrative office building and for the J. Graham Brown School. The Broadway Group (later called the Broadway Project Corporation) purchased the Brown Hotel in 1980. As part of a larger downtown revitalization initiative, Broadway Renaissance, a renovation of the structure began in 1983. In 1990, the Camberley Hotel Company and its president, Ian Lloyd-Jones, assumed management of the hotel, restored the Brown to its original splendor, and renamed it the Camberley-Brown Hotel.

The Brown Building, with the attached Brown Theater (formerly the Macauley Theater and now the W. L. Lyons Brown Theatre), was built in 1924–25. The structure is ten stories and composed of the same materials as the Brown Hotel. The theater sits at the building's rear. The interior and lobby have been completely refurbished. A marquee at the front of the building was added in 1983.

88. ST. FRANCIS HIGH SCHOOL
(YMCA)

233 West Broadway, Central Business District

McDonald Brothers, McDonald and Dodd; renovation by Potter & Cox

Landmark designation: NRHP, 1977

1911–1913

The seven-story brick and limestone-trimmed YMCA building opened on the northeast corner of Third Street and Broadway in 1913 as the organization's new central headquarters. The YMCA remained at this location until 1985, when a new central building was constructed at 501 South Second Street by the Louisville firm Bickel Gibson.

The YMCA is an example of the commercial Beaux Arts style found in Louisville architecture at this time. In contrast to the Weissinger-Gaulbert (1910), also designed by McDonald and Dodd, this building is modern in its starkness and spatial articulation. Dodd articulated the front surface of the building, U-shaped in plan, by pushing its two corners out beyond its center. However, the base responds to the shift volumetrically by pulling the center five-bay section away from the recessed upper portion, allowing a formal entry to exist. The lower level has a limestone water table topped with a limestone cornice. The body of the building, punctuated with sets of double-hung windows, has an otherwise stark massing. The top of the structure is patterned brickwork and a heavy cornice outlined with delicate ornamentation and layered dentils. The building has carved limestone modillions, ornate Palladian windows, and highly detailed scrolled plaster ceilings. These details remain.

In 1999, AU Associates of Lexington, Kentucky, was selected as the developer to adaptively reuse the former YMCA. They created an innovative mixed-use development that now includes St. Francis High School (a small private school for grades nine through twelve, founded in 1976 as an extension of St. Francis School of Goshen, Kentucky), as well as 58 apartments and commercial office and retail space.

In 2000, WW Architecture of Cambridge, Massachusetts, and GBBN of Lexington, Kentucky, won a limited design competition to design a sports complex and arts facility for the high school on an adjacent site. Project construction for this addition has not begun.

The architects for the building's complete renovation were the Louisville firm Potter & Cox. The developer of the property sensitively returned the building to its original splendor. Holly Wiedemann of AU Associates has led several award-winning adaptive-reuse projects in Kentucky.

89. WEISSINGER-GAULBERT APARTMENTS
709 South Third Street, Central Business District
McDonald and Dodd
Landmark designation: NRHP, 1977
1910–1912

The Weissinger-Gaulbert is the last remaining building of a group of three—the Main Building, the Broadway Annex, and the Third Street Annex—that formed, according to a 1912 *Courier-Journal* article, "Louisville's most elegant apartment complex of the early twentieth century." The Main Building was designed by the Louisville firm McDonald and Dodd, with J. F. Sheblessy, a Chicago native who studied with William Le Baron Jenney, as the chief architect. The Main Building was erected at the southwest corner of Broadway and Third Street in 1903 and razed in 1963. The Broadway Annex, built in 1907 just west of the Main Building, was designed by the McDonald Brothers; it was razed in 1955.

The Weissinger-Gaulbert, the Third Street Annex Apartment Building, was designed in 1910 by McDonald and Dodd and built on the site of the former residence of John M. Atherton. The Beaux Arts design has strong Chicago School influences, as evidenced by the vertical effect of the window placement and overall building organization. The building has a symmetrical W-shaped plan. It has three bays along Broadway and five bays along Third Street, and each bay has similar rhythmic undulations, resulting from an interplay of color and ornamentation. As in other Dodd-designed buildings, the exterior is treated plastically—ranging from applied ornamentation and detailed brickwork at the base (to introduce a pedestrian scale) to the placement of the vertically proportioned Chicago style windows (which exude a similar spatial quality to Burnham and Root's Monadnock Building of 1884) to the heavy cornice with overscaled dentils that wraps around the top of the structure. Occupied as both apartments and commercial space, the Weissinger-Gaulbert offers 85 residential units.

90. 800 APARTMENT BUILDING

800 South Fourth Street, Central Business District

Arrasmith and Tyler with Loewenberg & Loewenberg (Chicago)

1961–1963

The 800 Apartment Building was built as luxury apartments and was Louisville's first attempt at high-rise living. The six-sided, loz-enge-shaped building has three stories of parking below ground level and a fallout shelter on the lowest level. The structure was the first high-rise residential building in Louisville to use a continu-ous-pour concrete frame. It was Louisville's tallest building and one of the tallest buildings in the South at the time of its construc-tion. The developers of the property, Fritz W. Drybrough Sr. and Fritz W. Drybrough Jr., negotiated a contract with the Reynolds Metals Company of Louisville to supply the aluminum panels of the building's skin. Its aluminum curtain-wall system, made of tur-quoise aluminum, marble, glass, and masonry infill panels, is the second use of a curtain-wall system in Louisville (after the Liberty National Bank).

Honor Award for Superior Design, Federal Housing Administration, 1964; All Electric Award, General Electric, 1964

91. FIRST UNITARIAN CHURCH
(Church of the Messiah)
809 South Fourth Street, Central Business District
H. P. Bradshaw, rebuilt spire by John Grossman
1870–1871

The history of this building is ironic and tragic. Unitarians, perhaps the most liberal of Christians, reject the Trinity and emphasize religious tolerance. Yet parishioners chose an architect, H. P. Bradshaw, who designed an English Gothic church, after the precepts of A. C. Pugin and his son A. W. N. Pugin (known widely for recommending a strictly "correct" English-parish Gothic architecture, which specifically follows the liturgy of the Church). Bradshaw dutifully placed a soaring bell and entry tower of Kentucky limestone, with expressive "Trinitarian" windows, at, but not over, the crossing between the stone nave and transept. This contrasted with the "heretical" Wren churches in the English colonies, in which towers centered on the nave. The original interior, however, apparently looked like a New England meetinghouse with a Gothic interior, thus adopting a chaste Reformation space with details that contradicted meetinghouse architecture. The church burned in 1872 and was rebuilt in 1873. Another disastrous fire occurred in 1985, leaving only the original walls and the lower part of the tower. John Grossman replaced the spire with a steel spire outline, reused some of the walls, and lowered the roof of the transept, creating an oddly shaped side parapet and a false gable facade. Grossman also designed a courtyard by using a cacophony of structures, including the church, a stone and steel amphitheater, and the adjacent Italianate Heywood House. He also added an educational wing of glass and steel.

92. CALVARY EPISCOPAL CHURCH
821 South Fourth Street, Old Louisville
W. H. Redin, McDonald Brothers
Landmark designation: NRHP, 1978
1872–1889

Calvary Episcopal Church, built of Indiana and Pewee Valley limestone, is unusual in plan (it is not a central-aisle church). The stone spire of the tower and stone turret roof on the asymmetrical west front are unique among Louisville churches. W. H. Redin, who studied art and design in New York in the 1840s, came to Louisville before the Civil War to practice architecture and is known for his churches, residences, and the gate to Cave Hill Cemetery. In this church, Redin responded to the needs of ritual and the requirements of preaching by designing a sweeping "Akron" plan. Three aisles of pews are in an impressive octagonal auditorium space, created out of the crossing between the nave and transepts. The chancel is recessed from the crossing. The McDonald Brothers, at one time a firm of four architect brothers, completed the west front a decade later by closely following Redin's design. On the outside, the monochromatic limestone, the sparse Gothic ornamentation, the subdued buttresses, and the stone spire and turret roof give the church a solid, dignified, and confident expression. The tympanum of the main entrance is a simple, large quatrefoil with flowered bosses and surrounding tracery. On the inside, Redin designed the ceiling over the nave and transepts with magnificent hammerbeams, elaborated with quatrefoil tracery. The pointed, triangular, and hexagonal stained-glass windows include work from Tiffany Studios and the John B. Alberts Studio in Louisville, predecessor to Louisville Art Glass.

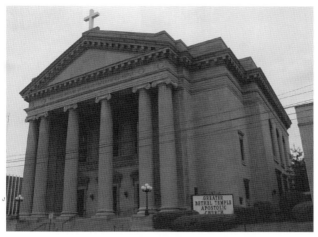

93. GREATER BETHEL TEMPLE APOSTOLIC CHURCH

(Temple Adath Israel)

834 South Third Street, Old Louisville

McDonald and Dodd

Landmark designation: NRHP, 1974

1905–1906

The Temple Adath Israel, codesigned by Kenneth McDonald and J. F. Sheblessy of the prominent Louisville architecture firm McDonald and Dodd, is an elegant classical revival Bedford-limestone structure. Six fluted columns dominate the entrance and support a portico with entablature and architrave, upon which the frieze is engraved, "Mine House Shall Be a House of Prayer for All People."

The interior is one large auditorium, based upon a modified Greek cross plan. The central square plan has bays extending on three sides, each with a gallery, creating a sanctuary. While ornament is kept to a minimum, rich moldings surround the arch. The classical revival layout is similar to the First Christian Church structure that was razed in 1911 to make way for the Starks Building. The building was dedicated in 1906 and served the Adath Israel congregation until 1977.

94. SPALDING COLLEGE
(Tompkins-Buchanan-Rankin House)
851 South Fourth Street, Old Louisville
Henry Whitestone
Landmark designation: NRHP, 1977
1871

In 1918, the Sisters of Charity of Nazareth purchased this five-bay, central-hall palazzo mansion of brick with limestone trim that Henry Whitestone designed for Joseph Tompkins in 1871. They turned it into a college and named it after Catherine Spalding, their founder. A 1941 college addition obscures the front elevation of the mansion today, but the side and rear elevations still present the serene Italianate exterior that is typical of Whitestone's work. Originally, the house had two stories, but in the 1880s a third story and an elaborate cornice were added. The exuberant Victorian interior is still intact and provides a display of varied details from 1871 and from the 1880s, which George Buchanan added after he bought the house in 1880. The first-floor hall is broad and long with elaborate doors, door surrounds, and hoods leading to the adjoining rooms, wood wall paneling, and a large carved-walnut staircase that winds to a third-floor stained-glass skylight. The ensemble of architectural gestures and hall furniture, such as the famous hat, coat, and mirror piece displayed at the 1884–85 World's Industrial and Cotton Exhibition in New Orleans, emphasize the important ritual of receiving guests in polite Victorian society. The second- and third-floor halls are the same size as the first-floor hall and are spacious rooms in themselves. Marble and ebony hearths with painted tiles, intricate electric light fixtures, mirrors, wallpaper, plaster cornices, a painted canvas ceiling in the parlor with a Japanese motif, lincrusta wainscoting, and a tooled-leather ceiling are among many interior delights created by the best craftsmen of the day.

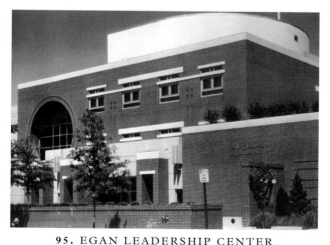

95. EGAN LEADERSHIP CENTER
(Spalding University Leadership Center)
901 South Fourth Street, Central Business District
Omni Architects (Lexington)
1992–1994

Named for former Spalding University president, Dr. Eileen Egan, the intent of this project was to create a new "front door" to the campus and house programs such as the Egan Leadership Medallion Program, which provides students with opportunities to develop leadership skills through a variety of professional-development seminars and community-service projects.

The brick-clad center contains a lecture hall, dining facilities, deli, bookstore, seminar and conference rooms, computer classrooms, and administrative offices. Louisville glass designer Kenneth von Roenn designed a unique circular stained-glass window (twenty feet in diameter) in the boardroom of the building.

Special Recognition Design Award, Kentucky Chapter of the American Society of Landscape Architects, 1992; Kentuckiana Masonry Institute Merit Award, 1995.

96. LAMPTON BAPTIST CHURCH
(First Christian Church)
850 South Fourth Street, Old Louisville
McDonald and Dodd
Landmark designation: NRHP, 1979
1909–1911

The First Christian Church was previously located on the site of what is today the Starks Building. The original church was razed in 1911.

The current building is an elegant limestone structure and one of the finest Beaux Arts churches in Louisville. The main body of

the church is a two-story structure with a pedimented portico supported by six fluted Corinthian columns and entablature. The roof is
topped with a dome on an octagonal drum. A monumental staircase
of two parts reaches the portico; the lower level is concrete and the
upper level is limestone. Classical motifs—egg-and-dart molding,
wreath-patterned reliefs, dentils, modillions, and roundels—accent
the entrance portico. A crown consisting of a blind arch caps the
central entryway. Each side of the main sanctuary consists of three
bays, articulated by pilasters. Corinthian capitals with double pilasters at their corners define the shallow-side transepts. The rear of
the building is a two-story structure with a truncated, low-hipped
roof and wide overhangs. The stained-glass windows of the banquet
hall depict the original razed structure.

97. LIMERICK NEIGHBORHOOD HISTORIC DISTRICT
Landmark designation: NRHP, 1978; LPD
1858–Present

The Limerick area was part of the rural countryside until 1858,
when the L & N Railroad established the Kentucky Locomotive
Works at Tenth and Kentucky Streets, followed by a depot, freight
yards, and repair shops. To fill these jobs, Irish Americans from
Portland built small brick and frame houses, often shotgun houses,
along the new street fronts, and African Americans lived in alley
houses. St. Louis Bertrand Church (1872) was the center of the Irish
community. After the L & N Railroad moved its yards to Highland

Park in 1905, many Irish slowly moved out and were replaced by African Americans who were moving out of the alleys. Eventually, the residents replaced many shotgun houses with more substantial brick and frame houses, using the variety of architectural expressions visible today. African Americans also renamed their neighborhood Limerick. Central Colored School was established at Sixth and Kentucky Streets in 1873, the first new school built for African Americans in Louisville and supported by taxes. The Kentucky Normal and Theological Institute, eventually to become Simmons University, was built at 1018 South Seventh Street in 1879, the first institution of higher education in Kentucky administered by African Americans. Simmons became the Municipal College for Negroes later and was eventually integrated into the University of Louisville. The west side of the neighborhood, near the CSX tracks, still shows the industrial origin and continuing nature of this working-class residential area. The neighborhood today is racially and economically diverse and possesses a wide variety of architectural types and styles.

98. ST. STEPHEN'S LIFESTYLE ENRICHMENT CAMPUS

(Simmons University and Bible College and
Louisville Municipal College for Negroes)

1018 South Seventh Street, Limerick

Architect unknown, Samuel Plato

Landmark designation: NRHP, 1976

1908–1924

In 1869, the Kentucky legislature granted the General Association of Colored Baptists of Kentucky permission to establish a school; in 1879, two brothers, Reverends Elijah P. Marrs and H. C. Marrs, opened Kentucky Normal and Theological Institute at the corner of Seventh and Kentucky Streets. The school was the first African American–controlled higher-education institution in the state of Kentucky. The institute was renamed State University in 1885 and renamed Simmons University in 1918, in honor of former President Reverend William J. Simmons. Simmons University closed in 1930 due to financial problems. The University of Louisville purchased the property and renamed it the Louisville Municipal College for Negroes in 1931. Municipal College closed in 1952 when the University of Louisville desegregated. The property is currently owned by St. Stephen's Baptist Church.

The campus, elevated above the street, consists of two primary buildings connected by a large grass courtyard. In 1908, the Baptist

Women's Educational Convention erected C. H. Parrish Hall (named for the president of the university, Charles H. Parrish Sr.), which served as a girls' dormitory and Domestic Science Building. Steward Hall, the boys' dormitory and classrooms, was designed by noted African American architect Samuel Plato (an alumnus of Simmons University) in 1924, named for the chairman of the Board of Trustees, William H. Steward, and served as the main building on the campus. The building's gymnasium was converted into a theater space and doubles, as a church and community space.

99. MARY D. HILL SCHOOL
(Central Colored School)
542 West Kentucky Street, Limerick
J. B. McElfatrick and Son
Landmark designation: NRHP, 1976; LL
1873

Education for African Americans was never prohibited in Kentucky, but it was not free until after the Civil War. Central Colored School was the first publicly supported new school built exclusively for African Americans in Louisville. Designed by J. B. McElfatrick and Son with a Renaissance revival expression based on Italian palazzi, this square brick school sits on a stone foundation and has four symmetrically organized facades divided into three stories by a horizontal water table, two limestone and brick corbelled stringcourses, and a corbelled limestone cornice. Doors on three sides are set in projected, rusticated wall planes, articulated further by engaged pilasters on all three floors. Two doors at the rear have more utilitarian details and purposes. Window sizes, shapes, and details differ from floor to floor, but all have terra-cotta keystones in the arches, as do all the doors. Each floor has four large corner rooms, with stairs and corridors filling the middle of the plan. By 1875, 1,000 elementary students attended, and in 1882 junior- and senior-high students also enrolled. By 1893, Central Colored School was so overcrowded that it moved to a new location at Ninth and Magazine and distributed some of its students to other colored schools, including the Eastern, Western, Portland, and Fulton Street Colored Schools. Sixth Street School became a school for white elementary students, was renamed the Mary D. Hill School in 1917, and closed in 1970. The interior has been extensively renovated for professional offices.

100. LOUISVILLE WAR MEMORIAL
AUDITORIUM
970 South Fourth Street, Old Louisville
Carrère & Hastings (New York) with E. T. Hutchings
Landmark designation: NRHP, 1977
1927–1929

Designed by Carrère & Hastings, architects of the New York Public Library (1897–1911), in association with Louisville architect E. T. Hutchings, the auditorium aligned with Hastings's belief that the architecture should incorporate the surrounding context and topography into a holistic whole. The classical style of the structure, influenced by Hastings's Beaux Arts training, introduced a grand scale to the neighborhood, which at the time of its construction was surrounded by Renaissance revival residential and commercial architecture. The scale and form of the building reflected national and regional trends for civic architecture of the time and further enhanced Louisville's search for respectability, sophistication, and national status.

Built on the site of two residences owned by James G. Carter, the auditorium commemorates the soldiers, sailors, and marines from Jefferson County who served the nation during World War I. The Fourth Street facade has ten fluted Doric columns and temple-like massing with a portico, lobby, and circular performance space. Unlike the limestone primary facade, clad with classical motifs, the remaining elevations are simple and undecorated. Opened on Armistice Day, November 11, 1929, the building continues to function as a cultural and architectural symbol as well as a memorial.

The auditorium is home to Henry Pilcher's largest organ and one of Louisville's most famous instruments, with 5,288 pipes, the Pilcher Opus 1454, which was constructed and installed in 1929. Artists such as Sergei Rachmaninoff, George Gershwin, Mikhail Baryshnikov, and the Peking Opera have performed on the auditorium's stage.

101. WATERFRONT DEVELOPMENT CORPORATION
(Ohio River Sand Company)
129 East River Road, Central Business District
Hartstern, Louis & Henry
1964–1965

Built as "a showcase for the raw materials that Ohio River Sand Company furnishes to the building industry," this concrete and glass structure cantilevers out above grade level, projecting thirteen feet toward Interstate 64 and the Ohio River. The two-story entry lobby is poured-in-place concrete with exposed concrete-block walls. To emphasize texture and to heighten the shadows, the architects varied the block patterns. The upper floors, which contain office space, cantilever off the central core and contain mechanical and electrical services. Concrete beams support walls of lightweight precast concrete. These sections have textured surfaces with exposed aggregate that can be easily cleaned.

102. WATERFRONT PARK

River Road at Brook Street, Central Business District
George Hargreaves (San Francisco), Bravura
1999

For much of its history, Louisville's link to the Ohio River had a vital economic component, and many of its major industries grew up along the waterway. By the latter portion of the twentieth century, though, the riverfront had fallen into neglect. The construction of I-64 was a double blow: it reinforced the barrier between the city and the river and allowed many people driving through the city to see its worst side, such that Louisville's name became Junk City to the CB radio culture of the 1970s.

Starting in 1986, the Waterfront Development Corporation assembled 55 acres, and by the mid-1990s construction began on a major recreational park. Noted landscape architect George Hargreaves's design calls for a series of loosely connected spaces devoted to a variety of outdoor activities. A great lawn, children's playgrounds, a plaza for festivals, inlets for boating, and trails for biking and jogging that extend further along the river comprise the first phase of the plan. Small-scale parking areas are largely hidden by landscaped berms and hills. A second phase was started in 2002, adding an amphitheater, rowing center, a spiral ramp to the abandoned Big Four Railroad Bridge for use as a pedestrian connection to Indiana, and additional diverse areas.

Waterfront Park has been a catalyst for other developments in the area, notably Slugger Field and the Extreme Park for skateboarders, both of which are adjacent. Recently, as the city has focused on increasing housing in its downtown area, several new residential developments, which overlook the park, have begun. There is speculation about rebuilding or removing the interstate highways, which would constitute a major improvement to the park.

103. HUMANA WATERSIDE BUILDING
(Belknap Hardware and Manufacturing Company)
101–23 East Main Street, Central Business District
Graham, Anderson, Probst & White (Chicago)
1923

At the time of its construction in 1923 (on the site of the second Galt House), the Belknap Hardware Building was the largest single-unit hardware plant in the world. It is one of three significant works in Louisville by the Chicago architecture firm Graham, Anderson, Probst & White. The firm also designed the Starks Building addition and the Heyburn Building.

The building has a strong horizontal emphasis: the limestone basement is two stories high, the body of the building rises nine stories in height, and the head is one story. Each section has similar details, with bays of industrial-style multiple-paned windows. The central entry is *in antis*, with an engaged limestone aperture, flanked by two fluted Doric columns that are two stories in height. The Belknap Building is now the Waterside Building and owned by the Humana Corporation.

104. LOUISVILLE BALLET
315 East Main Street, Central Business District
Bravura
1995

The performing arts are centered on Main Street, anchored by Actors Theatre and the Kentucky Center for the Arts on West Main Street. The new building for the Louisville Ballet extends the area to East Main Street and is linked to Waterfront Park, which has recaptured a portion of the riverfront for the public. New apartment buildings and a minor league baseball stadium have reinforced the revitalization of this section of downtown. Bravura, especially its founder, Jim Walters, has significant experience with a number of revitalization efforts across the city, including the Presbyterian Church headquarters and Waterfront Park.

The building is located in an area of older warehouses, some of which have been adapted to contemporary uses. The ballet reinforces this sense of adaptive reuse within the neighborhood through the use of simple, if contemporary, industrial construction techniques and forms. At the same time, the structure conflicts with its neighbors through its use of new materials, such as corrugated metal and diagonally staggered shingles. Different functions are separated into different volumes, and an extensive window overlooks Main Street from a large rehearsal space.

105. BRINLY-HARDY BUILDING
(Chesapeake & Ohio Freight Depot)
103 North Preston Street, Butchertown
Architect unknown
1902

Louisville struggled in the chaos of early American railroad building to make rail connections to other regional cities. The Louisville and Nashville Railroad completed a line between the two cities in 1859, and after the Civil War, Louisville competed for freight lines that would give the city and its countryside good access to northern and especially southern markets. The first railroad bridge crossed the

Ohio River in 1870. The second and third bridges followed in the early 1880s and 1890s, signifying the burgeoning demand for freight and passenger service and bringing many different railroad companies into an important nexus of traffic by 1900. The Chesapeake & Ohio Freight Depot, a Romanesque steel-framed shed faced with red brick, was built in 1902 and was one of many depots throughout the city. Freight cars passed under the broad central arches to be unloaded inside. An arcade of segmental, incised arches springing from corbelled capitals and engaged pilasters—reminders of early-nineteenth-century German Rundbogenstil architecture—indicate depot offices on the second floor. A limestone foundation and water table and a double limestone stringcourse bring a strong horizontal tie to the lively facade, which emphasizes a powerful vertical dimension in the cross gables on both the long and short sides. These gables have corbelled buttresses and broad, incised arches. Pinnacles with rounded limestone finials accentuate the four corners. The building is now part of Louisville Slugger Field.

106. EXTREME PARK
Witherspoon and Clay Streets, Butchertown
Stanley Saitowitz (San Francisco) with Zach Wormhoudt,
Luckett & Farley
2002

Regarded as one of the leading skateboard facilities in the country, Extreme Park is a major link in Louisville's diligent efforts to recapture its waterfront. Mayor Dave Armstrong took the lead in building the park after nearly 90,000 skateboard enthusiasts showed up for

Map 3: Buildings 101–115

ESPN's X-Games trials at a temporary facility nearby in 1999. The $2,500,000 project comprises 40,000 square feet of interconnected bowls, ramps, jumps, half pipes, and a 24-foot full pipe. Plans for an indoor pavilion have been discussed. It was designed by California architect Stanley Saitowitz with skateboard consultant Zach Wormhoudt, and, with its large curving volumes, reads as a gigantic homage to Jean Arp. Louisville's tradition of excellent concrete construction continues in this project.

The success of the park caught many people by surprise. On social terms, it reflected a meaningful commitment by the city to hear the voice of its younger residents. But it also took an overlooked and disadvantaged area in the shadow of an elevated expressway and gave it new life. Other businesses have moved into the area. The park, which is open 24 hours and free, is rarely empty. Bring a helmet if you plan to skate.

107. JEWISH HOSPITAL DOCTORS' OFFICE
BUILDING
250 East Liberty Street, Central Business District
Jasper D. Ward
1970

Jasper D. Ward's ability to make a most banal building type—the anonymous office building—into an interesting work of architecture is testimony to the talent of this under-recognized architect. The building is the simplest of programs: a ten-story office building, square in plan, economical in intentions. Yet it is located prominently at an intersection on a major approach to the north-south expressway that cuts through downtown Louisville. Ward started by hiding the scale of the building in disguising its height. Vertical panels of sandblasted white concrete are set against vertical runs of dark tinted glass; the effect makes it impossible to count the number of stories. This pattern of abstracted, overscaled pilasters also emphasizes the verticality in the composition of the elevation, which counters the blockish quality of the building itself. The panels thin at the top and bottom, providing the classical definition of base-shaft-cap to the elevations. Additionally, Ward disguised the mechanical systems and elevator shafts on the roof of the building by giving them a mask: a lined panel system that is proportioned to act as a cap for the building (and again emphasize its verticality). Inside, he found cause for invention: he put the structural system on either side of the building's corners, which opens those offices to views of the city.

108. UNIVERSITY OF LOUISVILLE HEALTH
SCIENCES CENTER
500 South Preston Street, Central Business District
Smith, Hinchman & Grylls Associates (Detroit), Louis & Henry,
Arrasmith and Judd
1970

The city of Louisville stepped gingerly into urban renewal in the late 1950s and early 1960s, clearing blighted areas east and west of the Central Business District. The plans for the western renewal district called for a complex of governmental buildings, but for the most part they never materialized (see Greyhound Lines). The area east of downtown, however, totaling 215 acres, was earmarked for a medical center complex, which has become a viable development and has grown in recent decades as the medical profession and its services have diversified.

The University of Louisville Health Sciences Center incorporates four separate but connected components: a medical school, a dental school, the Health Sciences Building (primarily teaching laboratories), and a library and commons building. The overall plan for the complex was designed by Smith, Hinchman & Grylls from Detroit. Two Louisville firms were associated for two of the individual buildings: Louis & Henry were the architects for the dental school (pictured here), and Arrasmith and Judd for the library and commons building.

The four buildings are located around a raised plaza and front onto it. The dental school is across Preston Street from the plaza, but a pair of elevated pedestrian walkways connect it to the laboratory building, library, and commons. The walkways continue through each structure, providing dedicated circulation through all the buildings in the complex.

The medical school dominates due to its size: a fourteen-story tower at the west edge of the plaza. The remaining buildings are lower, three to four stories. All are built in concrete, with paired cylindrical columns running through the entire elevation of each building to support the projecting roof. At the time, Louisville benefited from the presence of a number of local contractors with substantial experience in concrete construction; this kept costs down and provided elevated skills in working the material.

The plaza is an attractive component of the overall design. It is raised nearly a full story off Preston Street, which isolates it substantially in terms of visibility and sound. A geometric fountain, large-scale sculpture, and a number of landscaped areas moderate the scale of the buildings.

109. COMMUNITY HEALTH BUILDING
(Louisville Medical School)
101 West Chestnut Street, Central Business District
Clarke & Loomis
Landmark designation: NRHP, 1975
1891–1893

At the age of seventeen, Arthur Loomis joined Charles J. Clarke's firm as an apprentice, became head draftsman in 1885, and a partner in Clarke & Loomis in 1891, just in time to design Louisville's medical school in Richardsonian Romanesque splendor. The firm designed many other residences and buildings in this style, including the Conrad House, the Robinson House, the Levy Brothers Building, Manual Training School, and the Todd Building, a ten-story Chicago School structure that was demolished in 1983 for a parking lot. Loomis designed the J. B. Speed Museum in 1927 in a different style, indicating the ability of an "academic eclectic" architect to adopt almost any architectural expression. Loomis's four-story, monochromatic limestone medical school, with its corner stair towers and robust cross-gabled elevations, reflects the late work of H. H. Richardson, the most influential architect of the day.

The main entrance is set in a projecting plane that organizes its facade vertically in relationship to the tower. The facade also has a pronounced horizontal stringcourse over the main floor and an emphatic cornice, which strengthens the horizontal composition. The main door is recessed under a porch and behind a powerful limestone arch with articulated, ribbed voussoirs and held by squat columns and mixed floral capitals. Carved stone details of plants and animals provide focal points for corners, springs of arches, sills, and pinnacles. The interior has been extensively renovated but retains its tile floors and wainscoting and cap on the walls.

110. JEFFERSON COMMUNITY COLLEGE
(Louisville Presbyterian Theological Seminary)
109 East Broadway, Central Business District
Dodd & Cobb
Landmark designation: NRHP, 1978
1903–1909

Architect William J. Dodd partnered with engineer Arthur Cobb in 1896, and in 1902 designed one of their most significant commissions, the Louisville Presbyterian Theological Seminary. Dodd joined important national architects such as Ralph Adams Cram, Bertram Grosvenor Goodhue, and James Gamble Rogers by adopting the collegiate Gothic style for campus buildings. The seminary, made of brick faced with limestone, was built in a U-shape surrounding a quadrangle, bringing under one roof the seminary's lecture and seminar rooms, a chapel, library, dining room, student commons, and dormitory.

Dodd freely adapted the perpendicular Tudor style of Gothic architecture, featuring the ogee window formed by two convex and compound curves. Trefoil and quatrefoil tracery fill many of the arched windows, which vary in form from ogee to pointed to round. Octagonal turrets with niches and their canopies frame the main-entry block, with an off-center main door and center clock overhead. The west dormitory door also has octagonal turrets, which end in crenellations, and the battlements between the turrets are repeated prominently over the east dormitory door and on the parapet to the left of the main door, over the chapel's stained-glass windows. Bartizans with finials end the corners of the dorm wings. The chapel, now used as a theater, has dark double-hammer beams, with arched braces ending in pendants, and intricate wall braces, wall posts, and corbels that separate the tall stained glass. The inlaid herringbone brick floor, dark paneled entry, and wall paneling (to chair rail height) reinforce the medieval feeling of the space. Jefferson Community College renovated the interior in 2003.

111. ST. PAUL'S GERMAN EVANGELICAL CHURCH
213 East Broadway, Phoenix Hill
Clarke & Loomis
Landmark designation: NRHP, 1982
1905–1911

The Neogothic St. Paul's German Evangelical Church is among the finest ecclesiastical designs of Clarke & Loomis. The primary facade of the building unites into one volume an eclectic tripartite composition of Tudor and Gothic motifs. The main entry, a half story above street level, is under a large Tudor arch that frames a set of double doors. The center portion of the facade contains a shallow bay window, detailed with ornamental stained glass, above which rests a one-story lancet arch with stained-glass windows.

The church interior has an Akron plan, in which the axis of the building is turned on a diagonal, which aligns with the far west foyer of the building. The main chancel area has a sloping floor and an irregular octagonal plan and ceiling. A 1998 renovation converted the building into doctors' offices. The stained-glass windows and details remain, although a second-floor partition at the balcony closes off the choir loft from the main chancel. The adjoining parish house incorporates the same stone and detailing.

112. FIRST LUTHERAN CHURCH ELCA
417 East Broadway, Phoenix Hill
Mason Maury
Landmark designation: NRHP, 1982
1874–1904

German immigrants streamed early into Kentucky, and by the 1850s there were some 18,000 German Catholics and Protestants in Louisville. They settled primarily into the neighborhoods of Phoenix Hill, Butchertown, and Germantown, where they built a number of large, usually Gothic revival churches. Outside and inside, First English Lutheran Church, begun in 1874, is one of the most striking of these German churches because of its fully formed, symmetrically placed entrance towers. Unfortunately, the designer of the church is unknown. Mason Maury, an employee of W. H. Redin in the late 1870s and early 1880s and a partner of William J. Dodd from 1889 to 1896 (both known for their Gothic churches in Louisville), is credited with designing the front facade, probably after Cologne Cathedral. It was attached in 1904–05. First Lutheran is one of the few in Louisville with fully developed, hexagonal, twin Gothic spires, accentuated by sharply pointed windows, hood-molds, and many minarets with tall finials. These spires frame the gabled nave, with its stained-glass rose window held by heavy tracery. Three front doors, with smaller stained glass rose windows in the tympanums, lead to a double-aisled nave, with ten clerestory stained-glass windows that tell the story of Jesus. Dark hammer-beam trusses, with drops and corbelled wall braces, carry the roof of the nave above the clerestory windows. A large Tudor arch, held by compound, engaged columns and demarcated by a deep, compound wave molding, opens to the chancel, which supports a large pipe organ. Alois Lang carved the fine wooden sculpture of the Last Supper behind the altar. At the south end of the nave, stained-glass windows depict Philip Melancthon and Martin Luther and the German cities they made famous during the Reformation.

113. SAINT MARTIN OF TOURS

639 South Shelby Street, Phoenix Hill
Architect unknown
Landmark designation: NRHP, 1983
1853–1860s

One of several churches built for German Roman Catholics in Louisville during the nineteenth century, Saint Martin of Tours originally had an unencumbered soaring clock and bell tower, with two doors that entered into an octagonal narthex and steps to the nave level. The tower, articulated with pinnacles and gables, telescoped in stages to its full height, ending with a copper spire, finial, and cross. The central-aisled nave of stone, built in 1853, and the transepts of equal length, the five-sided chancel, and the tower, completed in the 1860s, house one of the most authentically German religious spaces in Louisville. Groined vaults, once a flat, coved ceiling, cover a rich and colorful imported interior design, which includes life-size statues of the Apostles made of zinc and plaster, polychromatic marbles, stained-glass windows, and painted windows, all imported from Germany. The Royal Bavarian Art Institute for Stained Glass in Munich made the stained glass. Painted windows in the chapels came from a seventeenth-century monastery. Skeletal remains of two martyrs, Saint Bonosa and Saint Magnus, donated by an Italian monastery in 1901, lie in glass reliquaries in the chancel. A great organ, built by a Cincinnati firm in 1861, rebuilt in 1875, and electrified and rebuilt in 1895 by a Detroit firm, retains its original pipe work. Marble altars and a communion rail were added in the 1890s. In 1903, a new stone entry gable and two side rooms were built to cover the original base of the tower. Two side buildings, a convent, and a school have been demolished. The Pfarrschule (1896) across the street was sold to pay for recent restorations and renovations. *Open 24 hours a day. Latin mass is offered at 12:30 P.M. on Sunday.*

114. UNITY OF LOUISVILLE—UNITY TEMPLE
(Adath Jeshurun Temple and School)
757 South Brook Street, Old Louisville
J. J. Gaffney
Landmark designation: NRHP, 1982
1918–1925

J. J. Gaffney is known for his use of a wide range of architectural styles and heavily decorated surfaces. For the Adath Jeshurun

Temple, Gaffney used Islamic and Byzantine motifs. The centralized structure sits on a smooth-coursed limestone base, and glazed yellow brick covers the rest of the facades. A singular large dome, covered with red glazed tiles, dominates the building mass. This volume is symmetrical in plan and elevation. The central portion contains three arched openings, adorned with decorative colored tile in the tympanum. The lower portion of each arch contains stained-glass window panels. Entry to the building is from the South Brook Street facade through three arched doorways that puncture a protruding one-story narthex. Decorative, colorful glazed tiles in the form of geometric motifs cover the tympanum of each patterned brick arched opening. With the exception of the addition of building lettering and a change in the style of the exterior light fixtures between the arched openings, little has changed on the building's exterior since it was constructed.

The interior of the narthex is simple, with two flights of stairs descending to the office area and three flights of stairs ascending to the sanctuary, which is entered off the narthex through three sets of doors. Within the sanctuary, a series of tapered Ionic columns support the dome. Heavy ribbing and cross braces accentuate the structure of the dramatic dome, which is decorated with religious iconography. The main chancel contains the original walnut pews.

The school-community building, which is more classically designed, connects to the temple in the front (by a decorative iron gateway) and in the rear forming an L-shaped complex. The building was sold to Unity of Louisville in 1957.

115. SPECTRUM BUILDING
(Louisville Male High School)
911 South Brook Street, Old Louisville
J. Earl Henry, Luckett & Farley
Landmark designation: NRHP, 1979
1914–1915

J. Earl Henry was a 1906 graduate of Illinois State University and had worked as a draftsman and designer for prominent architect Brinton B. Davis before serving as the architect for the Louisville School Board from 1912 to 1919. It was during this period that he built Louisville Male High School, along with the Albert S. Brandeis, Shawnee Elementary, and William R. Belknap schools. The Male High School building combines classical motifs with those of the Jacobean period, including Jacobean arches, planar red brick facades with decorative brick patterning, and sculptural elements in the towers, window bays, and ornamental details. The entryway is most impressive.

In 1990, the school moved to the Old Durrett High School property on Preston Highway, leaving the building at 911 South Brook Street abandoned. In 2000, three Male graduates purchased the building, adaptively reusing the old facility primarily as office space. It is now called the Spectrum Building. A complete historic restoration of the structure is in progress.

116. U.S. MARINE HOSPITAL
2215 Portland Avenue, Portland
Robert Mills
Landmark designation: LL, 1976; NRHP, 1978; NHL, 1997
1845–1852

Placed on the Eleven Most Endangered Historic Places list in 2003 by the National Trust for Historic Preservation, this U.S. Marine Hospital is the only extant example of seven inland hospitals that the U.S. erected to care for sailors who worked America's interior waterways. It functioned as a federal hospital during the Civil War and was closed in 1933 with the construction of a new hospital. At the behest of the Department of the Treasury, Robert Mills (1781–1855) designed prototype hospitals for 150 beds in the late

1830s, and they were routinely modified by subsequent government architects for specific sites. Located over the Ohio River to catch the breezes, this serene Greek revival brick structure, with three galleried stories and a basement, still testifies to the importance of the Ohio River and its sailors in the history of the city. Over time, Stephen Long, Charles Fuller, and Joseph Sawyer replaced Mills's classical columns with piers that hold the recessed open galleries with cast-iron railings on the north and south facades, retained the octagonal cupola (now lost), and added Italianate window treatments. The overall simplicity of the massing and cornice gives the hospital muscularity and solidity. In plan, the hospital has three main floors of equal size, which are divided into four wards by transverse halls. The pavilions at each corner of the building were designed for staircases, service rooms, and smaller wards. Although the interior is in poor condition, it has great integrity, with original wood finishes, staircases, coffered ceilings, a cast-iron ceiling vent with hemp-leaf details, and downside-up metal cornices with swags. A Save America's Treasures grant and Transportation Enhancement funding in 2004 will help guarantee the survival of this landmark.

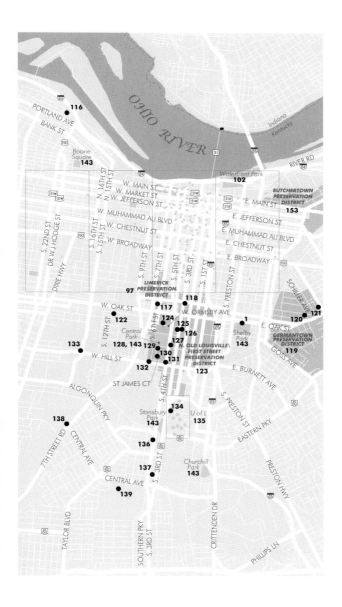

Map 4: Buildings 116–153

including Old Louisville, Limerick, Germantown, and Butchertown

117. ST. LOUIS BERTRAND CATHOLIC CHURCH
1104 South Sixth Street, Limerick
H. P. Bradshaw
Landmark designation: LL, 1975; NRHP, 1975, 1978
1873

Established in 1866 by the Dominican Order to minister to Irish Roman Catholics who had settled in the Limerick neighborhood next to the L & N Railroad, this stone church (made of Oldham County, Kentucky, limestone with White River limestone trim from Bowling Green) replaced the first church on Seventh Street in 1873. Designed by H. P. Bradshaw, it revives a late-thirteenth-century Edwardian English Gothic architecture in the details of its asymmetrical entrance facade, capped bell tower, corner turret, clerestory, buttressed side elevations, and five-sided apse. The orientation of the church is unorthodox with its east entrance and western apse. James Casey was the general stonemason, and John Healy was the stone contractor. The large nave, with a central and two side aisles, is lighted by large clerestory windows. Before the renovation (1947–48), the interior had elaborate and colorful walls, especially on the pendentives of the pointed arches that hold the clerestory, as shown in a photograph in the choir loft. The renovation also brought the installation of many fine German wood carvings from Oberammergau, Bavaria, including the white oak main altar, side altars, baldacchino, and stations of the cross. The stained-glass windows portray the fifteen mysteries of the rosary. The grotto dedicated to Our Lady of Lourdes (1887) is one of the oldest in the U.S. The renovation replaced the first floor with the current terrazzo floor, which contains radiant heating pipes. The solid brick Italianate school next door has three stories of round-headed windows and a mansard roof. It was closed in 1971, after 80 years of providing Roman Catholic parochial education to mostly Irish American children.

118. WALNUT STREET BAPTIST CHURCH

1101 South Third Street, Old Louisville
Kenneth McDonald
Landmark designation: NRHP, 1975
1900–1902

Squire Boone, brother of explorer Daniel Boone, founded the First Baptist Church of Louisville in 1815. Twenty years later, the church formed its first mission, the Second Baptist Church. In 1849, the two churches reunited and in 1854 built a new building on the northwest corner of Fourth Street and Walnut Street (presently Muhammad Ali Boulevard), a site now occupied by Meidinger Tower. In 1898, the structure of the church was near collapse, so the congregation sold the property for $120,000, holding its final service on the site on April 1, 1900. On May 2, 1900, the church purchased a lot at the corner of Third and St. Catherine Streets for $16,500. A design competition held in 1900 selected Louisville architect Kenneth McDonald from a field of fifteen entrants. McDonald's entry was a Gothic revival structure with a central entrance tower and corner minarets and seven side window bays, divided by pinnacled buttresses. The congregation maintained its Walnut Street name following its move in 1902 to the new church.

McDonald, one of four architect brothers, graduated from Virginia Military Institute in 1873 as a civil engineer. In 1878, he joined his brother, Harry Peake McDonald (and eventually his two other brothers) in an architectural practice. McDonald became the partner of William J. Dodd in 1906.

The present Neogothic form of the sanctuary is a result of renovations in 1923 and 1975. With its pedimented central mass, framed by layered, asymmetrical bell and stair entrance towers, an ogee arch with two side minarets forming the doorway, and colossal pointed stained-glass windows on three sides, this church has architectural roots in the Gothic details and massing of Canterbury Cathedral, Chartres, Rouen, and Reims. From the exterior massing, it is difficult to read the complex interior plan of the main church, which is laid out in the form of a Greek cross. The nave is composed of several aisles and pews that sweep in a circle around the altar. This sweep is repeated on the second-floor gallery of pews. The main sanctuary has 60 stained-glass windows, including a unique Tiffany-style window (the only one of its kind in the city) on the north wall that shows the Annunciation. A sleek hammer-beam truss system, which you can touch at the gallery level, holds the high roof over the chancel. A chapel and education center, built in 1954, complete the rear of the church. An elevated skywalk connects the main church building to the Pittigrew Memorial Activities Building across Hubbard Poole Alley. Another building at 1143 South Third Street serves as the parish's offices.

119. GERMANTOWN NEIGHBORHOOD
Barret Avenue and Goss Avenue
1850s

Butchertown, Phoenix Hill, and Germantown are neighborhoods where nineteenth-century German immigrants settled in large numbers around the industrial and railroad complex to the east of the Downtown Commercial District. The first wave of Germans came in the 1820s, settling first in Butchertown and Phoenix Hill. Many German Catholics, after the failed revolution of 1848, became the second wave of immigrants, who started settling in the 1850s in Germantown, a lowland neighborhood that also carried the nickname "Frogtown." There were numerous dairies here, but the last closed in 1936. By the turn of the century, shotgun houses, many of them camelback, became the predominant house type. Today, Germantown has one of the highest concentrations of shotgun houses in Louisville. Many corner grocery stores and taverns once served this tight-knit ethnic community, but few remain. St. Therese Catholic Church, at Kentucky Street and Schiller Avenue the Bradford Mills Building at 1034 East Oak Street, the Hope Worsted Mills building at 942 East Kentucky Street, Vine Street Baptist Church, and St. John's Episcopal Church represent a variety of institutional and industrial architecture.

120. ST. THERESE ROMAN CATHOLIC CHURCH

1010 Schiller Avenue, Germantown
Architect unknown (school), Fred T. Erhart (church)
Landmark designation: NRHP, 1975
1906–1928

The design for St. Therese "Little Flower of Jesus" Church responds to a challenging polygonal site, bounded by East Kentucky Street and Schiller Avenue at the junction of the Paristown and Germantown neighborhoods. The structure is built with buff brick, permastone detailing, and a red Spanish-tile roof.

The primary facade, composed of a series of screen walls that mediate between the two tall towers, is Spanish Renaissance revival, a style of architecture popularized in the 1920s by Bertram Grosvenor Goodhue after the Panama-California Exposition in San Diego in 1915. The entrance, through three arched doorways, leads into an open loggia and vestibule. An octagonal drum, topped by a zinc-covered cupola visible from Schiller Avenue, dominates the elevation. A twelve-foot tall wrought-iron cross rises above the cupola.

Ten columns cut from Scagliola stone (now painted a salmon color) support eight coffered arches and carry the load of the octagonal dome, which spans the rectangular-shaped chancel. While the sanctuary is cubic in proportion, it is crowned with a coffered ceiling that has tapered inlays, giving the appearance of an increased verticality. Below the ceiling datum are eight large windows, infilled with gold and white translucent glass panels that combine to illuminate the sanctuary. The resulting space is light, open, and without glare. The lower portions of the walls have niches carved into the spaces between the large windows. These niches contain marble sculptures that depict the fourteen stations of the cross.

A 1968–69 renovation by Lawrence Melillo included remodeling the interior to reflect the change in liturgical requirements put in place by Vatican II. Of the changes, the most significant is the relocation of the altar from the west to a more central location below the dome and the reformatting of the linear central-aisle seating to a more circular arrangement. Melillo also designed an elegant double-curved wrought-iron ornamental screen that separated the main altar and tabernacle from the 30-seat chapel beyond. The ornamental screen was removed in the early 1970s, although remnants of it remain in both wings of the church—one in front of the sacristy and the other in front of the devotional chapel.

In juxtaposition to the massiveness of the church, the rectory is a simple rectangular volume, capped with a low-hipped tile roof that helps provide an elegant transition to the scale of the surrounding neighborhood. The school is the oldest building of the complex and dates from 1906–07. It faces Kentucky Street, and while the exterior remains relatively unaltered since its construction, in 1988 the interior of the school and the adjacent convent were converted into low-income apartments. These buildings have Arts and Crafts detailing. Neither the school nor the convent are attributed to an architect.

121. LYNN'S PARADISE CAFE
(Key Market)
984 Barret Avenue, Highlands
Architect unknown
Date unknown

Lynn Winters is a creative fixture in Louisville, in large part due to the success of her fun and funky restaurant on Barret Avenue. Using the shell of a grocery store, Winters dresses up the interior by dressing down the environs and the furnishings. Bright colors, animal statuary, an interior tree decorated with hand-painted eggs, and knick knacks on every table are some of the highlights. The restaurant sponsors an Ugly Lamp contest at the Kentucky State Fair (several past winners are on display) and a Pajama Party brunch the morning after New Year's Eve. The lightheartedness of the decor belie Winters's serious commitments: she supports local farmers and business initiatives by women. The café has become a neighborhood institution, anchoring several new galleries and vintage stores. Winters has diversified her activities into plans for another restaurant and a graphics business, but her puckish style remains the same.

122. SUD CHEMIE
(Catalyst and Chemicals)
1227 South Twelfth Street, Algonquin
Norman Sweet
1965

In 1965, Catalyst and Chemicals emerged from the Girdler Chemical Company, and turned to Norman Sweet (a leading Louisville modern architect, known more for his innovative house designs than for his commercial architecture) to design an office space that reflected the company's forward-thinking initiatives. Because Sweet always tried to incorporate innovative technology in his architecture, he saw the advantages of precast and prestressed concrete construction, which were being investigated in office-building designs around Louisville at the time. Dolt and Dew, Kentucky's leading precast and pre-stressed specialists, assisted Sweet in the design and construction of the building.

This process, a sequential installation, allowing for floor and roof to go up simultaneously, saves time. The Catalyst and Chemicals Building took ten working days to construct using precast panels. Picking up on the context of large brick warehouses, Sweet used brick walls to provide a contrast to the concrete. The faceted panels create an undulating and rhythmic pattern.

One of the more interesting details of the building is found in the front lobby. Using small colored-glass tiles, Sweet designed a mosaic that depicts a chemical reaction. The striking colors offset the otherwise dark masonry walls of the interior.

123. OLD LOUISVILLE HISTORIC DISTRICT

Between Kentucky Street, Avery Avenue, Interstate 65, and Seventh Street; Old Louisville

Landmark designation: NRHP, 1975, 1984; LPD

1870

A major preservation success story, which became a catalyst for the local preservation movement, Old Louisville rose in the 1960s from a dilapidated district of abused and cut-up single-family dwellings and apartments to a superb example of a mixed residential and business Victorian neighborhood with a wide variety of architectural styles by the 1980s.

Louisville annexed this land in 1868 to develop its first suburb in the 1870s, and, urged on by the Southern Exposition sited there from 1883 to 1887, the upper classes built hundreds of large houses—especially large Italian Renaissance revival and Richardsonian Romanesque revival structures—during the Gilded Age. In the peak year of 1885, 260 houses were constructed, and by the 1890s St. James Court and Belgravia Court featured secluded parkways, foundations, statues, and an organic setting of trees, flowers, sidewalks, and mixed residential buildings, large and small, in an urban landscape.

The neighborhood became déclassé in the 1920s with the development of automobiles and fashionable suburbs in the eastern borderlands of Louisville. It slowly fell into decay until Restoration Inc. restored ten houses in 1961. The Neighborhood Development Corporation, established in 1968, pressed the preservation agenda further in Old Louisville, and in 1973 the city appointed its first Historic Landmarks and Preservation Districts Commission. Old Louisville now encompasses 101 acres and 1,271 buildings. Third Street is the main thoroughfare.

Visitors should park just south of Ormsby Street, walk down Third Street, go west to Central Park, and walk south down St. James Court.

124. SPEED HOUSE
(Belknap-Speed House)
505 West Ormsby Avenue, Old Louisville
Architect unknown
Landmark designation: NRHP, 1975
c. 1876

James Breckinridge Speed, the grandson of John Speed, was a leading nineteenth-century Louisville industrialist who presided over cement, telephone, and coal companies and wool and cotton mills. His second wife, Harriett Theresa Bishop, built the J. B. Speed Museum (1927). His asymmetrical three-story house has a stone trim, stringcourses, foundation, and water table, and the polychromatic brick window treatments bring life to the red brick exterior walls. A large front porch, held by clustered pillars on double plinths, shelters a door frame of carved stone and heavy double doors with beveled leaded glass. A three-story bay with a conical roof, a side porte cochere with stained-glass lights flanking the door underneath, and a music room designed by Arthur Loomis in 1916 connecting the house to a large carriage house in the garden, all add to the complex nature of this high Victorian labyrinth of rooms, porches, and halls. The public portion of the house has a reception hall with connecting parlor, drawing room, and dining rooms. A winding side staircase with a bronze newel post leads past a stained-glass window flanked by niches to the second and third floors. The bedrooms and dressing rooms on these floors present a variety of fine Victorian hearths. The bathrooms retain many of their earliest features, including a copper bathtub. The music room, built to entertain Louisville society and leased to the Louisville Academy of Music after Harriet Speed's death, has been altered, and its stage made into a separate room.

125. FILSON CLUB HISTORICAL SOCIETY
(E. H. Ferguson Mansion)
1310 South Third Street, Old Louisville
Dodd & Cobb
Landmark designation: NRHP, 1975
1902–1905

Edwin Hite Ferguson, born the son of a tobacco mogul in 1852, had a Midas touch, whether he invested in wholesale businesses or manufacturing. His attempts to corner the cottonseed-oil market in the late 1890s eventually led to his ouster as head of the Kentucky Refining Company in 1907. In 1899, however, when he married Sophie Fullerton Marfield, he was rolling in money, and they lived an extravagant life at 1314 South Fourth Street. Ferguson, then the president of the Louisville Soap Company, purchased the lot north of his house and hired Louisville architect William J. Dodd of Dodd & Cobb (who had trained with William Le Baron Jenney in Chicago and later with Solon S. Beman, on new buildings for the town of Pullman, Illinois) to design a new house there. Dodd proposed a fashionable Beaux Arts dwelling that at the time of its construction was the most expensive home in Old Louisville, costing more than $100,000 by the time it was finished in 1905. Beaux Arts architecture is based on the principles of symmetry, axiality, balanced composition, and functionality, resulting in a utilitarian plan more than in any particular expression, though usually it is neoclassical in style. The Ferguson Mansion is a three-story structure of red brick and limestone, with rusticated limestone on levels one and three. This house presents a projecting central entrance mass and portico, carried by fluted columns and pillars with Ionic capitals, which are flanked by two wings. These three masses are tied together horizontally by a two-part rusticated base of cut limestone. Walls of Roman brick above this base differentiate the public space on the first floor from the private space on the second and third floors. Limestone quoins, a wide frieze, and a heavy classical cornice complete the balanced framing of the design, permitting a variety of neoclassical details on the exterior.

The mansion was purchased in 1926 by C. D. Pearson, who converted the lower floors of the structure into a funeral home while maintaining the upstairs as a family residence. The lavish interior was significantly altered between 1924 and 1927, including the removal of a large stained-glass window and the rerouting of a central staircase. Filled with finely crafted mosaic floors and walls, paneled walls, elaborate hearths, coffered ceilings, art, and sculpture, it maintains much of its original quality, despite its modification.

The Filson Club Historical Society, which purchased the mansion in 1984, currently occupies the site. The Louisville firm Grossman Chapman Kingsley won a 1984 competition to redesign the Ferguson Mansion into a new home for the Filson Club Historical Society. The design was completed in 1986 with the design (by project architect John Grossman and chief designer Robert Kingsley) of the main building, and remodeled the interior for use by the Filson Club. Original photographs of the building hang in the main lobby. Houses to the north and south of the current house were demolished in 1950.

126. FIRST CHURCH OF CHRIST SCIENTIST

1305 South Third Street, Old Louisville
Brinton B. Davis
Landmark designation: NRHP, 1974
1927

In 1913, the First Church of Christ Scientist purchased a site at the southeast corner of South Third Street and Ormsby Avenue in Old Louisville; by 1916, construction had begun, and in 1917 the cornerstone was laid. Completed in stages, the church did not welcome its congregation until 1927. Christian Science churches are not officially dedicated until all indebtedness is paid off, so the building was not dedicated until 1951.

The exterior is native Kentucky limestone, quarried in Bowling Green. Twelve Ionic columns support the pedimented portico and flat-roofed entrance canopy; they were all carved from the same block of limestone. The lettering cut into the stone entablature is of the same style used on the Kentucky State Capitol in Frankfort.

Inspired by the Tomb of Napoleon in France, the sanctuary interior contains a barrel-vaulted skylight, large clerestory, and segmented arched windows.

127. LANDWARD HOUSE
1385 South Fourth Street, Old Louisville
Henry Whitestone, addition by Arthur Loomis
Landmark designation: NRHP, 1973
1872

This stately three-story brick Italianate mansion, originally with 22 rooms and six bathrooms, was one of the first houses in Old Louisville. It was also the office of Dr. Stuart Robinson, M.D. A brick structure faced with limestone creates the five-bay entry facade and projecting entrance. In 1910, Arthur Loomis designed the large rear addition, with its gallery and cast-iron columns, and the side porch leading to the garden that Frederick Law Olmsted Jr. designed in 1929. The garden is divided into three parts: an informal side lawn with edge plantings and three disbursed trees, a formal labyrinth garden, and a vegetable garden that has been transformed into a parking lot. The large carriage house in the rear, now a landscape-architecture firm, once sheltered horse stalls and carriage storage areas on the first floor and provided living space for servants and a hay loft on the second. The plan of the house has a traditional central hall with adjoining library, parlor, dining room, and doctor's office and waiting room.

128. CENTRAL PARK
Fourth and Magnolia Streets, Old Louisville
Olmsted Brothers (Boston)
Landmark designation: NRHP, 1974, 1982
1903–1925

Understandable confusion abounds about the work of Frederick Law Olmsted in Louisville, mostly because his son, Rick, changed his name to Frederick Law Olmsted Jr. and followed in his father's footsteps. He employed the same principles of landscape architecture that his father made famous. Young Olmsted designed Central Park in the year of his father's death, and it took more than 20 additional years to complete the park's design. The Louisville Parks Board purchased Central Park in 1902 from the DuPont family, who had extended the trolley lines from Oak to Magnolia Street, spurring residential development that had begun in the 1870s. The site of the park had been part of the Southern Exposition of 1883–87, but only some statuary remain. In 1905, Olmsted Jr. designed the Tuscan pergola as a formal element in the park as well as a picturesque English landscape that accentuated existing natural elements, especially the large trees, already in place. He planted additional trees, often in clusters, leaving open spaces articulated by trees and meandering sidewalks with benches for sitting and contemplation. Many of the old trees remain. Old postcards show a manicured hedge, defining the edge of the park and distinguishing it from the surrounding streets. Neither Olmsted liked parks with formal recreational areas such as baseball diamonds or football fields, although they acceded to their clients' wishes. In their view, parks were supposed to provide a natural retreat from the ills of the city. This park is a soothing oasis that leads into St. James Court, an exquisite turn-of-the-century development with a central fountain, circle drive, handsome plantings, and variety of large houses.

129. CONRAD-CALDWELL HOUSE
(Theophilus Conrad House)
1402 St. James Court, Old Louisville
Clarke & Loomis
Landmark designation: NRHP, 1975
1893–1894

Built for a tanning merchant and his family at a cost of $35,000, this elaborately detailed limestone mansion, designed by Arthur Loomis on St. James Court, is the epitome of the highly variable residential architecture in the high Victorian neighborhood of Old Louisville. Heavy corner towers and turrets with hexagonal, coned, or pyramidal roofs give the house a vertical framework, within which a variety of architectural elements, fenestration, intricate foliation, and carved faces, shells, lions, fish, and other creatures gleefully operate according to their own rhyme and reason. Squat columns, twisted and carved near their organic capitals, carry the two segmented arches of an off-center porch with a balustrade above. The heavy stringcourses, which stretch across the facades and around the corners, and the monochromatic stonework tie the contrasting masses, planes, and exuberant incrustations together so that the whole becomes more than the sum of its parts. The interior presents the rich complexity that was required to receive Victorian society: a great staircase in the reception hall and carved arched doorways lead into parlors and dining rooms with high ceilings, parquet floors, inlaid window moldings, stained-glass windows, and elaborate fireplaces with carved marble mantels. For 40 years, this house— once called Conrad's Folly—served as the Rose Anna Hughes Presbyterian Retirement Home. Since 1987, the house has belonged to the St. James Court Historic Foundation.

Open to the public Sunday, Wednesday, Thursday, and Friday from noon to 4 P.M. and Saturday from 10 A.M. to 4 P.M.

130. WILLIAM JAMES DODD RESIDENCE
1448 St. James Court, Old Louisville
William James Dodd
1911

The architect William James Dodd designed this house for his own use. At the time it was built, Dodd was in partnership with Kenneth McDonald, and together they designed several commercial and residential buildings in Louisville, including the Western Colored Branch Carnegie Library (1908); the First Christian Church (1910–11); and the YMCA, now the St. Francis (1912–13). The Arts and Crafts house is stucco, with a red tiled roof, and was constructed in 1911 for Dodd and his wife, Ione Estes. Today it is a private residence.

131. TOWNHOUSE GROUP
(Joseph Werne House)
1468 South Fourth Street, Old Louisville
Dodd & Cobb
Landmark designation: NRHP, 1975
1897

These five townhouses, with all their exuberant idiosyncrasies, still present a sophisticated urbane whole that transcends their robust differences through scale, form, material, and insistent horizontal ties at their bases, over the windows, along their stringcourses, and at the cornice level. Their spiked verticality, created through an abundance of finials, dormers with boisterous pediments, and several forms of pyramidal roofs, produce a vaguely chateauesque expression, a variation on the Second Empire Baroque style that Richard Morris Hunt made fashionable in the U.S. after he returned to New York in the 1850s from his studies at the Ecole des Beaux Arts in Paris. As a young architect of 22, William James Dodd came to Louisville in 1884 from Chicago. Having worked with the engineer William Le Baron Jenney and the architect Solon S. Beman (with whom Frank Lloyd Wright also apprenticed), Dodd was well prepared to design in any style and with an imaginative flare. He was also familiar with an apartment plan that had spread from Paris to New York and from there to other American cities like Chicago. With French stylistic precedents and Beaux Arts functionality in mind, Dodd raised the brick townhouses on limestone bases and trimmed the fine red massings with equally fine red terra-cotta details. He gave each house a basement, eight limestone steps to a porch that sheltered the entrance to a reception hall, parlors, and a winding stair to two floors of private rooms above. These townhouses have been divided into numerous apartments and are no longer single-family dwellings.

132. BETHLEHEM EVANGELICAL UNITED CHURCH OF CHRIST

1480 South Sixth Street, Old Louisville
Gray and Wischmeyer
Landmark designation: NRHP, 1975
1915

The Bethlehem United Church of Christ is a three-story brick building, founded by a thriving German congregation. During its heyday in the 1940s and 1950s, more than 300 members would attend Sunday services. But, like many urban churches, Bethlehem United lost membership to suburban flight in the 1960s and 1970s.

The church building sits on a slope above Sixth Street. Detailed with terra-cotta tile (manufactured in Chicago), stained glass, and brown brick in various bond patterns, it presents a hybrid of Mediterranean and mission influences. From the front elevation, the church is one story in height, but three stories are visible from its west elevation. The plan is symmetrically arranged with a bell tower, side aisles, and transepts. The main facade has entrances leading directly into the side aisles, with no direct external entry into the bell tower. All the facades have brick arched openings with limestone keystones. These windows, between limestone-capped brick buttresses, are in pairs and triples and provide clerestory light into the main chancel. All gables have corbelled arches with patterned details and limestone spring stones. Significant alterations include new central heating and air-conditioning and mechanized wheelchair access, yet the building has retained its initial quality and character throughout the years.

133. LOUISVILLE FIRE ACADEMY—FIRE ENVIRONMENT BUILDING

1501 West Hill Street, Parkhill

Arrasmith, Judd, Rapp, Chovan, Inc.

1990

Located on six acres of industrial land in the Parkhill neighborhood of downtown Louisville, the Fire Academy features a complex for fire training, technical support, and administrative facilities. The Fire Environment Building, the first and most prominent building of the master plan, is a unique blend of diverse functional needs with a variety of physical forms, intended to simulate different building types in the city. The resulting design is a cohesive, functional, six-story building. The concrete and galvanized-steel structure steps back at each floor, providing different configurations of balconies, terraces, ladders, stairways, windows, fire escapes, and doors. The interior is unfinished, unheated, open, and provides a two-story loft space with movable partitions, balconies, a stair tower, and an elevator shaft. The plan is flexible to accommodate a variety of spatial arrangements, ranging from residential to commercial to industrial types of buildings.

Merit Award for Excellence in Architectural Design, AIA Kentucky, 1994

134. SPEED ART MUSEUM
(J. B. Speed Memorial Art Museum)
2035 South Third Street, Old Louisville
Arthur Loomis
1925–1927

Named in honor of a Louisville businessman who was active in many charitable organizations and built in his memory by his widow, the J. B. Speed Memorial Art Museum is Kentucky's major art museum. The Speeds were notable collectors of painting and sculpture, although the first major gifts to the museum were from other collectors. Public outreach has been a guiding mission of the museum since its inception, and it has maintained a policy of not charging admission to the public.

The museum is sited on the University of Louisville's Belknap campus in Old Louisville, although it has no formal affiliation with the university. Its original building was designed by noted Louisville architect Arthur Loomis, who was selected for the commission by Mrs. Speed. Its neoclassical design, inspired by the Cleveland Museum of Art, takes the form of an elongated pavilion, built of carved limestone blocks. A ceremonial entrance, framed by two Tuscan columns, faces Third Street. Inside, the galleries are laid out symmetrically; classical details are rendered in marble and bronze. Additions to the museum were anticipated and appear in the form of two wings, extending from either end of the original building.

Dr. Preston Pope Satterwhite was an early supporter of the Speed Art Museum, donating a major collection of fifteenth- and sixteenth-century French and Italian decorative arts in 1941. Three years later, he donated a seventeenth-century room of carved wood in an English Renaissance style, from an estate in Devonshire, England. In 1954, the room was disassembled, moved, and reassembled in a new pavilion added to the original museum; Dr. Satterwhite provided the funding for the addition.

The Satterwhite Wing incorporates the patron's own collection of decorative arts and tapestries and remains a favorite among many of the museum's members. The gallery was renovated as part of the 1995 master plan, and new lighting was installed.

In 1973, reacting to an expansion of programmatic activities, the Speed Art Museum hired Brenner, Danforth, and Rockwell of Chicago to design a major addition for an auditorium, sculpture court, and assorted administrative and support functions. The modern design was a striking departure from the historical style of the original museum.

Gallery space was substantially increased in 1983; a significant addition to the museum included upgraded services and an education center. Unlike the first two additions, located at the edges of the original building, the south addition, by Geddes Brecher Qualls Cunningham of Philadelphia, is directly on axis with the 1927 structure. The exterior of the addition is visible only from the backside of the museum; in keeping with the postmodern idiom, it echoes the proportions and detailing of the original building.

Recognizing deficiencies in its administrative services, the museum undertook a significant master-planning effort in the mid-1990s. Architect Peter Rose, who had recently completed the Canadian Center for Architecture in Montreal, led the master plan and subsequently provided the first designs. These projects were not glamorous but crucial to the operation of a professional contemporary exhibition facility: art storage and security were upgraded; delivery areas were vastly enlarged; and space for support staff was increased. There were improvements to the public areas as well: the Satterwhite galleries were renovated; the educational area was upgraded into an interactive learning center; and a parking facility, shared with the university, was built.

The Speed Art Museum has grown significantly since its inception. The various additions reflect the priorities of the periods in which they were built and have served the museum well. Yet they do not work together; the museum is at this time an interesting agglomeration of pieces, rather than an integrated whole. Realizing this discord, the museum is presently exploring options to address a more comprehensive facility for itself, either through addition to and renovation of the present structures or by moving some significant portion of its activities to a separate location.

135. UNIVERSITY OF LOUISVILLE, BELKNAP CAMPUS
South Third Street, Old Louisville
Multiple architects
1927–Present

Feeling pressures to expand, the University of Louisville moved from a downtown location to the Belknap Campus in Old Louisville in the mid-1920s. The site had been used as a House of Refuge for girls in the middle of the nineteenth century and as the Industrial School of Reform in the early twentieth century. A commitment by the university to provide facilities for higher education for African Americans led to the approval of a bond issue for new buildings, allowing the university to embark on a building program. Among the first were the Administration Building (pictured), modeled after Thomas Jefferson's University of Virginia Library (it was designed by Frederick Morgan and Arthur Tafel Sr. in 1927, renovated by Jasper Ward in 1975, and renamed Grawemeyer Hall in 1988), and the J. B. Speed Scientific School. The Speed Art Museum, on the grounds of the

Belknap Campus but not directly affiliated with the university, was built in 1927.

After World War II, the university went through a substantial period of enrollment growth, which culminated in a number of new large buildings in the late 1960s and the next decade. One notable building of the postwar period is the Natural Sciences Building of 1954, a brick classroom structure with exceptional limestone detailing, especially at the entrance colonnade and the stairs leading up to it, facing onto Eastern Parkway. It was designed by W. S. Arrasmith of Arrasmith and Tyler.

An academic quadrangle was created just north of Grawemeyer Hall in the early 1970s, when a new library, life-sciences building, and humanities building were completed. Each of these buildings composed one side of the quad; the fourth side is Gardiner Hall, the oldest building on the Belknap Campus (1871). All of the new buildings utilize cantilevered portions of upper floors to create a modern interpretation of a cloistered academic quadrangle. Consistency of materials brings the buildings together, while variations in volume and circulation paths establish individual qualities for each. Noted modern architect Pietro Belluschi served as a consultant on the design of the quad.

Ekstrom Library was designed by the Louisville firm Louis & Henry and completed in 1981. It is the largest of the buildings on the quadrangle. The main entrance faces east onto the quad. The plan utilizes diagonal geometries to link different rectangular volumes. These geometries are accentuated by the surface of the building: brick, concrete, and glass panels are completely flush, emphasizing the tautness of the plan's geometry.

Across the quad is the Humanities Building (now the Bingham Humanities Building). Designed by Sasaki, Dawson, DeMay Associates (Watertown, Massachusetts) and completed in 1973, it has its own courtyard, with thirty classrooms and departmental offices located around it. An open walkway defines the entrance to the courtyard, and individual classrooms cantilever out of the main body to provide covered walkways at the edge of the quadrangle.

The first of the quadrangle buildings to be built was the Life Sciences Building (1970), also designed by Louis & Henry. The three-story structure has a concrete frame, with brick and glass panels; like the library, each material is flush, emphasizing the taut qualities of the exterior of the building. A true colonnade runs the entire front of the building, with selected classrooms cantilevered even further beyond its edge. This circulation route works well for students arriving from the fraternities and dormitories along Third and Fourth Streets. Finally, a path runs through the center of the building, directly into the center of the quad.

The School of Music (1980) was designed by James Lee Gibson of Bickel Gibson. This large building wraps partially around a central raised courtyard, protecting it from the traffic on nearby Cardinal Lane and creating the ambience of a small Italian campo. The materials and volume of the building resonate with the academic work of the noted English architect James Stirling. The recital hall inside the School of Music is a remarkable accomplishment in both design and acoustics. The warmth of its wood interior finish is matched by the quality of its sound and accordingly has developed quite a following in the city's cultural circles. It is the home of the Chamber Music Society of Louisville.

Louis & Henry have carried out more work for the university than any other architect, and four of their campus projects provide a useful overview of the changing sensibilities of the firm. Crawford Gymnasium, from 1964 (when the firm was named Hartstern, Louis & Henry), demonstrates the firm's facility with concrete construction, which was the material of choice for most major projects in the city at the time. The roof was the first thin-shell concrete structure in the region, spanning 125 feet in each direction and forming a flattened dome. The thickness of the material was just four inches.

For the College of Business and Public Administration (1985), Louis & Henry utilized Pietro Belluschi as a consultant. Together they developed a large building that opened onto an inner courtyard. Circulation through the courtyard moved in an irregular manner, creating the ambience of a small piazza. At the same time, the firm geometries of the plan played diagonal lines against orthogonal volumes; well-crafted details, such as sharp-edged exterior stairs, resolved these different organizing systems with skill.

Lutz Hall (1996) provides room for an array of liberal arts programs. Two massive steel arches, rising nearly three stories, frame the entrances to the building. The lobby is compromised slightly by the intrusion of the elevator systems into the monumental volume, yet the effect remains grand. A rusticated-limestone base supports a taut rectangular brick volume.

The Gheens Science Hall and Rauch Planetarium (2001) replace an earlier structure, which was razed to allow space for a parking garage to serve the university and the Speed Art Museum. The design uses a distinctive circular geometry to create an enclosed yet exterior forecourt to the new planetarium. The building itself is a truncated conical shape.

One final noteworthy campus building is Evelyn Schneider Hall (formerly the University Library). It is used by the Fine Arts department, as well as by the Art Library and Dario Covi Gallery. The building was completed in 1957 by the New York firm O'Connor and Kilham (known for its library designs). Its simple brick volume is augmented by an asymmetrical glass and limestone entry pavilion and by a deep brise soleil on the south side of the building, facing the Cochran Fountain.

136. REYNOLDS METALS BUILDING
(Ford Motor Company Building)
2500-2520 South Third Street, University
Albert Kahn
1915

The Ford Motor Company Building, a four-story reinforced concrete structure sheathed in ornamental brick was designed by Albert Kahn and constructed in 1915 on the two-and-one-third-acre site across Third Street from the University of Louisville.

The building's footprint is eleven bays wide and is designed to accommodate both the angle of Third Street and the railroad tracks that cross in front of it. The building pays homage to the image of the traditional factory building with its ornamented brickwork, while exhibiting modernistic tenets such as a dominant horizontal reading of its facades, a functionalist program-driven setting, and simple design and construction. Albert Kahn is noted for designing more than 1,000 industrial buildings for Ford and hundreds for General Motors and Packard. Each structure was open, bright, airy, simple, efficient, and well proportioned. This building prototype became synonymous with Albert Kahn and the Ford Motor Company. A one-story building with identical detailing to the original structure was added in 1923 and removed in 1935 when the buildings were sold to the Reynolds Metals Company. Reynolds altered the windows, infilling the upper two floors with glass blocks, and added corrugated-aluminum awnings.

The building is currently owned by the University of Louisville and used for storage.

137. HOLY NAME CHURCH
2914–16 South Third Street, South End
Architect unknown (church), J. J. Gaffney (school and rectory), and
Thomas J. Nolan (convent)
Landmark designation: NRHP, 1982
1902–1953

The Holy Name complex comprises of four distinct structures, which consist of a church, school and rectory, and convent. J. J. Gaffney, a prominent Louisville architect, is noted for such dynamic ecclesiastical projects as the Temple Adath Jeshurun (now the Unity Temple) and St. James Roman Catholic Church.

The Holy Name school was built in 1902 and included an auditorium. Constructed as a two-and-a-half-story red brick structure, the auditorium served as a temporary church until the church proper was completed in 1912. The church, consecrated in 1924 and easily the most impressive structure in the complex, is a steel-framed Romanesque revival building with Byzantine details, brown glazed brick, and cream-colored brick trim. The primary facade consists of a central gabled section that is flanked by two towers: a bell tower to the south and a slightly smaller tower to the north. Both towers are covered with red tile. The church is arranged in a Latin-cross plan, with five pairs of slender Corinthian steel columns supporting ribbed vaults that span the nave and side aisles. Tall stained-glass windows and sculptured stations of the cross surround the interior walls of the sanctuary.

The church has undergone two significant interior renovations: one in 1938 included the laying of new terrazzo floors, the renovation of the pews, and the installation of new lighting; another in the early 1960s incorporated the liturgical changes, including the removal of the marble-trimmed communion rail and conch-shell pulpit. The original church had exquisite ceiling ornamentation, which was eventually removed because the expense to restore and maintain it proved to be prohibitive. The central altar used today came from the chapel in the convent (1938), which is now the headquarters of Catholic Charities.

The rectory, also designed by Gaffney and built in 1927, is an orange-glazed brick residence. The convent, by Thomas J. Nolan, is similar in style and materials used.

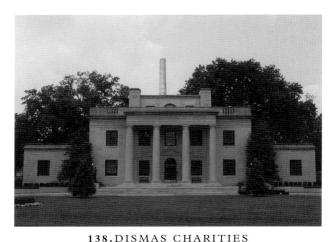

138.DISMAS CHARITIES
(Seagram's Distillery and Administrative Offices)
2400-2600 Seventh Street Road, South End
Joseph and Joseph
1933–1936

The Seagram's Distillery campus includes the administration building (1933), which served as Seagram's headquarters and is of the Regency revival style. Four large limestone columns support a portico, marking the entry to the limestone-faced building. The interior has marble floors and walnut paneling.

The distillery warehouse complex provides a dynamic, over-scaled backdrop to the administration building. The brick ware-houses, constructed in 1936, have art deco limestone detailing. They have connecting tunnels below ground, so that the barrels were never visible to the public as they moved from building to building. During World War II, the set of buildings was converted for the production of industrial alcohol, used to make synthetic rub-ber and various medicines. Seagram's closed the complex in 1983. The buildings are now occupied by various tenants, which include storage and manufacturing facilities as well as office space.

139. CHURCHILL DOWNS
(Louisville Jockey Club and Driving Park Association)
700 Central Avenue, Oakdale
John Andrewartha, Joseph Baldez
Landmark designation: NRHP, 1978; NHL, 1978
1875

Churchill Downs is a 147-acre parcel of land that Meriwether Lewis Clark Jr. purchased for the Louisville Jockey Club and Driving Park Association from the Churchill family to replace the Oakland Race Course that began operating in Old Louisville in 1833. John Andrewartha designed the original entrance lodge, grandstand, clubhouse, and stables on the southeast curve of track in time for the first running of the Kentucky Derby in 1875 (none of his work remains). Officially known as Churchill Downs only since 1937, the racetrack has undergone a myriad of changes into the twenty-first century. In 1882, the Jockey Club had the grandstand lengthened and added three towers and a promenade. All of these original structures were replaced between 1895 and 1896 with a brick and metal girder grandstand on the west side of the track that included the famous twin spires designed by Joseph Baldez, a draftsman for D. X. Murphy & Brothers. Some of this grandstand is still extant, and part of the classical clubhouse (1902) stood until 2003. By the 1940s, the grandstand stretched around the first curve, and in the 1960s VIP skyboxes were erected where the old clubhouse stood, giving the grandstand, especially the west facade, the appearance of a giant ship. This was mostly removed in 2003. With a new museum in 1985, a new entrance in 2000, and extensive remodeling as late as 2004, Churchill Downs will have more than 51,000 seats and will offer new services such as an expanded Turf Club, luxury suites, integrated simulcast wagering, a Millionaire's Row, and premium box seating. The new facility, along with infield and backside standing capacity, can entertain 165,000 fans for America's most famous stakes race, which occurs on the first Saturday of every May. The place rather than the main building gives Churchill Downs its National Historic Landmark status. No matter the building, racing fans and visitors love to witness the most exciting story here, the running of the horses and the winning of bets on a close race.

140. EASTSIDE CHRISTIAN CHURCH–FAMILY LIFE CENTER
1732 Thames Drive, Jeffersonville Indiana
Omni Architects (Lexington), Michael Jacobs, Eric Zabilka
1996

When Eastside Christian Church moved from Clarksville to Jeffersonville, Indiana, the church hired Omni Architects to design a master plan that would incorporate a new church and an activities building. When the master plan was completed, finances dictated that the Family Life Center be built first. The center includes administrative offices, classrooms and educational facilities, and a gymnasium that also serves as a worship space. The congregation wanted the facility to communicate its "contemporary Christian message" with a nontraditional design solution. The dominant feature of the building is a conical skylight enclosure at the front entrance. Inside, the space expands vertically toward the skylight and horizontally toward the gymnasium and worship space.

The gymnasium, surrounded on three sides by circulation corridors and placed at the center of the building, allows for future expansion of classrooms to the north side of the building. To visually anchor the building into the flat site, the architects used a stepped flat-metal system at the pedestrian level to create a plinth. Above it, the exterior facade has a heavy corrugated-metal skin, which further defines the building's primary programmatic spaces. Instead of using a vertical cap detail at the corners, which would have dominated the facade, the building has mitered corners, suggesting a more continuous surface. The facade gradually arcs in the vertical dimension, hiding the rooftop mechanical units behind the wall.

The future church, to sit in front of the Family Life Center, will further define the courtyard as a center for outdoor fellowship. *Metal Architecture Awards Program, National Merit Award and Award of Merit, AIA Kentucky, 2000*

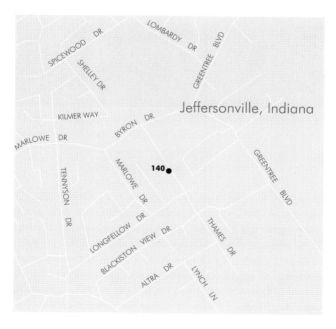

Map 5: Building 140 (Jeffersonville, Indiana)

141. PORTLAND NEIGHBORHOOD HISTORIC DISTRICT

Northwestern Parkway

Landmark designation: NRHP, 1980

1811

Surveyed in 1811, Portland developed along the Ohio River next to Shippingport and Louisville, and when the Louisville and Portland Canal opened in 1830, Portland had grown into a thriving town, filled with wharves, warehouses, taverns, hotels, and working-class residences on small lots. Annexed in 1834, then declared independent in 1842 over a controversy about a railroad connection to its wharf that was never realized, Portland was settled in the 1850s by Irish immigrants who voted successfully in 1852 to make Portland part of Louisville again. The neighborhood retained its maritime focus until 1871, when the wharves and warehouses were empty as a result of the widening of the canal for larger ships.

Significant architecture includes vernacular warehouses, residences, the U.S. Marine Hospital (1852) designed by Robert Mills, Notre Dame du Port Church (1871), Portland School (1855), and the Carnegie Library designed by Val P. Collins (1913). The Portland Museum at 2308 Portland Avenue exhibits a history of the neighborhood that once helped ferry escaped slaves on the Underground Railroad across the river to New Albany, Indiana. The neighborhood still possesses a rich brick industrial fabric and working-class houses of many types. The exteriors of these houses provide a history of building materials, especially the manufactured stone that dots the long east-west thoroughfares, an element that gives Portland a variable and robust urban texture, enhanced by decorated and fenced yards.

142. PORTLAND ELEMENTARY SCHOOL
3410 Northwestern Parkway, Portland
Jasper D. Ward
1967–1968

Portland Elementary includes a renovation of the original simple four-room schoolhouse that dates from 1853 and an addition that wraps around the original structure, integrating it into the design.

The pedimented roof of the original structure is visible above the new arched entry.

The modern structure was designed in 1968 by Jasper D. Ward, a leading architect in Louisville, known for his contextually sensitive building and community activism, and is a monumental building with large arched openings and pure geometric forms. The windows and volumes of the addition evoke the paddle-wheel steamships that used to frequent the Portland area at the turn of the twentieth century. The design respects the old building while including elegant and imaginative details: the windows of the original structure have been transformed into door openings to the new addition or infilled with chalkboards and bulletin boards. Programmatically, the addition provides new light-filled classrooms, recreational areas, an administration suite, and dining spaces.

A separate structure, the "playtorium" (a gymnasium without spectator space), was added in 1988 and is linked to the main structure by a glass-enclosed passageway. Subsequent renovations, to bring the entire complex up to current Kentucky Education Reform Act (KERA) standards, were completed in 1991.

Design Award, AIA Kentucky, 1968

143. METRO PARKS
(Olmsted Parks and Parkway System)
Frederick Law Olmsted Sr., Olmsted Brothers
Landmark designation: NRHP, 1982
1891–1940

In 1891, the city asked Frederick Law Olmsted Sr., already in his 69th year but still the most well-known landscape architect in America, to design a park and parkway system according to the precepts he wrote down in a proposal titled "What Louisville Needs."

In the form of a so-called "emerald necklace," Olmsted designed six of the parks and parkways, including Cherokee Park (1891), Shawnee Park (1892), and Iroquois Park (1892). By mid-1895, Olmsted could no longer work, and his son, Rick, and stepson, John, continued their father's work as the Olmsted Brothers, who by 1940 had designed and built twelve more parks, including Chickasaw Park (1921) and Seneca Park (1928). Olmsted Sr. took advantage of existing natural settings, making them accessible to the public through winding roads that pay special attention to the topography and scenic views. At Cherokee Park, a one-way road loops through thick woods, meanders along Beargrass Creek, and curves around clearings and hills, taking visitors to Big Rock and into formal collecting points, such as Hogan's Fountain and Christiansen Fountain. Iroquois Park has a mountainous, wooded setting that provides spectacular views of the city. Shawnee Park, used primarily for various forms of recreation, is a flat site bordering the Ohio River, which Olmsted addressed with a road from one end of the park to the other. He formed a great open space with an encircling parkway that leads to three organic concourses and a lily pool. See Susan Rademacher's essay, "A Living Legacy: Louisville's Olmsted Landscapes," for more information (p 45).

144. MEAD CONTAINER COMPANY BUILDING
(Ford Motor Company Plant)
1400 Southwestern Parkway, Parkland
Albert Kahn
Landmark designation: NRHP, 1983
1924–1925

The success of the Model T and its variants resulted in an increase in production and employment that was too much for the Third Street plant (2500 South Third Street) to handle. A new plant was completed in 1925 on the site of the old Kentucky State Fairgrounds. The plant is a one-story decorative-brick building and is an excellent example of the industrial architecture fostered by Albert Kahn in the U.S. Typical of other industrial plants by Kahn for the Ford Motor Company, everything is under one roof. The building, constructed of steel and faced with brick in ornate patterns, has a series of standard-designed sawtooth skylights, which allow natural light to penetrate deep into the work environment. The Mead Corporation purchased the plant in 1959 and subsequently renovated the interior. This renovation, however, is reversible: the original building fabric still exists behind drop ceilings and removable partitions.

145. PARK DUVALLE
(Cotter Lang Homes)
1804 Russell Lee Drive, West End
UDA Architects (Pittsburgh), Louisville Development Authority,
William Rawn (Boston)
1999

In 1992, the federal government approved the Urban Revitalization Demonstration Program. Hope VI, as it is now called, allows cities to implement extreme solutions to the problem of severely distressed public housing, including the replacement of existing structures with an entirely new plan. The goals for the program were to promote mixed-income development, stable social and physical environs, and residential oversight. Louisville received a $51,000,000 grant in 1993 and applied it to the neighborhood of the Cotter Lang Homes. A broad consortium of public and private interests brought another $140,000,000 to the project.

A master plan was developed by the Louisville Development Authority and consultant Ray Gindroz of UDA Associates, leading to the involvement of local residential builders who agreed to follow architectural guidelines set forth by the planners. From the time ground was broken and the first model houses completed, Park DuValle was a success, providing both public and market-rate housing together in one development. Over 450 private homes have been sold, and another 760 rental units are occupied. A town center with roughly 25,000 square feet of retail space began construction in 2004.

The social values of the Hope VI program were an important hypothesis for the Park DuValle project; by all accounts, it has achieved its goals. A distressed and often dangerous housing project has been replaced with a stable, mixed-income neighborhood. Many of the area residents have made the transition from Cotter Lang to Park DuValle and benefited from it.

146. CARTER DUVALLE EDUCATION CENTER
3500 Bohne Avenue, Park DuValle
Tyler and Associates, Voelker Winn Architects
c. 1940

The Carter DuValle Education Center juxtaposes old and new construction to create a lively component of the Park DuValle redevelopment. The project combines two 1940s school buildings by Tyler and Associates that were converted into a community and service center in the 1980s into a single structure, providing for an elementary school and neighborhood service facility. Voelker Winn Architects utilized different portions of the old Cotter Elementary School and DuValle Junior High School to provide space to relocate Carter Traditional Elementary School to the site and add a community center (including the Head Start program) and a neighborhood family and health facility.

The architects added a new wing for Head Start, which enclosed a space between the two former schools as an interior court for the preschool children. Another courtyard was also created by new construction. Strong geometric forms are used throughout the project to reinforce basic learning concepts in the educational programs. The former auditorium of the middle school has been renovated into the media center/library and is an important resource for the community.

The project was the last element of the Park DuValle neighborhood redevelopment.

Honored by the National Trust for Historic Preservation in its Historic Schools Success Stories project, 2004; Brick Award of Honor, Kentuckiana Masonry Institute, 2004.

147. LOUISVILLE PATRIOTS PEACE MEMORIAL

Thurman-Hutchins Park (River Road and Indian Hills Trail), Indian Hills

David Quillin (Berlin, Maryland)

2002

The tragic peacetime death of a local soldier led to a design competition for a pavilion that honors local military personnel who "gave their lives in the line of duty for the United States at times other than those of declared hostile action." The design competition was guided by noted Louisville architect Jim Walters of Bravura. The winning project was designed by architect David Quillin, a one-person firm from the Eastern Shore of Maryland; forty other entries were considered. Humana Corporation chair David Jones donated the land for the project, which is adjacent to a major recreational park along the Ohio River.

Quillin's design is a roofless square pavilion, built of brick, which is intended to act as a lantern. The pavilion is lifted off the ground on a series of piers; a square spiral of stairs takes the visitor away from the noise of the adjacent park up into the pavilion, where the names of those honored service men and women are engraved on glass bricks. The lantern metaphor is apt; the structure changes dramatically in different qualities of light. Look carefully at the facade that faces River Road: in the right light, a slight variation in the type of brick creates an American flag across the front of the structure.

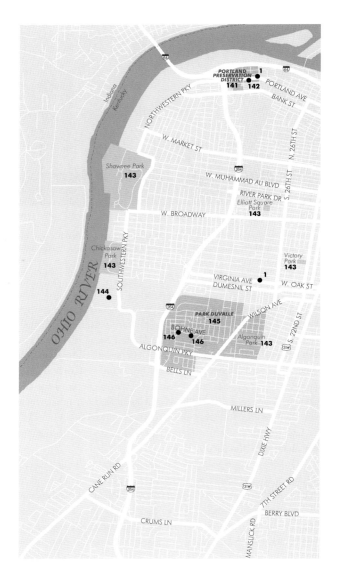

Map 6: Buildings 141–146

148. LOUISVILLE VISUAL ARTS ASSOCIATION

(Louisville Water Company and Pumping Station)

River Road at Zorn Avenue, Mockingbird Valley

Theodore R. Scowden

Landmark designation: NHL

1858–1860s

The Kentucky legislature granted a charter to the Louisville Water Company in 1854, and this classical revival complex pumped its first water in 1860, saving Louisville from typhoid and cholera epidemics and providing fire protection. Theodore Scowden, an engineer and architect who also designed waterworks for Cleveland and Cincinnati, may have modeled his white waterworks after Benjamin Latrobe's famous Philadelphia Waterworks, built in 1800. Some scholars suggest that C. N. Ledoux's Royal Salt Works (1775) at Arc-et-Senans, France, was Scowden's model.

The original waterworks consisted of a wooden standpipe, a 158-foot painted brick engine and boiler room, two offices, two coal houses, and two smokestacks. After an 1890 tornado destroyed the complex, it was rebuilt with a 169-foot Doric tower and belvedere made of riveted cast iron. The base of the standpipe is a Corinthian peristyle with entablature, balustrade, and ten zinc figures. Nine figures are classical gods and goddesses. The tenth figure, of an American Indian and his dog, replaced a classical figure destroyed by the tornado. Behind the standpipe sits the two-story temple-like engine and boiler building, with a portico held up by four Corinthian columns with terra-cotta capitals. The delicate white exterior of the classical complex stands in contrast to a later waterworks, with its muscular limestone tower and buildings. Still owned and maintained by the Louisville Water Company, the waterworks was retired in 1909, renovated from 1978 to 1980 and again in 1993. The Louisville Visual Arts Association now uses the structure for an art gallery.

Open Monday to Friday, 9 A.M. to 5 P.M. and Saturday, 12 P.M. to 4 P.M.

149. MERRIWETHER HOUSE
6421 Upper River Road, Harrod's Creek
Harry Hall Merriwether
Landmark designation: NRHP, 1989
Late nineteenth century

Harry and Isaac Merriwether were early African American residents of the Harrod's Creek area. They sited their house on a knoll overlooking a tributary that frequently swelled outside its banks, but only once in the memory of family members has water entered the house. This two-story, side entry–hall house has a hipped roof, a wraparound porch, and is sheathed with clapboard. As a vernacular structure, it grew by slow accretion over the years with the additions of a lateral hall, a kitchen on the rear elevation, and three rooms on the far-side elevation.

150. STITES RESIDENCE
(Speed Residence)
34 Mockingbird Valley Drive, Mockingbird Valley
Samuel Calvin Molloy
1938

The site of the Speed Residence is immediately adjacent to the Louisville Country Club in Mockingbird Valley. While his wife was traveling, Evarts Speed commissioned Louisville architect Samuel Calvin Molloy to design a modern home that would reflect European influences of the time. Upon her return, Mrs. Speed was quoted as saying, "Evarts! I'm not living in any damn filling station."

The house plan and cubic massing is clearly modern. The original program called for a strict separation of public (living/dining) and private spaces (bedrooms), with three bedrooms, a living room, dining room, kitchen, and entrance hall. This portion of the building had Masonite floors (now hardwood) throughout, a painted white brick exterior, and a flat, built-up membrane roof. A cantilevered overhang sits just above door height at the front entry. A narrow entrance hallway leads to the main public living space, which combines the living and dining areas, the path of circulation serving as a transition between them. The entry-hall and living-room windows were originally glass block but have been replaced (along with those in the dining room) with vertical clear-glass fixed windows, creating a space that is visually transparent from front to rear. In the bedrooms, large double-hung windows meet at the corners and spatially extend the interior cubic massing of the room into the exterior.

From the front, the house appears to be a one-story house nestled into the hillside, but it is much larger from the rear, with a walkout basement. Sitting on a high red-brick plinth, the house becomes a jewel in the landscape. A rear sun porch and freestanding garage were added in 1960. The original attached garage was converted into a residential wing. The sun porch was enclosed in the mid-1970s and extends from the kitchen, continuing the vertical fenestration of the other living spaces. The garage has horizontal siding with a ten-inch exposure and proportions similar to the original house.

151. SHEARER RESIDENCE
(Miles Residence)
32 Mockingbird Valley Drive, Mockingbird Valley
Grossman Martin Chapman
1975–1978

The leaders of Louisville's banks were among the first advocates for modern architecture, and that influence extended beyond their business activities. In 1975, Stephen Miles, then president of the First National Bank, commissioned H. Stow Chapman to design a modern house in Mockingbird Valley. Chapman's design used two overlapping grids—one at 90° and another at 45°—to organize the house in both plan and section. The project, which pivots on a centrally located fireplace, is essentially one continuous volume, unified under a series of steeply sloping roofs and high ceilings, each relating to the programmatic elements below. The first floor has an entry, living room, dining room, kitchen, master bedroom, and three-car garage. The second floor has a children's bedroom and guest bedroom. The master bedroom borrows light from an interior skylight that extends from the bedroom to an exterior skylight in the living room, thus maintaining visual privacy. The exterior of the house is a white-stained red cedar vertical siding. A pool at the rear of the house continues the grid orientation, as a primary ten-yard swimming pool crosss at a 45° angle.

152. NORMAN RESIDENCE
(DeCamp Residence)
615 Club Lane, Mockingbird Valley
Design Environment Group Architects (DEGA)
1969–1971

Located on a cul-de-sac on what was formerly the Bigelow Estate, this modern house sits halfway down a steeply sloping wedge-shaped plot of land in Mockingbird Valley Estates. The placement of the building allows the three sloping roofs of the house to sit just above street level, masking the two-story volume of the actual house. Low concrete garden walls at the street prevent a direct view of the house and shelter the main entry from public view above.

Poured-in-place concrete foundation walls step down the hillside, allowing the J-shaped plan to clearly divide the programmatic elements at both the upper and lower levels. The first floor contains a living room, master bedroom, den, dining room, guest bedroom, and kitchen, all connected by a circulation spine. Three staircases—two inside and one outside—lead to the three bedrooms and mechanical space below. One staircase is a square tower, fondly known as the "silo," which links the living room with the lower-level common room. The exterior staircase links two distinctly different decks. On the lower level, a covered eating and cooking deck, made with aggregate-concrete flooring, provides private dining with views of the woods. The upstairs deck links views between the living room, dining room, and kitchen, providing an open-air informal dining space. The location of this deck visually extends the space of each of the rooms, making them appear larger. The master-bedroom suite contains clerestory "moon windows" that reflect the evening light deep into the room. The original house had exposed vertical cedar panels with a painted standing-seam metal roof. The roof has since been replaced with an asphalt shingle roof, and the siding has been painted gray-green; however, the original character of the house remains.

153. BUTCHERTOWN HISTORIC DISTRICT
Washington Street
Landmark designation: NRHP, 1976
1820s

This area began to fill with German immigrants in the late 1820s, and the Bourbon Stock Yards, established in 1834, brought more immigrants before and after the Civil War, who worked in the neighborhood's meat-packing, soap-making, and beer-making industries well into the twentieth century. Animals were driven to the stock yards on Frankfort Pike as late as the 1940s, but many other manufacturing buildings were established along the railroad, including four breweries. By the 1870s and 1880s, the tall steeples of large Roman Catholic and Protestant churches, such as St. Joseph's Catholic Church, symbolized the variety of religious beliefs held by the community. The flood of 1937 was devastating, and in the 1960s the neighborhood was re-zoned to industrial status, even though much of it was still residential. The construction of I-64 cut off part of the neighborhood, and the expansion of that thoroughfare threatens Butchertown today. Preservationists worked hard to keep it a mixed industrial-residential working-class neighborhood, and parts of it have been populated with artists and young professionals. The historic district is composed of 724 parcels on 129 acres and is made up of about 45% commercial and industrial buildings and 30% residential structures. Many camelback shotgun houses, mixed with numerous other house types, line the streets. The Hadley Pottery Company on 1570 Story Avenue owns one of the oldest warehouses, which has remained almost unchanged since the mid-nineteenth century.

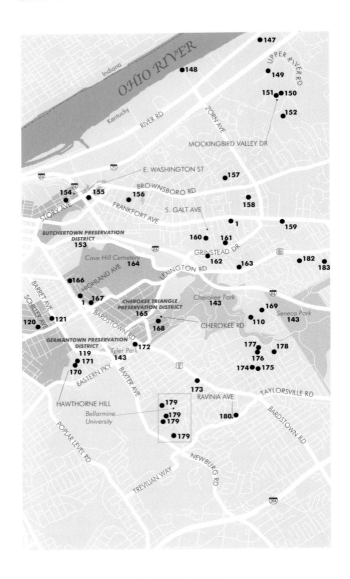

Map 7: Buildings 147–180

154. ST. JOSEPH'S CATHOLIC CHURCH
1406 East Washington Street, Butchertown
A. J. Schelling
Landmark designation: NRHP, 1976
1883–1905

The twin spires of this brick Gothic church, like many church tow-ers in Germany, are visible for a long distance, providing a hallmark of the neighborhood of Butchertown. The area was settled mostly by German Roman Catholics and Protestants before and after the Civil War to fill factory and railroad jobs nearby. The current church replaced an original edifice in 1883, though its towers were not fin-ished until 1905. A. J. Schelling put his name on the building as the architect, but A. Druiding of St. Louis may be responsible for the interior plan. Louis Hodapp was the master brick mason, and Urban Stengel built the limestone foundation. The nave has white walls, a flat interior ceiling fashioned as an ogee arch and liernes, and blue wood and plaster trim. A ribbed vaulting with liernes bursts over the chancel. The altar and two side altars are astounding hand-carved wooden Baroque pieces designed by H. Allard and carved at the Josephinum Orphanage in Columbus, Ohio. The towering main altar portrays Louis IX, St. Joseph, and a pelican finial symbolic of the church feeding its young. One of the side altars presents St. Michael driving out the devil, sculpted with the stereotypical pointed ears, fire-red body, and tail. Many details throughout the church are edged in gold leaf. The communion rails divide the chancel from the nave and the pews on each side of a central aisle and are original. Adjacent to the church is the Grotto of Lourdes (1922) and the rectory (1939).

155. HADLEY POTTERY COMPANY
1570 Story Avenue, Butchertown
Landmark designation: NRHP, 1976
c. 1855

The Bourbon Stock Yards opened in the Butchertown neighborhood in 1834 and closed in 1999. To transform the by-products of the slaughterhouse into many useful products, enterprising people built factories and warehouses near the stockyard. These structures were built according to precedents set for industrial architecture during the mid-eighteenth century in England and later in the U.S., such as Slater's Textile Mill in Pawtucket, Rhode Island, and textile

mills in Lowell and Waltham, Massachusetts. Like these, the Hadley
Pottery Company Building is a long, thin brick and stone structure
with many windows, which allow plenty of light and ventilation into
the manufacturing space. It has three floors and a basement, with an
interior structure of heavy wooden beams that hold the floors. This
building has accommodated a number of different manufacturers
since about 1855, including the Butchertown Candle Company,
the Louisville Saddle & Girth Mills, the Semple Cordage Mill, and,
since 1945, the Hadley Pottery Company. The accommodations
have often required changes and additions to the original structure,
resulting in the current accretive, vernacular building that, as one of
the oldest surviving industrial buildings in Louisville, has given service to several generations of manufacturers for the last 150 years.
The longest and present occupant has been Hadley Pottery, founded by Mary Alice Hadley to produce her award-winning pottery.
Open Monday to Friday, 8:30 A.M. to 5:00 P.M. and Saturday, 9:00
A.M. to 1:00 P.M.

156. KENTUCKY SCHOOL FOR THE BLIND
(Kentucky Institution for the Education of the Blind)
1867 Frankfort Avenue, Clifton
Jasper D. Ward and Robert Kingsley
1975

Dating to the first half of the nineteenth century, the Kentucky
School for the Blind was the third institution of its kind in the U.S.

It was housed initially on Broadway and moved to the Frankfort Avenue site in 1855, in a notable building designed by Elias E. Williams. That structure was razed in 1967.

In the 1970s, Jasper Ward was retained to design a new auditorium on the campus. Working with Robert Kingsley, he created a severe brick volume. The only relief in the brick walls is a colonnade of piers that runs entirely around the perimeter of the building; a limited number of windows and doors are located behind the colonnade and thus are largely invisible from the exterior. The square piers and the spaces between them are equal in size; this narrow spacing is echoed in the space between the piers and the building itself. The ground floor slopes as it follows a swale in the landscape.

Ward and Kingsley's goal was to translate the experience of the primary occupants of the building to the public at large: that is, the auditorium is a building that is intended to be felt, not seen. The complete lack of visible openings from the exterior, the close spacing of the piers so that one could literally move from one to another without losing touch with the building, and the sloping floor as an orienting system are manifestations of this idea. In its materials and form, the style of the architecture resonates with a number of the later works of noted Finnish architect Alvar Aalto and demonstrate the architects' professional aspirations for the building.

There are other interesting buildings on the campus as well. Bickel Gibson carried out a library and bridge just west of the auditorium in 1982. In that project, the architects reinforced the modernist style of the auditorium and sited their building in a manner that emphasized the auditorium's importance as the public face of the school.

157. HENRY REED HOUSE
(Selema Hall)
2837 Riedling Road, Clifton Heights
Architect unknown
Landmark designation: NRHP, 1978
1837

Selema Hall, built as a plantation house in 1837 on an estate
that originally entailed 6,000 acres, shows some similarities to
Farmington—built 30 years earlier on the other side of Louisville—
but it is significantly larger in plan and scale. Selema Hall's core is
a five-bay brick square with Flemish and English bond walls, which
rise from an English basement and are capped by a white cornice
of dentils and modillions, a low, pyramidal roof, and a lantern. The
roof has a wood structural system, held together by lapped mortise
and tenon connections. Paired fluted columns and Ionic capitals
carry the flat-roofed portico that leads to a large federal door, surrounded by a frame with rose medallions, sidelights, and a transom
of cut glass. Underneath, the portico shelters a porch and outside
entrance to the basement. The portico on the rear elevation creates
a sheltered entrance to the main floor and to the basement. On the
main floor, the central-hall plan provides a wide hall with high ceilings and tall doors that open into spacious double parlors, a drawing
room, and a dining room. Gigantic wood-paneled doors between
the double rooms complement the expressive Greek revival wall

paneling, the dark wood floors with boards of various widths, and carved marble hearths that are the foci in the four main rooms. A curvaceous balustrade, set in the middle of the hall not far from the rear door, surrounds a stairwell and delicate stair and railings that lead down to a wide central hall in a basement with three rooms. On the main and basement floors the wide back porch has been filled in to create transverse halls and connections to a large servants' wing, which stretches into the backyard.

158. MILAM TANDY HOUSE/JUDGE EMMETT FIELD HOUSE

2909 Field Avenue, Crescent Hill

Jonathan C. Wright

Landmark designation: NRHP, 1982; LL

1878

The development of new architectural expressions in the nineteenth century, based on loose references to medieval and classical architecture, resulted in a succession of fashionable images in American domestic buildings, which gave the upper class and a growing middle class many choices. One of the most popular styles was the Italianate, which swept across the U.S. from the 1840s to the 1880s. The forces of capitalism, new efficiencies of production, an increasing availability of money, the standardization of parts, an incipient consumer mentality, and effective railroad connections between urban industrial centers and their hinterlands increased the widespread distribution of this style. Its application was particularly heavy on the facades of thousands of commercial main streets and later on houses in newly emerging suburbs. The classical core of the Milam Tandy House, built late in the heyday of this fashion, is a brick square that admits a number of picturesque extrusions, such as a projecting cross-gabled entrance, a back ell for the kitchen below and sleeping porch upstairs, a wraparound porch, a side porch, and a widow's walk with balustrade. The front elevation is bilaterally symmetrical on both floors and has a central projecting bay and two bays on each side. Details—such as the quoins, a relatively flat roofline articulated by brackets, and imaginative dentils repeated along the porch rooflines and over windows—associate the house with its neoclassical predecessors, such as the pivotal Queen's House (1616), built in England by Inigo Jones.

159. WATERWORKS CRESCENT HILL RESERVOIR
(Crescent Hill Waterworks)
3006 Frankfort Avenue Reservoir at Frankfort Avenue, Crescent Hill
Charles Hermany
Landmark designation: NRHP, 1979
1876–1879

Jefferson County's population grew 160% from 1860 to 1900, and its first classical waterworks on River Road, which had never provided more than muddy water to its patrons, could not keep up with the city's needs by the 1870s. Charles Hermany, chief engineer of the waterworks, enlarged pumping and reservoir capacity enormously in 1879 when his stone Gothic revival pumping station began bringing Ohio River water into the new 100-million-gallon reservoir. Zorn Avenue marks the underground line that cuts into Crescent Hill and runs to the river. In contrast to the earlier pumping station's Roman-temple image, which appeals to the magic of gods and goddesses for water, the new one is a Gothic structure that appeals first to the observable organic world, another basic tenet of Romanticism. The building's mix of Italianate details and its human scale give the structure a domestic expression that would fit well into any late-nineteenth-century Victorian suburban neighborhood in the U.S. A small stone superintendent's house near the reservoir adds to a charming setting, which is a destination point for many bikers and joggers.

160. PETERSON-DUMESNIL HOUSE
301 South Peterson, Crescent Hill
Henry Whitestone
Landmark designation: NRHP, 1975; LL
c. 1869–1870

Designed by Henry Whitestone as a summer residence for Joseph Peterson's family, this asymmetrical Italianate villa made a powerful statement with its large mass, heavy cornice of brackets, dentils, and medallions, hexagonal lantern and finial, and wraparound Victorian porch on one of the highest hills in the Crescent Hill neighborhood.

The exterior walls of brick have round-headed floor-to-ceiling windows with stone-carved hood moldings and scroll braces. The interior has been altered, but it retains a central hall with a winding stair to the second floor. This serene and beautiful house is the headquarters of the Louisville Historical Society, the Crescent Hill Community Council, and the Peterson-Dumesnil House Foundation.

161. CLAY-MCCANDLISS HOUSE
330–32 Wildwood Place, Crescent Hill
Architect unknown, renovation by Mark Hawkins
c. 1920

On April 3, 1974, a massive tornado touched down near the Louisville airport and tore through eastern Louisville into Oldham County for twenty minutes. Two people were killed, thousands of houses damaged or destroyed, and tens of thousands of trees leveled. One structure that was lost was a shotgun house, the center building in a line of five shotgun houses, on a narrow lane in Crescent Hill. The adjacent houses remained largely intact.

Noted urban-affairs author and critic Grady Clay and his wife, forester Judith McCandliss, purchased the complex, including an adjacent property with a large stand of trees and spring house on a steep hillside. Architect Mark Hawkins joined the two westernmost houses together and utilized the site of the missing house as a forecourt to the renovated and expanded complex. Over the years, Clay and McCandliss have cultivated the lot to the point that it has become a miniature urban forest, and the view through the entrance gate to the house frames a vista of that landscape. Clay and McCandliss are presently renovating the two shotgun houses at the eastern end of the group for use as an artist's residence. The complex can best be glimpsed through the trees from Bayly Avenue.

162. CHARLES CASH RESIDENCE
(Maurice Miller Residence)
500 Upland Road, Crescent Hill
Samuel Calvin Molloy
1938

In 1938 Louisville architect Samuel Calvin Molloy designed a three-bedroom residence for Maurice Miller. The house, one of the most modern in the region at the time, embraces the International Style tendencies championed by architects such as Le Corbusier and William Lescaze yet dilutes them for livability and comfort.

The house fronts on three streets: Grinstead Drive to the north, Upland Road to the east, and Cross Hill Road to the south. The entry is from the motor court located off Upland Road. Inspired by Edward Durrell Stone's Collier's House (1936), the true 'front door' of the house faces the motor court at the rear, by the one-story two-car garage that connects to the house by a breezeway. The two-story residence applies an industrial aesthetic to both exterior and interior, with freestanding steel columns, metal pipe rails, and horizontal windows. The structure has a columnar grid of steel and an exterior skin of concrete block sheathed in white painted stucco. Ribbon windows infilled with glass block allow a maximum of light into the first-floor dining room and upstairs bathrooms while maintaining privacy.

Every room in the house opens to the outside, making the boundaries between inside and outside thin and permeable. The architect placed the public living and dining spaces on the first floor along the Grinstead facade, protecting the private study and kitchen spaces to the rear. A corridor centered on a figural staircase continues up to the second floor. At the second floor, three bedrooms extend off the corridor, and a large master-bedroom suite opens onto a private porch above the dining room. A large bedroom on the north side and a smaller central bedroom are linked on the inside by a wide corridor and on the outside by a second-story balcony that broadens into a roof deck above the study on the east.

Although there have been renovations, recent efforts have been sensitive to the original design and construction. Many features remain, such as the dark-stained oak floors throughout. The red-striped black "battleship linoleum" floors in the kitchen, did not survive. Louisville architect Jasper D. Ward, to meet the standards of the then owner, a local restaurateur, remodeled the kitchen. The bathrooms are detailed in black and tan Carrara glass tiles. The current owner, architect Charles Cash, opened the kitchen to an adjacent maid's room and bath, creating a breakfast room and mudroom, rebuilt the exterior dining terrace in the spirit of the original drawings, and restored the French doors leading from the dining room. Originally designed with a pergola supported by a stucco wall, the dining terrace now has a seat wall and planter of concrete block and stucco, terminating the exterior flagstone paving.

163. SOUTHERN BAPTIST THEOLOGICAL SEMINARY

2739 Lexington Road, Crescent Hill

Arthur Loomis, James Gamble Rogers, Olmsted Brothers (Boston)

1926–1959

The Southern Baptist Theological Seminary moved to downtown Louisville in 1877 from Greenville, North Carolina, where it was established in 1859. Under the direction of president E.Y. Mullins, the campus moved from its downtown site to its present location, on the former Rudolph Fink estate, in 1926. The entire campus contains refined examples of the colonial revival style with the majority of the buildings designed and built between 1926 and 1959.

The Olmsted Brothers (Boston) designed the campus master plan, the focal point being the Seminary Lawn, affectionately known as the Josephus Bowl. The primary campus buildings—Norton Hall, Mullins Hall, Boyce Library, and Honeycutt Hall—frame and anchor the Seminary Lawn. This area is composed of three defined outdoor rooms that pay homage to Thomas Jefferson's design for the University of Virginia campus. Unlike Jefferson's Lawn, this plan clearly separates the functions of living (housing), gathering (library and classrooms), and administration (offices), providing a vital community organized around learning.

Norton Hall houses the Seminary's administrative offices, classrooms, and Broadus Chapel. It was built in 1926 by Arthur Loomis and James Gamble Rogers (1867–1947), a Kentucky-born architect noted for the Sterling Memorial Library and Harkness Memorial Quadrangle at Yale University, his alma mater. The chapel was modeled after the first Baptist church in America and named for John A. Broadus, the second president of the Seminary (1888–95). The primary worship center for the community is the colonial revival Alumni Memorial Chapel. Designed by the Louisville firm Nevin, Morgan, and Kolbrook and completed in 1950, the chapel hosts dramatic and musical events, as well as graduation ceremonies. The firm also designed the James P. Boyce Centennial Library (named for the first president of the Seminary), which was completed in 1959 on the 100th anniversary of Southern Seminary. The library holds one of the world's largest and most extensive theological collections. In 2002, the Louisville firm Louis & Henry designed the Grinstead Apartments, at Grinstead Drive and Seminary Drive, to accommodate the growing number of students.

164. CAVE HILL CEMETERY
701 Baxter Avenue, Cherokee Park
W. H. Redin
Landmark designation: NRHP, 1979
1848

Cave Hill, a 296-acre tract that includes a national cemetery for fallen Union soldiers and a private one for 200 Confederate soldiers, is one of many rural cemeteries established in the U.S. during the nineteenth century that followed the picturesque landscape designs of precedent-setting Mt. Auburn Cemetery in Watertown and Cambridge, Massachusetts. Taking advantage of topography, existing natural resources, and other site characteristics such as water, designers of rural cemeteries provided beautiful English park–like settings near the centers of cities for burial of the dead and for the benefit of the living, who used them for family outings, picnics, and escape from the stresses of city life. As Reverend E. P. Humphrey said in his dedicatory address in 1848, "Let the place of graves be rural and beautiful. Let trees be planted there. Let the opening year invite to their branches the springing leaf and birds of song....Let the tokens of fond remembrance in the shrub and flower be there." Cave Hill is not only a natural setting. It presents a panoply of funerary art and sculpture that dazzles the eye and moves the spirit. The Renaissance revival entry gate and campanile are attributed to the architect W. H. Redin. The numerous mausolea represent a striking history of architectural expression in the older sections of the cemetery.

Pick up a map at the main gate to find your way to the Satterwhite Temple of Love, the Tingley Memorial Fountain, the Wilder Monument, the Tiffany Vase, and the Irvin Mausoleum by architect Henry Whitestone. Open from 8 A.M. to 4:30 P.M.

165. CHEROKEE TRIANGLE HISTORIC DISTRICT

Cherokee Parkway

Landmark designation: NRHP, 1976; LPD

1866–1913

Cave Hill Cemetery opened in 1848, and by 1864 enough people had traveled to the cemetery and bought property around it to warrant a mule trolley, which ran from downtown via Broadway and Baxter Avenue to turn around in front of W. H. Redin's cemetery gate. James W. Henning and Joshua S. Speed were the force behind much of the suburban development that clustered near the cemetery. They became partners in 1851 and laid out a large tract of hilly land, called the Henning and Speed Highland Addition. In 1870, they purchased another large tract of wooded land, which eventually became the Cherokee Triangle. At first, the residences there were rural villas built for the upper class, who favored a variety of big Victorian (especially Italianate) residences with servants' quarters and carriage houses. A good example of one of these rural villas is the Hillard House at 1074 Cherokee Road, built between 1871 and 1872. It was the first house in the new suburb. In 1889, an electric trolley replaced the mule trolley and was extended down Bardstown Road. When Olmsted Sr.'s Cherokee Park opened in 1892, many middle-class families moved to Cherokee Triangle in the Highlands, away from the river. There was a strong demand for property, which was filled by a wide range of house styles and sizes, built along shaded streets. The automobile eventually eliminated the extensive Louisville streetcar system in 1948, but many of the businesses along busy Bardstown Road and Baxter Avenue in the Highlands owe their existence to that dismantled, yet efficient transportation technology. Baxter and Highland Avenues form a rich nexus of restaurants, bars, pubs, antique stores, and boutiques that give a sense of the variety of buildings in this robust neighborhood.

166. CHURCH OF THE ADVENT
901 Baxter Avenue, Cherokee Triangle
Frederick C. Withers
Landmark designation: NRHP, 1976
1887–1888

Frederick C. Withers, an architect from New York, designed one of the most picturesque Gothic revival churches in the city; it responds to a complex triangular site where Baxter Avenue meets Cave Hill Road. The northern elevation, which faces a small yard with trees so large that most of the year the church lies somewhat hidden behind them, presents buttressed limestone walls that recede visually under the massive slate roof. This elevation becomes more complicated with two entries, one small and the other large; a gabled extension that protrudes from the walls; and a hexagonal Lady chapel that reaches into the yard and toward the floral exuberance of Cave Hill Cemetery. An off-center spire rises from the Lady chapel, not from the nave itself. The western elevation, facing noisy Baxter Avenue, is a much simpler, fortress-like wall, with a gable leading to a narthex.

The interior, which is seldom open to visitors, boasts a dark, simplified hammer-beam truss system, held by contrasting white walls and expressive stained-glass windows. Beautifully sculptured angels of wood hold the lectern and adorn the altar. The pews, floors, and beaded wainscoting are original. The Church of the Advent is an excellent example of an early suburban church, designed to mediate, through architecture and symbol, that complex and important place where the busy street brings the living face to face with eternal questions answered at the cemetery.

167. HILLARD HOUSE
1074 Cherokee Road, Cherokee Triangle
Architect unknown
Landmark designation: NRHP, 1976
1871–1872

In 1871, James Henning gave this commodious brick house, carriage house, and two lots to his daughter as a wedding gift. Though its Italianate character has always been clear, the plan of this three-story structure has evolved significantly since Henning built it. Initially, it had a traditional side entry–hall plan, with a spiral stair in the hall leading to four bedrooms upstairs, and a sitting room, dining room, and kitchen with three pantries in an ell downstairs. The architect made the side-entry plan clear on the Cherokee Road front elevation by stepping back the hall door and placing the formal public rooms under a steep gable and dark wood cornice. The front door is also recessed in a foyer and has an etched-glass window, depicting a stag, typical of Bavarian folk art. The tall, thin proportions of the windows and doors accentuate the exterior's vertical dimension. Inside, the ceilings and doors, with their heavily layered plaster moldings, create voluminous spaces, responding to a Victorian belief that health was promoted by abundant air, which should not be breathed more than once. In the 1890s, a large three-story wing and porch, held by octagonal limestone columns, greatly expanded the house, giving it a central-hall plan, replacing the spiral stair with a winding side stair in the new wing, and providing projecting bays. In the 1920s, two second-story sleeping porches with colonial revival details were added because of the tuberculosis scare, and in the 1930s Frederick Lindley Morgan designed paneling for the library. The carriage house, originally for servants and hay on the second floor and for carriages and horses on the first, is an apartment and office today.

168. 1444–48 CHEROKEE ROAD
Cherokee Triangle
Grossman Martin Chapman
1977

In 1975, Louisville businessman and landowner Jim Kaiser approached H. Stow Chapman of Grossman Martin Chapman (and the firm's design and construction company, Atelier Construction) to design a five-unit townhouse complex on a site in Cherokee Triangle that overlooks Cherokee Park. After a heavily debated review with the neighborhood association and the Louisville Landmarks Commission, Chapman reduced the design to one volume with three distinct units and minimal, side-yard setbacks.

The intent of the design was to maintain a volumetric reading consistent with the neighborhood's yet without mimicking the context. The design, completed in 1977, reinterprets its context through massing and height alignments that allow the three single-family townhouses to read as one unit on the same scale as the adjacent homes. Following neighborhood deed restrictions, the project has masonry construction finished with white stucco and steeply pitched slate roofs. The front facade of each unit has a two-story skylight-covered cylindrical form, as well as the architect's interpretation of a shutter system: double-hung windows that peel back from the primary surface of the front facade. While designed to read as one volume, the units vary in plan, section, and relationship to the cylindrical front massing. Both the 1444 and the 1446 units use the front volume to provide light to the two-story dining room below, while the 1448 unit uses the volume to provide light to a second-story master bedroom and lower-level dining room.

The 1444 unit, originally designed with an open atrium, now has an enclosed interior court. Number 1446 has undergone two significant interior renovations, one in 1987 by Jasper D. Ward for Judy and Bob Hanekamp and one in 2003 by the current owners, Stephen Vance and David Eckert. The latest renovation includes a fountain sculpture designed by Kentucky artisan Dave Caudill. H. Stow Chapman designed the art-glass windows in the 1448 unit, and Fenestra Studios constructed them.

169. LOUISVILLE PRESBYTERIAN
THEOLOGICAL SEMINARY
1044 Alta Vista Road, Cherokee Park
Hartstern, Louis & Henry
1961–1969

The Louisville Presbyterian Theological Seminary is located at the crown of two heavily wooded hilltops overlooking Cherokee Park. The Seminary needed a larger space and moved from its collegiate Gothic downtown campus to the suburbs when Interstate-65 was built immediately adjacent to it. In 1959, the Seminary purchased 38 acres from Dr. Duke McCall of the Baptist seminary and acquired the adjacent Norton Estate, with its classical revival house (1903) and extensive gardens designed by Frederick Olmsted Jr. (in 1991 the Olmsted Foundation employed Art Richardson to oversee a renovation).

The main campus consists of seven buildings, with an academic core on one hilltop and residence halls on the other. Despite the physical separation caused by a 90-foot ravine, the campus is unified by the architects' choice of materials—Bedford limestone with precast concrete window spandrels—rather than by its form. The shape of the administration building and library roof, a thin-shell concrete hyperbolic parabola, is clearly influenced by Eero Saarinen's Irwin Union Bank in Columbus, Indiana. The chapel, sited on the brow of the hill, is the dominant symbol, the jewel of the campus. A campanile with an electronic carillon punctuates the exterior of the chapel. The roof of the chapel is covered with pyramidal cast-aluminum panels and is finished in a medium bronze color to match the extruded aluminum work on the rest of the project. William Schickel of Loveland, Ohio, designed the stained-glass windows.

170. JAMES M. KASDAN RESIDENCE

7 Hawthorne Hill, Cherokee Park

Keck and Keck (Chicago)

1936

The Chicago architectural firm Keck and Keck designed a modernist residence for James M. Kasdan in 1936. George Fred Keck and William Keck are widely known for their House of Tomorrow and Crystal House designs at the 1933–34 Century of Progress World's Fair in Chicago. In the Kasdan Residence, the International Style is evident despite the red brick construction. Keck and Keck deployed several of their early-modernist tenets in this house—a flat-roofed cubic building mass, bands of casement windows, passive solar heating, and a second-floor porch enclosure that completes the building volume. This house predates three other significant modern homes in Louisville, two by Samuel Calvin Molloy (the Speed Residence and the Miller Residence) and one by Bruce Goff (Triaero).

Similar in style and proportion to the Keck and Keck–designed Leigh House in Kaukauna, Wisconsin (1933), this residence is surrounded by deep-forested terrain and sits fifteen feet below street level. The main entrance is asymmetrically located and has a short, curved, projecting roof that cantilevers from a brick fin wall, providing a covered entry. A row of glass blocks, ten units high, flanks both sides of the entrance. A flat built-up roof covers the building. The interior is minimalist. Keck and Keck were early advocates of solar architecture. It is unclear if they experimented with shallow rooftop pools intended to cool the house in summer by evaporation, but the location on the site clearly shades the house from the summer sun yet admits winter sun for passive heating. It is one of two Keck and Keck–designed projects in Kentucky, the other being the M. S. Dix Residence in Lake Barkeley (1970).

171. HOWARD-GETTYS HOUSE
(Caldwell/Guthrie House)
1226 Bates Court, Highlands
Architect unknown
Landmark designation: NRHP, 1978
1810–1865

This is the epitome of a vernacular composite structure built, rebuilt, and expanded many times over a period of almost two centuries. The first section of the house, built in 1810, appears as a side porch that leads to a long shotgun house. In 1825, the owners built the raised brick central-hall house with engaged pilasters and capitals, which divide the facade. A raised portico, with a full pediment and entablature held by a set of double pillars, leads to a federal entrance with an elliptical fanlight. In about 1865, this new house was connected to the old shotgun house with a hall and side entrance. Eventually, the porch in front of the shotgun house was filled in, and a second story, probably built at some other time over the porch, wraps

around the roof of the 1825 house. The interior has been restored
and renovated several times, most recently in 2002–03.

172. ST. JAMES ROMAN CATHOLIC CHURCH
1826 Edenside Avenue, Highlands
J. J. Gaffney
Landmark designation: NRHP, 1983
1912–1913

With notable Baroque influences and Byzantine characteristics—
such as contrasts of color and light and decorative surface elements,
a cruciform plan, round arches, and circular windows—St. James
Roman Catholic Church is one of the finest existing examples of
the work of Louisville architect J. J. Gaffney. The church, which
sits on a rusticated-limestone foundation, has an exterior of bright
orange-glazed brick with single courses of red-glazed brick every
sixth row. A bell tower is suggestive of an Italian campanile. The
main entrance is a tripartite arched opening, decorated with cream-
colored terra-cotta panels. Original renderings and drawings of the
church by Gaffney are framed and hanging in the church rectory.

The interior of the church is under a gold-colored dome that is supported by four large arches. The pendentives of the arches are decorated with stained-glass panels that bear symbols of the four evangelists. The center of the dome has an oculus that symbolizes the eye of God. The iconography of the windows that line the nave contain patterned stained glass and represent the resurrection and the descent of the Holy Spirit and were manufactured by F. X. Zettler Company of Munich, Germany. Venetian gold mosaics cover the Carrara marble altar.

The two-and-a-half-story rectory is made of materials similar to those of the church. St. James Elementary School, located to the south of the church and rectory, is a two-story red brick structure with buff-brick banding and decoration.

173. ST. FRANCIS OF ASSISI CATHOLIC CHURCH
1960 Bardstown Road, Highlands
Fred T. Erhart
Landmark designation: NRHP, 1987
1926

The St. Francis of Assisi complex represents more than a century of architectural design. The Reverend William George McCloskey purchased the two-acre site in 1885. The original structure, no longer in existence, was a wooden church with a stone foundation.

Adjacent to the church was a rectory and two-room school, both made of wood. Founded as a German-speaking parish, St. Francis of Assisi expanded and renovated the church in 1910. Among the valuable relics obtained during this renovation were a particle of the True Cross and a relic of St. Francis of Assisi.

The Ursuline Sisters constructed a brick structure in 1912–13 on the north side of the church. In 1924, the diocese commissioned Louisville architect Fred T. Erhart to design a new building, to combine a school, a temporary church (currently the auditorium), and residential quarters for the Ursuline Sisters. The building was dedicated on July 4, 1926. Two years later, the rectory was completed. The use of materials such as brown brick is reminiscent of the St. Francis Church in Assisi, Italy. The style of the rectory follows the stylistic tendencies of the school, namely the Spanish mission style. A new church and Chapel of the Blessed Virgin was planned in 1939; however, plans were delayed until 1949, when the church commissioned Louisville architects Walter Wagner Sr. and Joseph Potts to design a new modified English Gothic church.

The original drawings of the church detailed an elaborate entryway, including an elevated staircase and a stained-glass window of St. Francis of Assisi. After comment and review by several of the older parishioners, the architects removed the staircase and redesigned the entry to its current setting. The church is made of stone from St. Meinrad, Indiana. The cornerstone contains a copper box with historical data, a leather-bound book of the history of St. Francis of Assisi Church, dust from the tomb of St. Francis of Assisi in Italy, and American coins marked with the year's date, 1952. The interior of the church is laden with symbolism; the seven beams that support the vaulted ceilings are symbolic of the seven sacraments, and the circular stained-glass window above the main altar has twelve divisions, which represent the twelve Apostles, branching out from the center. The marble altar was fabricated in Italy.

174. HUMPHREY-MCMEEKIN HOUSE

2240 Douglass Boulevard, Highlands
Gray and Wischmeyer
Landmark designation: NRHP, 1983
1914–1915

The Humphrey-McMeekin House is considered one of the finest colonial revival examples in Louisville. Lewis C. Humphrey and his wife, Eleanor Belknap, commissioned the design for the house, and the Alfred Struck Company executed Gray and Wischmeyer's plan. The 7,000-square-foot house is based on a central-hall plan and is made of quality materials, including a brick massing, slate roofing, and wood trim on the exterior, and hardwood and marble flooring and elaborate plasterwork on the interior. The exceptional details reflect the period of its construction and incorporate splayed jack arches with stone keystones over the windows, elliptical transoms, and leaded-glass sidelights. The building mass is covered with decorative brickwork, especially at the chimneys, which rise above the roofline to create "bookends." At each end of the house are two semicircular porch projections, supported by colossal Corinthian columns.

Samuel H. and Isabel McMeekin purchased the property in 1973. McMeekin had gained recognition as an author of 26 books, including the best-seller *Show Me a Land,* published in 1940.

175. CONGREGATION ADATH JESHURUN
2401 Woodbourne Avenue, Highlands
Braverman and Halperin (Cleveland)
1957

Adath Jeshurun was founded in 1851 and was known at that time as Beth Israel. In 1894, the congregation acquired a vacant church at the corner of Floyd and Chestnut Streets for use as its synagogue and changed its name to Congregation Adath Jeshurun. From 1919 to 1957, the congregation was located in the Byzantine synagogue on the corner of Brook and College Streets designed by J. J. Gaffney in 1918–19. In 1957, the congregation moved again to its current location, a four-and-a-half-acre site in the Highlands. Like other post-1950 synagogues in Louisville, the Adath Jeshurun building has a doorless ark wall facade. The exterior of the building is a buff brick, accented by Bedford limestone. The entrance is along a five-bay limestone pergola, which rises above the carved landscaping designed in 1966 by Miller, Wihry & Lanz.

The J. J. Gittleman Educational Center, a religious school dedicated in 1966 and named in honor of the Rabbi Emeritus who had served the congregation since 1917, has seen no significant changes since its construction. In 2003, the congregation hired New Jersey architect Michael Callori to renovate the synagogue with a new office wing adjacent to the boardroom and Switow Chapel and with extensive changes to the Shapira Sanctuary and Anne G. Lipski Auditorium.

176. AXTON HOUSE
2192 Millvale Road, Highlands
Architect unknown, renovation and addition by Michael Koch
1953

Tracy and Gayle Axton hired Michael Koch and John McIntyre to "modernize" their 1953 California-style ranch house. The resulting design was a dynamic volume that transformed and enlarged the existing stone-veneered structure into a contemporary house, simultaneously masking and revealing the original structure.

A copper-skinned wall serves as a protective shield, closing the house to the street, while a floor-to-ceiling glass wall behind the house opens up the interior to the hillside and natural spring beyond. The front wall serves two functions: first as a visual buffer to traffic along Millvale Road, and second as a guide leading visitors into the spacious two-story entry vestibule. Inside the brick-veneered house, the plan unites the programmatic elements of the first floor in one contiguous open volume. The dining room, living room, central kitchen, and family area each have floor-to-ceiling glass panels that visually extend the inside space to the outside. Light-colored maple and oak floors and brightly colored walls highlight the interior. The second floor contains the private spaces of the house and uses a bridge to connect the master bedroom and bath to the bedroom, bathroom, and office space across the entry vestibule. Glass blocks in the master bathroom provide light and privacy. Clerestory windows on the upper level allow natural light to penetrate deep into the body of the house.

177. NOLAN RESIDENCE

2181 Millvale Road, Cherokee Park

Robert A. Nolan

1947

The site of the Nolan Residence has a 45-foot vertical drop from the front of the house to the street. To account for this, the owner and architect, Robert A. Nolan, of the Louisville architecture firm Thomas J. Nolan & Sons, set his new house on the stone foundations of the garage and stable of the former Van Cleave estate. The uniquely modern house has thick stone walls and a concrete floor. The exterior materials are brick and marine-grade plywood. The main body of the house is on the second floor, with a utility room, maid's room, and recreation porch at the first level. The three-bedroom house is entered from the rear through a cantilevered concrete sidewalk, parallel to the garage that sits a half story above the first floor. The common space is contained in a living and dining room (fifteen feet by thirty-three feet) outside the kitchen.

178. BICKEL RESIDENCE
(Valletta House)
2324 Valletta Lane, Seneca Gardens/Cherokee Park
Edd R. Gregg
1954–1956

The original 1954 design for the Valletta House was based on creating a house for two musicians. Modern home designs by John Rex in California at the time were the inspiration for owners Benjamin and Doris Owen. Among the notable musicians and composers who have performed in the house are musicians Brooks Smith, John Browning, Rosalyn Tureck, Gary Karr, Andras Schiff, and Igor Kipnis and composers Norman dello Joio, Wallingford Riegger, Aaron Copland, and Kent Kennan. The house is located on a steeply sloped lot in a valley midway between two historic mansions bordering Cherokee Park. The architect's design engages the hillside, calling for an L-shaped plan to divide the program of the house into two components. The first includes a lower-level carport with a bedroom and bath, laundry, and storage rooms; the other is a second-story entry and kitchen immediately adjacent to a two-story music hall and living room. The exterior utilizes brick construction with stained fir siding.

The renovations have been both elegant and beautifully detailed, enriching the house's overall quality. A 1977 renovation converted the carport into a lower-level garage, workshop, and garden storage room. Beginning in 1985, Doris and her second husband, Louisville architect John H. Bickel III, designed a series of renovations that increased the square footage to approximately 5,000 square feet. The intention of the renovations was to respect the character and quality of the original design while adding needed improvements for the retiring couple. The 1956 screened-in porch was transformed in 1987 into a solarium and swim room, with a swimming pool and fountain occupying what was the back patio. In 1994, a second-story painting and design studio was added over the garage.

179. BELLARMINE UNIVERSITY
(Bellarmine College)
2001 Newburg Road, Belknap
Thomas J. Nolan & Sons, Al J. Schneider, Grossman Martin Chapman, Nolan & Nolan, Inc.
1950–2003

Located seven miles east of downtown Louisville, the Bellarmine campus stands on property that was once part of a royal land grant from King George III to James McCorkle for his service in the French and Indian War. After the American Revolution, Thomas Jefferson retitled the land. During the antebellum period, this land was a plantation owned by the Griffin family, who, impoverished by the Civil War, sold the estate to Bishop William George McCloskey for a seminary, Preston Park, which was in operation between 1871 and 1909. During the Civil War, the Griffin estate house served as a military hospital. Old Preston Park also served at times as an orphanage staffed by the Sisters of Charity of Nazareth: St. Vincent's for Girls (1892–1901) and St. Thomas for Boys (1910–38). Under the sponsorship of the Roman Catholic Archdiocese of Louisville, Bellarmine College opened on October 3, 1950. In 2000, the Board of Trustees voted to change the name of the institution from Bellarmine College to Bellarmine University to reflect more accurately its educational status. Today the campus has twenty-seven buildings set on 135 acres.

The Science Building (named Pasteur Hall in 1961), designed by Thomas J. Nolan & Sons in 1950 and built by Al J. Schneider, is a modern, utilitarian, rough-textured buff-brick building with limestone trim. The interior has terrazzo floors and red oak cabinets and worktables. A May 7, 1950, *Courier-Journal* article described the building as "strikingly beautiful." The addition to the Science Building in 1968 doubled its size to contain eleven labs, nine offices, a classroom, and a 300-seat auditorium (later named the New Science Theater). The building had further renovation in 2002 and is now used by nursing and the health sciences.

The Administration Building (named Horrigan Hall in 1961), designed by Thomas J. Nolan & Sons in 1953–54 and built by Al J. Schneider, is also a modern, rough-textured buff-brick building with limestone trim. The floors of the halls and lounge are terrazzo. The three-story building has a six-story tower and was intended to crown the top of the hill. The cornerstone was placed in 1953 and features three inscribed fleurs-de-lis, in commemoration of the 175th anniversary of Louisville's founding. Inside the cornerstone were placed a medal of St. Robert Bellarmine, a list of current students, copies of the college catalog, a student manual, a college brochure, and a map of Louisville. The building—with its 300-seat cafeteria, 350-seat chapel, and 150-seat lecture hall—quickly became the center of campus activity. The building has been renovated three times: in 1961 for technology upgrades, in 1970 for an air-conditioning upgrade and the design of a new chapel, and in 1986–87 when an elevator and an entrance in the Newburg Road facade were installed.

In 1982, Grossman Martin Chapman were selected to design a large college activities center and fine arts–humanities complex. The buildings form a new core for the campus known as the Maurice D.

S. Johnson Quadrangle. Built between 1983 and 1984, they include the George G. Brown Activities Building and the George W. Norton Fine Arts Complex, which consists of two buildings: Alumni Hall (1984) and the Wilson W. Wyatt Sr. Lecture-Recital Hall (1984). In 1997, the W. L. Lyons Brown Library (1997) completed the quad.

Nolan & Nolan, Inc. designed the Our Lady of the Woods Chapel (1999–2001). The chapel is sited on a secluded, wooded hillside just past Horrigan Hall and Miles Hall. It is made of brick and Cor-ten steel, with wood floors and large expanses of glass that frame the view of the Bear Grass Creek Valley below. The arrangement of the chapel is a transformed crucifix cathedral plan, with Gothic-like flying buttresses of steel on the exterior. Below the main level are a mechanical basement and undercroft, with an outdoor ceremonial and meditation grotto space. Guy Kemper designed the art-glass windows.

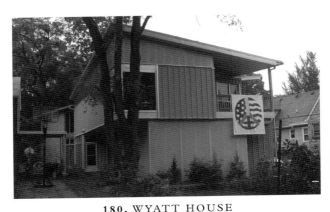

180. WYATT HOUSE
2077 Ravinia Avenue, Lakeside
Mockbee Coker Architects (Mississippi)
2001

This controversial house was not completed before the resolution of a substantial legal conflict regarding its alleged violations of the Lakeside neighborhood deed restrictions. Lakeside was laid out by the Olmsted Brothers' firm in the 1920s, and a limited array of exterior materials is permitted (primarily brick, stucco, and stone). The house departs substantially from those listed materials, utilizing corrugated-metal panels, translucent plastic, and concrete to define a series of large, interlocking open spaces. Sited on a small cul-de-sac, it is considerably larger than the surrounding houses.

Questions of decorum aside, the house is an exuberant architectural accomplishment. Two axes, defined by mature trees in the front and back of the house, provided the organizing spine for the plan. A carport tucked behind a service area allows for privacy from the street, and a large enclosed porch opens to the rear yard. An asymmetrical butterfly roof sits above a clerestory of Lexan panels, increasing both volume and natural light for the rooms underneath. Qualities of space and light and views of nature predominate inside the house.

The owners sought out unorthodox architect Samuel Mockbee after studying his projects in Alabama that use simple building materials to build inexpensive houses for the rural poor; Coleman Coker, Mockbee's longtime collaborator, became the project architect as Mockbee's health declined (he died in 2001).

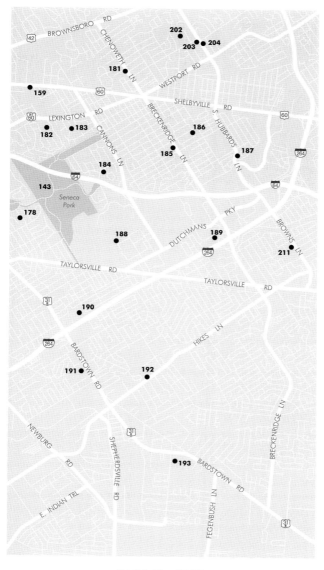

Map 8: Buildings 181–204

181. THORPE INTERIORS
224 Chenoweth Lane, St. Matthews
Taliesin Associated Architects (Scottsdale, Arizona)
1963

In 1963, Thorpe Interiors made a request to Kenneth Lockhart of Taliesin Associated Architects to design a new front for the building, a place for a reception area, and a direct access to the second-story attic space of their wood clapboard office (1905–07). Lockhart was in Louisville to sign contracts for two projects—a chiropractic hospital (unbuilt) and the Lincoln Income Life Insurance Tower and Liberty National Bank & Trust Company (Kaden Tower). Six months later, Skip Thorpe received a roll of drawings with an idea for a new front, resulting in a magnificent addition, which Taliesin architect William Wesley Peters described in a conversation with the owner as a "bold attempt to show architecture and interior design working together."

To visually dislodge the structure from the surrounding Victorian homes, Peters extended the slope of the existing house down to the tops of the existing windows and sloped the earth up to the top of the foundation. The residual facade was then covered over by suspending an undulating screen of vertical wood members from the cantilevered overhang. The loss of light due to the placement of the screens was offset by the addition of two skylights. The new front of the office has large arched openings surrounded by shallow, terraced reflecting pools, with fountains on both the inside and the outside. On the interior, the original front porch and facade were replaced with another vertical undulating screen. Rather than hanging in a fashion similar to that of the exterior facade, the internal screen becomes a load-bearing wall that supports the second-story attic space. The floor material is smooth concrete with circular patterned areas of exposed aggregate concrete at the entrance.

In 1970, it became apparent that, while the building was meeting the requested programmatic requirements, the material selections were not capturing the image of the emerging interior-design firm. William Wesley Peters's response was the design of a storefront showcase window that continues the horizontal character of the 1963 facade. This area was later incorporated into the 1983 addition and only visible from the inside.

In 1983, Thorpe Interiors acquired the six-room house (c. 1910) on the adjacent lot. Thorpe returned to Taliesin for a design scheme that would connect the two properties. Referred to as the "bridge" between the two houses, Peters designed a gallery space with clerestory windows, which punctuate the area around the bridge, and floor-to-ceiling insulated glass panels. A 1995 addition to the rear of the 1910 building by Larry Leis of Louis & Henry follows the vocabulary of the Taliesin interventions. A 1995 renovation added a secondary entrance to accommodate the expanding business as well as a second-story parapet to mask the rear mechanical unit.

182. WHITEHALL
3110 Lexington Road, Crescent Hill
John C. Marshall
1855

Whitehall underwent a significant renovation in 1909 and 1910 probably as a delayed response to the Chicago Columbian Exposition of 1893, which more than 20,000,000 people visited. The exposition profoundly changed American views of how cities, parks, and architecture could look and inspired many alterations to old buildings. Whitehall was originally built around 1855 as a two-story central-hall house. A separate summer kitchen stood in the backyard, far from the house. New owners enlarged the house from eight rooms to fifteen, adding a massive portico with pediment, full Doric entablature, six gigantic fluted columns with Corinthian capitals, two wings with smaller porches, a two-story ell, and a small back porch.

The renovated first-floor plan eliminated a partition, one room, and two hearths to create a large parlor on one side of the hall. The door at the end of the hall was closed with a new hearth, and the stair was taken out of the hall and placed in a lateral position to the hall. The old central hall became a twentieth-century room, but it retained its historic reception functions. Downstairs ceilings were raised about two feet to enhance the monumentality of the interior.

Imperatives from the Columbian Exposition also demanded landscape changes, in this case from informal and organic to formal and refined Florentine gardens. The Historic Homes Foundation, the tenth owner of the house, unabashedly interprets all of these developments for what they are, including the change from house to museum. The idea that change is the nature of history and of most buildings, too, lends Whitehall a refreshing authenticity.

Open Monday through Friday, 10 A.M. to 2 P.M.

183. SPRING STATION
3241 Trinity Road, Cherokee Park
Norborne Beale
Landmark designation: NRHP, 1977
1805–1808

This Greek revival dwelling, like Ridgeway and Oxmoor, has a five-part Palladian plan. The house belonged to Norborne Beale, who came to Kentucky from Albemarle County, Virginia, reportedly with a drawing by Thomas Jefferson, who had designed several plans similar to Spring Station's. Beale built a raised two-story, symmetrical brick temple with full pediment and lunette on a stone foundation and attached a muscular portico with hefty Doric columns and a balustrade above. This imposing porch received guests according to the rules of hospitality that were transplanted by Virginians who came to Kentucky to live out Jefferson's agrarian vision. Beale and many others succeeded in a plantation economy buoyed by the hands of slaves. He soon extended the central core of the house with two hyphens and end pavilions, which repeat the pediment and lunette motif. An emphatic cornice acts as a compositional device to unite the five sections of the facade. The main door leads to a multipurpose space, used as a living room, ballroom, parlor, reception hall, and passage through the house.

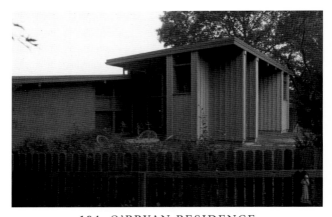

184. O'BRYAN RESIDENCE
(Klotter Residence)
1103 Old Cannons Lane, Rockcreek Gardens
Sweet and Judd
1960

This house is one of several designed by Norman Sweet and Arnold Judd Sr. throughout the Louisville area. Typical of their aesthetic, the building is constructed of double Douglas-fir roof beams that rest on wood structural columns, between which both fixed and operable windows are placed. Sweet's horizontal and vertical modules are based on a four-foot increment with cubic subincrements of sixteen inches. This proportion is maintained in both horizontal and vertical dimensions. The building is covered with transparently stained vertical cedar siding and Roman-brick veneer with similarly colored mortar. The loftlike interior centers on a pass-through central hearth of Roman brick that separates the kitchen from the dining and living area. This house, designed for Louis and Katie Klotter and their family, follows the modernist tenet of division between public (living, dining, and kitchen) and private (bedroom, bathroom). However, this house is unique from other Sweet homes in the impressive way that it addresses the street and site, on a steep hillside with a walk-out lower level. It is entered from the rear of the property, allowing the primary views to extend uninterrupted across the street below and the park beyond.

The house has undergone several minor renovations, but all changes have been constructed in a manner complementary to the original design. A 2002–03 addition by the current owners, architect Mark O'Bryan and his wife, interior designer Mary Lee O'Bryan, replaces the rear carport and storage area with a monumental structure. It also includes a dining room and social space with glass walls on three sides, clerestory windows to the west, and a freestanding storage shed made of salvaged wood from the carport.

185. OUR LADY OF LOURDES CATHOLIC CHURCH

512 Breckinridge Lane, St. Matthews
Thomas J. Nolan & Sons, Grossman Chapman Klarer
1950–1995

Thomas J. Nolan & Sons designed Our Lady of Lourdes Church in 1961–65. The church seats 900 parishioners and reflects the liturgical changes put in place by Vatican II. The design allows all parishioners to be within 90 feet of the altar. The main volume of the church, as seen from Breckinridge Lane, has an interior height of twenty-six feet. The side aisles have twelve-foot-high ceilings. On the exterior, exposed concrete and limestone detailing accentuate the building's bays. The structure is concrete with a steel frame and a buff brick exterior facing. An undulating concrete roof covers the narthex. Originally, people entered the building through a loggia and passed through the single-story narthex before entering the double-height chancel. Grossman Chapman Klarer altered this entrance sequence in the 1993 renovation.

The interior of the church has mosaic tile and plaster walls, terrazzo floors with marble wainscoting, and walnut trim throughout.

Conrad Schmitt Studios of Milwaukee designed the mosaic tile, the crucifix, the stations of the cross, the statuary, and the stained-glass windows within the church. The August Wagner Studios of Berlin, Germany, created all the other mosaics and hand-carved icons. The sacristy once had four stained-glass windows. During the 1997 renovation, one of the panels was removed and stored so that the church could be connected to the adjacent gathering space.

In 1971, Nolan & Nolan designed a two-story rectory parallel to Breckinridge Lane. In 1993, a new activities center and the Parish Life Center, designed by Grossman Chapman Klarer and built by F. W. Owens Construction Company, unified the complex. The Parish Life Center has the same exposed concrete and limestone detailing as the school (Christian Formation Center), rectory, and church.

186. MOORE HOUSE
4032 Norbourne Boulevard, St. Matthews
Donald L. Williams and George E. Rolfe
1964

The clients owned the two-story Neogeorgian house adjacent to this corner lot and wanted to stay in the neighborhood. Donald L. Williams and George E. Rolfe, of the firm McCulloch and Bickel, designed the project. The couple desired a compact, one-floor, easy-to-care-for house; the architects responded with a volumetric 2,600-square-foot structure. The house is essentially three cubic brick volumes, linked by gallery spaces, with three large pyramidal roofs, which increase the apparent mass of the building and contextually fit the building, despite its modern character, into the large, two story Georgian context of the neighborhood. Located in Norbourne Estates, the house's main entry is from South Sherrin Avenue. An asphalt-shingled pyramidal roof with light scoops covers each of the volumes, allowing light to penetrate deep into the private spaces of the house. The vaulted ceilings create a sense of openness and height despite the building's small footprint.

The program of the house revolves around two axes—one major and one minor—which create variety in both the internal and external views. Flooring material and color provide orientation. The house has a minimal number of openings to the street, but the two private courtyards (one off the master bedroom and the other off the guest room) have floor-to-ceiling glass and provide extensive light to the interior of the house. Redwood privacy fences and high brick walls surround three sides of the courtyards and act as a screen to the neighboring properties.

187. THEODORE BROWN HOUSE
(Woodhaven)
Theodore Brown
Landmark designation: NRHP, 1983
1853

At the height of A. J. Downing's influence, which had spread far and wide through his books *Cottage Residences* (1842) and *The Architecture of Country Houses* (1850), Theodore Brown built a small Gothic cottage following many of the rules Downing set down for a middle-class residence. In contrast to the rules for a villa, Brown's house is a two-and-a-half-story, symmetrical, five-bay, central-hall house with a projecting cross gable over the porch entrance, which is marked by a Tudor arch and a squared-off hood molding. Diamond-shaped glass with quatrefoil tracery fill all the windows. An oriel (which comes from the Latin word *oratoriolum,* meaning "a little place for prayer"), an oculus, raking bargeboards of Gothic tracery, and a pinnacle at the apex of the roof center the composition of the front facade. Paired windows with square heads and hood moldings differentiate the second floor. Tudor arches, beveled posts, elaborate balustrades, and a tracery parapet articulate the two side porches. Clustered chimneys complete the medieval image. The plan forms a Latin cross, resembling Design XXVI in Downing's *The Architecture of Country Houses.* In response to the requirements of a bed-and-breakfast establishment, Brown's house has evolved with the addition of outside stairs to a garret room, and the dark wood details have been painted white. The carriage house, with its octagonal lantern, has been adaptively reused as a guest house. Other new buildings fill up what was once a picturesque yard that provided a proper natural prospect for the house.

188. BOWMAN FIELD ADMINISTRATION BUILDING

2710 Moran Avenue at Bowman Field
Wischmeyer & Arrasmith
Landmark designation: NRHP, 1988
1935

The Bowman Field Administration Building sits at the center of one of the oldest continuously operating airfields in America. Bowman Field opened in 1919 as a flying field on the site of the Baron Von Zedwitz estate, a property seized by the federal government under the Alien Property Act of World War I. It has attracted many notable aviators, including Charles Lindbergh, with the *Spirit of St. Louis*, in 1927. During the 1937 flood in Louisville, the airfield served planes delivering supplies and medicine to the area. Throughout World War II, it was one of the country's most important training bases. The Bowman Field Administration Building was constructed in two stages. The first section consisted of a two-story central section flanked by two single-story wings. The north wing was torn down in 1935. William S. Arrasmith, a Louisville architect nationally known for his streamlined moderne–inspired Greyhound bus stations, designed a new central pavilion and two side wings under the Works Progress Administration (WPA). The interior of the center pavilion remains intact as a lobby, and the east wing is currently occupied by Le Relais, a fine French restaurant, which offers an intimate setting and views of the runway.

189. KADEN TOWER
(Lincoln Income Life Insurance Tower and
Liberty National Bank & Trust Company)
619 Dutchman's Lane, St. Matthews
Taliesin Associated Architects (Scottsdale, Arizona)
1965–1966

With the death of Frank Lloyd Wright in 1959, William Wesley
Peters became chief architect of Wright's firm, Taliesin Associated
Architects. Peters designed the Lincoln Income Life Insurance
Tower and the adjoining Liberty National Bank & Trust Company to
be a community landmark. The design for the Lincoln Tower has its

roots in three Frank Lloyd Wright projects: the Sarabhi Calico Mills Store in Amehabad, India (1946, unbuilt), the Rogers Lacy Hotel in Dallas, Texas (1946, unbuilt), and the Price Company Tower in Bartlesville, Oklahoma (1952). Like Wright's design for the Price office building, the Lincoln Tower is constructed of a reinforced concrete mastlike core, with floors cantilevered from large, deep steel trusses that enable a column-free interior space. The original design by Peters had a turquoise concrete shaft with a decorative gold-anodized-aluminum modular-panel system. The layout of the panels was fabricated to prevent birds from nesting on the facade's surface. Peters modified the skin to be prefabricated concrete when the manufacturer could not guarantee the resilience of the anodized surface. The tower's skin is not hung like a continuous curtain wall; rather, it is composed of structurally independent sections, which act as filigreed brise soliels that divert the sun's rays from the offices immediately behind them, without inhibiting views.

The overall parklike siting of the building complex on the seventeen-acre property is innovative and demonstrates Wright's ideas about integrating nature into the architecture. At the base of the tower, a large reflecting pool and fountain not only "square the circle," but also double as a cooling tower for the air-conditioning system. To the northeast of the building, Peters integrated a one-story concrete circular building for the Liberty Bank offices (Citizen's Union Bank currently leases this building). At the top of the tower, a restaurant (now Ruth's Chris Steakhouse) offers a spectacular view of downtown Louisville and the Indiana knobs beyond.

The building's current name, Kaden Tower, comes from combining the last names of the present owners, Jim Karp and the Blieden family, who purchased the building in 1986. An extensive renovation by Grossman Chapman Klarer in 1986–87 updated the office spaces, upgraded the auditorium, and repainted the exterior concrete panels their distinctive salmon color. In 2003, the exterior mounted glass elevator was modernized to provide air-conditioned cars, as originally intended.

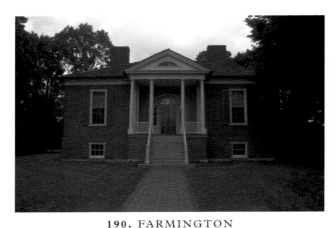

190. FARMINGTON

3033 Bardstown Road, Wellington
Paul Skidmore
Landmark designation: NRHP, 1972
1815–1816

Built by a master builder and skilled slaves for Judge John and Lucy Fry Speed, Farmington was the center of a 554-acre hemp plantation that young Abraham Lincoln frequently visited. In plan, form, and details, this raised federal mansion bears awkward relationships to the work of Thomas Jefferson, whom Lucy knew during her childhood in her Virginia home, which was also called Farmington. The Speeds selected Paul Skidmore, an itinerant "gentleman architect," to draw up a Jeffersonian plan of mixed Palladian and neoclassical origins.

The central-hall plan begins on a high piano nobile, reached by nine steps leading to a portico with a full pediment, carried by four Doric columns and an entablature. A Palladian door opens into a six-sided hall that separates a large octagonal dining room, parlor, and squared front chambers. A rectangular hall leads to a stair, two back chambers, and a rear porch. The English basement houses a winter kitchen, a traveler's room, and office. The newly restored period interior has original trimwork, hearths, brass, and windows. A summer kitchen, springhouse, smokehouse, reconstructed stone barn, and re-created nineteenth-century garden also remain on the current eighteen-acre estate.

Open Tuesday to Saturday, 10 A.M. to 4:30 P.M. with the last tour at 3:45 P.M., and Sunday 1:30 P.M. to 4:30 P.M. with the last tour at 3:30 P.M.

191. SHOWCASE CINEMAS
3408 Bardstown Road, West Buechel
Architect unknown
1965

This mid-century movie theater was built after the heyday of the great American movie palaces of the early twentieth century and before the bland multiplex boxes of the century's end. Like its precursors, Showcase Cinemas used its architectural style to attract an audience, although that style was distinctly modern, in contrast to the faux period extravaganzas evident in the palaces. But in its use of three screens (since enlarged to thirteen), the Showcase foreshadowed the use of multiple smaller, and relatively anonymous, screening rooms that are so prevalent today.

The two best features of Showcase Cinemas' architecture worked together to enhance the prominence of the theater in the neighborhood. First, its siting is close to Bardstown Road, rather than set back in acres of parking. Second, the building's largely glass facade makes the life inside the cinemas visible to passersby, especially at night. The building form is restrained, utilizing geometric patterns—gridded tile, linear fenestration, horizontal overhangs—and a uniformly white color to reinforce its allegiance to the International Style.

192. HIKES POINT CHRISTIAN CHURCH
(Southeast Christian Church)
2601 Hikes Lane, Buechel
Design Environment Group Architects (DEGA)
1967–1969

Located in the eastern suburb of Buechel, the initial phase of the Southeast Christian Church congregation included a church and sanctuary and provided a long-range development plan. Two existing buildings were first incorporated but eventually razed to allow the remainder of the master plan to be realized. According to Donald L. Williams of DEGA, the challenge was to "create a building that reflected the changing liturgy of the denomination and to design a building that strengthened the church in the world today and tomorrow." The narrow site, adjacent to an encroaching subdivision, informed the architect's response. DEGA designed a poured-in-place sandblasted concrete structure, with painted standing-seam metal roofing to hold the street edge, while creating an enclosed courtyard for liturgical activities and education behind. The tight clustering about the courtyard makes it the focal point for the entire complex. The interior of the structure is essentially devoid of applied ornamentation; however, dramatic natural lighting, combined with the architecture, becomes the central focus and is, itself, a work of art. The non-loadbearing walls and ceiling finish use varying patterns of ship-lapped Arkansas pine to create a rhythmic oscillation in the scored concrete panels. The central axis of the chancel terminates with a light scoop reminiscent of Le Corbusier's pilgrimage Chapel at Ronchamp. Williams designed the sculptural concrete iconography behind the altar. The flooring of the interior and central courtyard is patterned concrete.

To meet the expanding needs of the church, the parish eventually left Buechel for a new, larger facility at 920 Blankenbaker Parkway. The Buechel site was purchased in October 1998 by the Hikes Point Christian Church. A 1998–99 renovation maintained the original concrete in the sanctuary but added new movable seats and carpeting.

193. WESTMINSTER TERRACE RETIREMENT CENTER
2116 Buechel Bank Road, Buechel
H. Carleton Godsey Associates
1975

This project comprises both a renovation of an existing structure and the construction of a major new wing. H. Carleton Godsey composed a series of complimentary volumes of clearly separated functions. The best feature of the building is its detailing. Taut brick walls are used to enclose the volumes but also to separate the balcony spaces of the apartments, preserving a degree of privacy not usually seen in this type of structure. These partition walls have articulated ends, emphasizing the vertical qualities of the walls as piers and off-setting the horizontality of the balconies. The roof at the top of the piers is concrete, not brick, shaped into a taut, flattened arch. These qualities owe not a little to the work of Louis Kahn (brick) and Le

Corbusier (concrete roof), but the high quality of their synthesis represents the great degree to which local architects were looking broadly for inspiration at this time.

194. ROSEWELL
(Barbour-Middleton-Blodgett House)
6415 Transylvania Avenue, Harrods Creek
Henry Whitestone and Isaiah Rogers
Landmark designation: NRHP, 1980
1854

Rosewell, a country villa, is so elegant that only a few architects in Louisville could have designed it in 1854. Its architect, Henry Whitestone, apprenticed in Ireland with James Paine and came to Louisville in 1853 with Isaiah Rogers, the most noted hotel architect in the U.S. at midcentury. Whitestone is primarily known for his serene Italianate buildings, but he was fully schooled in all the revival styles and could execute any of them with ease. In Ireland, he designed the Greek revival County Clare Courthouse, and his replacement building for Gideon Shryock's Medical Institute of the City of Louisville, which burned in 1856, was an excellent example of Greek revival in Kentucky.

Rosewell, presented as an exquisitely formed object in a manicured landscape, is a raised, pink brick cube with similar front and back symmetrical elevations. The front elevation is framed with engaged pilasters at the corners, a white cornice with a full entablature and modillions under the eaves, and a water table that helps terminate the brick wall as it meets the ground. The raised portico, supported by double fluted columns with Corinthian capitals, entablature, and modillions under the overhang, carries a classical balustrade and is attached to a projecting wall plane, accentuating the portico's centralizing effect. The central-hall plan, with three flights of stairs, opens to large double parlors on each side. This house was recently in jeopardy because of the planned construction of two new bridges across the Ohio River, but eventually officials agreed to minimize any adverse effects and possibly acquire it for preservation.

195. STICH RESIDENCE
(Gilores House)
7425 Woodhill Valley Road, Prospect
Sweet and Warner
1957

Norman Sweet, a leading modern architect in Louisville, designed this house for his wife, Graeme Gilores, and their two children. The Sweet design, contemporary for its time, included window walls with large expanses of glass and a built-up flat roof with deep overhangs. The architect's integration of the landscape and his use of aggregate block and redwood siding exude a strong Wrightian influence, similar to several Sweet-designed houses of the 1950s and 1960s. Emphasizing its transparency, the house has an open-air courtyard at its core, incorporating a creek, a small bridge, and bamboo plantings. There is a see-through fireplace in the living room, which has a glass window on its exterior side. The original design had one hallway at the entry, which was later expanded to incorporate a sitting space for the children. The current owners use this space as a library. The house and its two-acre site underwent an extensive but sympathetic renovation in 1996. The exterior observation deck, off the living and dining rooms, was rebuilt, and the color of the house was changed from mauve to greenish brown.

196. LEIGHT HOUSE

6 Glen Arden Road, Glenview

Jasper D. Ward & Associates, Frederick DiSanto, Winona S. Chamberlin

1966–1968

The house Jasper D. Ward, Fred DiSanto, and Winona Chamberlin designed for Adel and Leonard Leight is composed of a series of pure geometric volumes that negotiate a gently sloping two-acre terraced site and is reminiscent of Edward Larrabee Barnes's house for Andrew Rockefeller in Greenwich, Connecticut (1965).

Like the Barnes design, the vertical, wood-sided Leight House steps down a densely forested hillside, while peaked ribbed-metal roofs bring sunlight to the rooms below. Thus the house is a series of clustered volumes that are united by a single horizontal volume. Four primary hoods project above the roofline, the function and scale of each unique to the room below.

Ward subdivided the house into two programs: a bedroom wing and a living area that includes the kitchen, living room, and dining room. A gallery space links the two volumes together. Ward, DiSanto, and Chamberlin successfully played off the Leights' request for a place to exhibit their contemporary-art collection by providing natural light in each room. The architects also deployed saturated color, combined with the projecting walls of the building, to create a dynamic expression of art in its own right. In 1984, Ward designed a semicircular addition to house the owner's art collection and to expand the kitchen.

197. PRIVATE RESIDENCE
1 Arden Drive, Glenview
Herb Greene
1966

This house sits on a steeply wooded site in Glenview. Like other Herb Greene houses, the design presents a composition of form and surface that responds to the site and the vernacular context. The architect developed a scheme that uses conventional materials (painted vertical wood siding and like-colored brick), while producing dynamic terraces. The contemporary structure steps down the hillside, creating patio gardens at all levels. The entrance is unassuming and hidden from view. The back of the house, however, opens up, extending the interior of the house with views of the forest. Deep overhangs cover large expanses of glass, allowing filtered sunlight to enter the home. An external freestanding 100-foot-long switchback ramp, projecting into the trees, connects the first and second floors.

198. TEMPLE CONGREGATION ADATH ISRAEL BRITH SHOLOM
5101 U.S. Highway 42, Prospect
Arrasmith and Judd, Joseph and Joseph
1980

Located at the intersection of Brownsboro Road (U.S. Highway 42) and Lime Kiln Road, in the heart of Louisville's residential East End, the Temple Congregation Adath Israel Brith Sholom sits in the corner portion of a ten-acre wooded site. The building's distinctive style and brown brick exterior has become a prominent architectural marker in the neighborhood.

In 1976, Adath Israel had begun designs for a new synagogue. Shortly after beginning its design review, Adath Israel and Brith Sholom consolidated to form the Temple Congregation. Officiants of Adath Israel who were managing partners of two Louisville architectural firms—Arnold M. Judd Sr. (Arrasmith and Rapp) and Alfred Joseph Jr. (Joseph and Joseph)—formed a joint venture to build a new temple and develop a campus master plan.

The complex reflects changes in practice since World War II, which expands the traditional role of the synagogue to include assembly halls, social halls, classrooms, administrative offices, auxiliary chapels, and a library. The shape of the building presents an ark-wall facade on one side and an entrance on the other. The design of the synagogue reflects the nature of the worship within, and exquisite faceted stained-glass windows, designed by Robert Markert, incorporate religious symbolism. The synagogue's auxiliary chapel has a hidden circular stairway that connects the building's mechanical room to the bimah.

In 1999, Arrasmith, Judd, Rapp, Chovan, Inc. began developing a design for the expansion of the original complex to include additions to the administrative offices, preschool, and classrooms, and two new additions, a freestanding social activity hall and the Klein Center for Celebration and Lifelong Learning. The design for the new additions, completed in 2002, reflects the architectural character, materials, forms, and details of the original structure.
Award for Masonry Design Excellence, Kentuckiana Masonry Institute, 1981

199. LOCUST GROVE
561 Blankenbaker Lane, Locust Grove Historic District
William Croghan
Landmark designation: NHL; LL
c. 1790

Locust Grove, a stately two-and-a-half-story plantation house with a four-room Georgian plan, was originally sited on 387 acres next to the Ohio River, which belonged to Major William Croghan from Philadelphia and his wife Lucy Clark Croghan (sister of George Rogers Clark, who founded Louisville on Corn Island in 1778). Croghan came to Kentucky as Clark's surveying partner. The architectural richness of the house reinforced the elevated status of several generations of the Croghan family, who entertained the most important visitors to early Louisville. The components of federal architecture in this house are worth examining carefully. The exterior is distinguished by front and back Flemish bond-brick walls raised on a limestone foundation and basement, a molded water table, jack arches, four end chimneys, five bays symmetrically composed around a delicate, attenuated federal entrance with a transom, and an unusual double stringcourse (found in Philadelphia) that separates the two main floors. Its central hall leads to parlors, dining rooms, George Rogers Clark's room on the first floor, and to an enclosed stair that opens onto a second-floor traveler's room, a bedroom, and a ballroom. The attic has a hall and four rooms for the children. Walnut paneling, ash floors, a stair rail, doors, hearths, wallpaper, and brass are among the original appointments.

The house was restored in 1964 to the period between 1790 and 1822, when Clark lived there and Zachary Taylor, James Monroe, Andrew Jackson, Aaron Burr, Meriwether Lewis, William Clark (General Clark's brother), and John James Audubon visited. Meriwether Lewis and William Clark exhibited trophies from their overland voyage to the Pacific when they returned to Louisville in 1806. The connection of this plantation to so many significant people is the reason for its National Historic Landmark status and is one of the main reasons that this place is so revered by Louisville citizens. At the time of the restoration, a wing (1837) was demolished. The current property of 55 acres possesses a number of restored and reconstructed dependencies, such as a summer kitchen, servants' quarters, icehouse, springhouse, smokehouse, log cabin, dairy, stable, stone barn, quadrant garden, herb garden, cutting garden, and split-rail fence.

Open Monday to Saturday, 10 A.M. to 4:30 P.M. and Sunday, 1:30 P.M. to 4:30 P.M. with the last tour at 3:30 P.M.

200. SPRINGFIELDS
5608 Apache Road, Indian Hills
Richard Taylor
Landmark designation: NHL, 1961; NRHP, 1966
1785

Having received 400 acres as pay for his heroic service in the Revolutionary War, Colonel Richard Taylor moved his wife and three children from his Virginia estate, Hare Forest, to a log cabin on this frontier site. One of many upper-class Virginians who settled in Kentucky, Taylor had passed by the Falls of the Ohio as early as 1769, on an adventure down the river to New Orleans. Eventually, he owned more than 8,000 acres in Kentucky. His third child, Zachary, who later became the twelfth president of the United States, came here as an eight-month-old child, lived on this site from 1785 to 1808, returned often, and is buried in the family plot at the Zachary Taylor National Cemetery, nearby at 4701 Brownsboro Road. Shortly after the family arrived, Colonel Taylor replaced their log house with a substantial two-and-a-half-story brick house. Between 1810 and 1820, Taylor added three bays to create a full Georgian house with a central hall and hearths in each room for a family of nine children. Although this house was heavily damaged by a tornado in 1974, it was fully restored and retains some of its original interior appointments, such as stained walnut and poplar floors, and door surrounds and painted corner blocks in the addition.

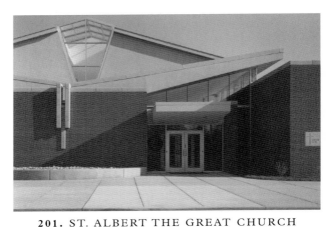

201. ST. ALBERT THE GREAT CHURCH
1395 Girard Drive, Westport
Al J. Schneider, Omni Architects (Lexington)
1960–2000

The addition to St. Albert the Great Church creates a sensitive exchange with the existing church structure and the surrounding community. The new Omni-designed campus includes a sanctuary, a renovation of the existing church, and classroom and educational facilities.

The sanctuary sits in the front yard of the existing church building, which Al J. Schneider designed in 1959–60. Using a similar palette of materials—brick, concrete, stucco, and metal windows—helped reduce the massiveness of the new building and its butterfly-shaped roof to a more human scale. The focal point of the new church is the central assembly space. The sanctuary uses a fan-shaped seating arrangement to increase the sense of community among the congregation. Two pivot doors (twenty feet tall) separate the narthex from the sanctuary. During Christmas and Easter services, these doors open to provide overflow seating for as many as 200 more parishioners. Louisville glass designer Kenneth von Roenn, of Architectural Art Glass, designed a unique, patterned stained-glass rose window, which creates a dynamic moiré effect when viewed from different vantage points. Von Roenn also designed the stained-glass panels located in the "metaphor wall" along Girard Avenue. This highly articulated facade wall incorpo-

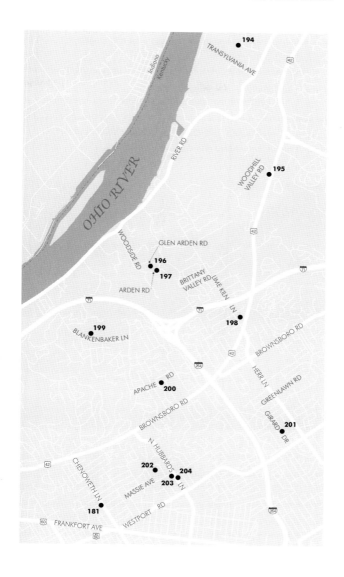

Map 9: Buildings 181–204

rates the fourteen stations of the cross and has niches for statues, candles, and other religious iconography.

The renovation of the existing church uses a racetrack concept plan to organize the new library, conference rooms, and work rooms in the center of the space. Offices located at the perimeter of the double-loaded corridors have views to the exterior. A courtyard amid the churches and new classrooms unites the campus.
Merit Award, Kentuckiana Masonry Institute, 2003

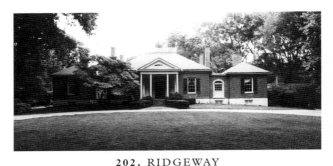

202. RIDGEWAY
4095 Massie Avenue, Woodlawn Park
Henry Massie
Landmark designation: NHL, 1973
1816–1818

Considered one of the most architecturally significant houses in Louisville and originally sited on 434 acres, Ridgeway is a finely designed federal, raised, brick dwelling with a five-part Palladian plan and striking neoclassical architectural details. Owing to close family, political, economic, and cultural relationships among the owners, who were members of an elite class from Old Virginia, Ridgeway, Farmington, and Oxmoor have many architectural features in common. Ridgeway is also similar to the William Morton House (1810) in Lexington, the Grange (1818) near Paris, and the Homewood (1801) in Baltimore. At Ridgeway, four tall chimneys soar above the single-story main block of Flemish bond walls, hipped roof, and railing. Four attenuated columns carry an entry portico with a full pediment and fanlight, which shelters a recessed entry similar to those at Farmington and Oxmoor, with double doors, sidelights, and lunette. Two hyphens with neoclassical false doors connect the main section of the house to wing pavilions, which also have hipped roofs and central chimneys. A square entry hall has an arched doorway and light, opening into a lateral hall that reaches the rooms in the end pavilions. A large dining room and parlor, which boast exceptional federal hearths and hand-carved mantles, are situated behind the lateral hall and are connected by a wide arched door. A covered walkway connects the main house to the brick summer kitchen, which is now a guest apartment. Renovated and restored several times, this house has been under almost continuous restoration since 1985, but it retains high architectural integrity and significance.

203. ST. MATTHEW'S EPISCOPAL CHURCH
330 North Hubbards Lane, Windy Hill
Olmsted Brothers (Boston), Louis & Henry
1952–1953

The St. Matthew's Mission was established in 1948 with 50 communicants, and it became a full parish in 1950. An eight-acre site was purchased in a suburb north of St. Matthews called Windy Hill, between Brownsboro and Lexington Roads. In 1950, the Olmsted Brothers were hired to design a fifteen-year development master plan for the site. In 1951, Frederick Louis, a communicant of the church and partner in the architecture firm Louis & Henry, was hired to design a structure that included a 200-seat sanctuary and auditorium space, kindergarten, nursery, office space, and class-rooms. In 1952, ground was broken. This first phase of the extensive Olmsted plan included a temporary church and parish hall.

A tall leaded-copper spire tops the Roman-brick, glass, and California-redwood edifice. Inside, pierced wood screens, which depict "the unfolding of the Word" in 42 biblical scenes, decorate the auditorium space. As the congregation continued to expand, Hartstern, Louis & Henry, was hired to design an addition to the complex. This second phase of the Olmsted plan called for a new sanctuary that could accommodate 450 communicants and demonstrate changes in the liturgy. In 1961, after a tour of European churches, Fred Louis and Larry Leis, the project architects, designed a dynamic chancel that is spanned by a parabolic roof structure. The canopy roof, free of walls, is constructed of laminated wood, carried by valley beams that support a system of A-frames sheathed with wood decking. Like the spire of the original structure, the roof is covered with lead-coated copper. The main congregation area is located on the first floor. The layout of that space is in the round, allowing for physical proximity among the congregation, and is symbolic of the Last Supper. The church was completed in 1964 and dedicated in 1965.

204. LUSTRON HOUSE
325 North Hubbards Lane, St. Matthews
Carl Strandlund
c. 1950

To address the housing shortage of post–World War II America and to provide returning war veterans with inexpensive housing, inventor Carl Strandlund designed affordable prefabricated houses called Lustron Homes. His intention was to create a new housing industry, similar to the automotive industry in scope and output, which, like fast-food restaurants and gas stations, could be built in 72 hours. The resulting products were sturdy steel structures that never needed painting, siding, or roofing. Of the 2,500 Lustron homes built, fifteen are in Louisville, and Louisville historian Joanne Weeter tallied fourteen still standing in 2000.

The Lustron Corporation offered three different house models. The house on North Hubbards Lane has the typical Lustron appearance—a one-story ranch house with a grid of enameled panels and inset aluminum windows—but it is atypical for its double-wide configuration. The exterior is gray, one of the eight pastel colors that were standard choices for a buyer. A local dealer was responsible for erecting the house, once it arrived by truck from the factory, and assembly typically took seven to ten days. The cost was substantially more than a conventional house of the period, with a cap of $10,000, but the company argued that the permanence of the steel framing, wall construction, and interior finishes, as well as the built-in cabinets and appliances, made it a worthwhile investment. Despite considerable public interest (Weeter notes that as many as 96,000 people visited the Louisville dealer's offices), the corporation filed for bankruptcy in 1950.

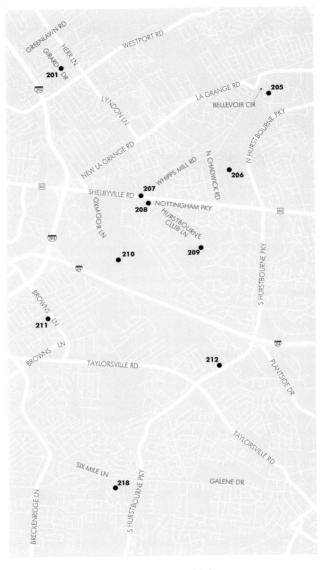

Map 10: Buildings 205–212

205. BELLEVOIR

1 Bellevoir Circle, Moorland

Hamilton and Edmonia Ormsby

Landmark designation: NRHP, 1980; LL

1864–1867

Bellevoir, owned by the Jefferson County Fiscal Court (now Louisville Metro Government) since 1912 , is an outstanding example of a brick, central-hall, Italianate villa or country house that A. J. Downing might have recommended for the upper classes in his book *The Architecture of Country Houses* (1850). By 1866, his book had gone through nine editions. Once part of Maghera, an estate of 800 acres that belonged to Judge Stephen Ormsby, Bellevoir is now confined to a small tract of land. The villa is square at its core and has a low-hipped roof, projecting entrance wing, two side wings, an elaborate two-story cast-iron front porch, two side porches, and other extensions in the rear. The facades have symmetrical, balanced openings, but the protruding masses and porches lend the house the organic effect that Victorian fashion and philosophy demanded. Bellevoir possesses classic Italianate elements and detailing, including paired chimneys; tall, thin floor-to-ceiling sash windows, with round pediment hood moldings and dentils; paired windows on the second bedroom, leading to a balcony; paired brackets under the wide eaves; and small attic windows in a frieze articulated by a horizontal stringcourse, dentils, heavy cornice, and stone quoins. A recessed entry under the porch leads to a large double door that opens into a central hall with a winding stair to the second floor. The Jefferson County Fiscal Court has used Bellevoir for various purposes. Between 1920 and 1968, it was part of the Louisville and Jefferson County Children's Home for dependent and delinquent children. In 1987, the Court sold most of the property to an office-park development that now surrounds the house.

206. UNIVERSITY OF LOUISVILLE—SHELBY CAMPUS
(Kentucky Southern College)
9001 Shelbyville Road, St. Matthews
Perkins and Will (Chicago)
1960–1969

The University of Louisville's Shelby Campus sits on land previously owned by Leroy Highbaugh Sr., a local developer. It was founded as Kentucky Southern College, a private co-educational Baptist college. The long-range master plan for the campus included 30 buildings, but only nine were built. In 1969, it merged with the University of Louisville.

The Classroom and Administration Building (1963) is now Burhans Hall, named for the former president of Kentucky Southern College, Rollin Burhans. It sits on a tall plinth and utilizes poured-in-place reinforced concrete and brick to create a clean-lined aesthetic. A central colonnade physically and visually ties together the two parts of the building. The staircases are self-supporting towers, surrounded by glass cages that provide protection without destroying the openness of the colonnade. The central colonnade was designed to allow the Administration Building to stand prominently on axis with the Shelbyville Road entrance, while framing what was intended to be the "real heart of the College," the Tower of Light and adjacent chapel in the quadrangle behind the building.

When the college merged with the University of Louisville in 1969, the School of Music moved from its cramped quarters in Gardencourt and the Old Reynolds Building (Belknap Campus) to the Shelby Campus. A subsequent master plan by Bickel Gibson had the School of Music as the new focal point of the Shelby Campus. This master plan was not realized, and in 1985 the Music School returned to the Belknap Campus, where Bickel Gibson designed an award-winning building for the school. The current uses for Burhans Hall include the Office of Continuing Studies and External Programs and the National Crime Prevention Institute.

207. EIGHT MILE HOUSE
8113 Shelbyville Road, Lyndon
Architect unknown
Landmark designation: NRHP, 1976
1790s–1800s

During the federal period, stops were built approximately every five to ten miles along Kentucky pikes. One of these stops, Eight Mile House, functioned as a tavern, stage stop, and tollhouse where fees were collected from travelers on Shelbyville Road. This location, situated on the edge of the Oxmoor plantation and along a well-traveled road, was excellent for travel and tavern business in a state known for carrying out traditions of hospitality inherited from Virginia, employing copious amounts of its own noble bourbon. The three-bay house represents a common single-pen house type, with a dirt-floor basement and kitchen. It has luckily survived because of its stout, random ashlar limestone walls and, more recently, because of its landmark status, which protects it from alteration. The wing addition and dormers are twentieth-century modifications. Oxmoor Toyota, the current owner, uses the house for its financing operation.

208. OUR SAVIOR LUTHERAN CHURCH
8305 Nottingham Parkway, Hurstbourne
Design Environment Group Architects (DEGA)
1966–1968

Our Savior Lutheran Church and School is located in the heart of a Hurstbourne residential subdivision. The church is a dynamic and inspirational space that emphasizes through its planning and seating arrangement total participation in worship activities.

Designed by DEGA, a leading modern-architecture firm in Louisville during the 1960s and 1970s, the church, according to Donald L. Williams of DEGA, embodies a "theologically conceived and religiously oriented" composition. Unique to church design of the time, parishioners arrive by car, passing under the nave through an approach bridge, effecting a sense of arrival before they have actually entered the parking area. A concrete cross anchors the entrance ramp to the church, while a shorter bell tower defines the access between religious education on the first floor and worship on the second floor.

A standing-seam metal roof covers the sanctuary. The central axis culminates at the altar and pulpit, behind which stands a large wooden cross as a focal point. The proportion and detailing of the cross repeat the dimensions of the concrete icon outside the building. While the interior chancel is devoid of extraneous ornamentation, the building's simple geometry and detailing, in particular its materials, resonance, and floor-level stained-glass bands, create a dramatic aura, by which the exterior walls appear to float above the floor. The church was completed during the first phase of the master plan, making the church a focus of the community.

To complete the original master plan for the site, Our Savior Lutheran School was connected to the original structure in 1985 by the Louisville architecture firm Godsey and Associates. The final form of the complex differs from the intent of the DEGA design but does define a U-shaped courtyard, around which the classrooms open. *Honor Award for Design Excellence, AIA Kentucky, 1969*

209. HURSTBOURNE COUNTRY CLUB
(Lynnford)
9000 Hurstbourne Club Lane, Hurstbourne
Jacob Beaverson
Landmark designation: NRHP, 1985
1852

Richard Clough Anderson, an early Louisville politician and diplomat, originally owned both this land and the now demolished Soldier's Retreat. In 1842, John Jacob Sr. bought the property (today several of the original stone outbuildings from the Anderson farm are extant). After John Jacob Jr. inherited his father's estate in 1852, he asked Jacob Beaverson to design and build Lynnford, a Gothic villa. A. J. Davis had made famous the picturesque Gothic villa, a large rambling country house for the upper classes, with the Lyndhurst mansion (1838–65) in Tarrytown, New York. Lynnford, which is now the central-gabled core of the Hurstbourne Country Club, was much less asymmetrical—and therefore less organic—than what Davis and A. J. Downing considered correct for a villa. Lynnford does have the clustered chimneys, the low pointed windows with diamond-shaped glass, pointed hood moldings, an oriel, and two side piazzas, which are all elements expected in Gothic revival structures of the period.

In the late nineteenth century, the house was the center of Hurstbourne Farms, a leading Kentucky horse farm that was home to the famous stallion Ten Broeck, for whom the extant horse barn was built. The house became more asymmetrical and received Tudor Gothic features in 1928, when the architect E. T. Hutchings enlarged the house and renovated the interior for Mrs. Alvin T. Hert. She also hired the Olmsted Brothers to design a nine-hole golf course, which is now half of the eighteen-hole Country Club course, a manicured but picturesque setting, with wandering roads that cross stone bridges over the meandering Beargrass Creek.

210. OXMOOR
720 Oxmoor Avenue, Oxmoor
Alexander Scott Bullitt
Landmark designation: NRHP, 1976
1790

Oxmoor began in 1790 as a jagged central-hall Virginia clapboard frame house, with one-and-a-half stories, end chimneys, four rooms with corner hearths on the first floor, and two rooms above. By the early twentieth century, it had become an expansive Palladian dwelling with colonial revival details. As the plantation house of Alexander Scott Bullitt, and his wife, Priscilla Christian, it served as the business and social center of 1,000 acres of land that Priscilla had inherited from her father. For his mixed-farming operation and numerous slaves, Alexander Bullitt created an array of substantial dependencies, including an extant springhouse, brick slave quarters, a slave wash and cookhouse, summer kitchen, smokehouse, overseer's house, icehouse, family cemetery, and a long tree-lined road to the house. In 1829, his son, William Christian Bullitt, attached a raised brick federal addition with a recessed portico, three unusually proportioned rooms, a connecting space to the old house, and a full basement. His grandson, William Marshall Bullitt, had a hyphen and kitchen pavilion built in 1916, elevated the 1829 section to two stories in 1926, and finally added a hyphen and an impressive library pavilion, designed by the New York architect F. Burrall Hoffman, in 1928. The house, each stage of which retains high integrity, remains in the Bullitt family. The Kentucky Heritage Council has a historic easement on the 80 acres immediately surrounding the main house and its outbuildings. The Filson Club Historical Society has the opportunity to use the property for educational and historical purposes.

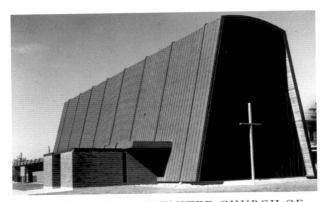

211. ST. ANDREW'S UNITED CHURCH OF CHRIST

2608 Browns Lane, St. Regis Park
McCulloch and Bickel
1964

St. Andrew's United Church of Christ was built on the site of an old farmhouse in St. Regis Park, a growing Louisville suburb. It is one of the notable ecclesiastical designs to emerge from Louisville's modern period. Another is the hyper-parabolic design by Louis & Henry for St. Matthew's Episcopal Church and the pyramidal design by Design Environment Group Architects for Our Savior Lutheran . Where St. Andrew's and St. Matthew's resolved the mathematical geometries of the sanctuary space with ribs of wooden timbers, Our Savior spans the sanctuary with steel.

The congregation of St. Andrew's desired a traditional center-aisle chancel to accommodate 300 to 400 parishioners, and a simple structure, to complement and intensify the worship experience. This program was achieved by combining a wooden frame with a thin copper membrane, to form a uniquely shaped roof.

The relief-sculptured brickwork on the west wall behind the altar dissipates as it reaches the sky. The architect intended this patterning to be open to personal reflection and meaning. In contrast, the east wall of the sanctuary is a composition of steel and stained glass. The lightness and solidity of this facade provide an interesting dialogue with the opposite end of the sanctuary.

A 2002 addition by Grossman Martin Chapman complete the 1964 master plan by adding classrooms and a multi-purpose gymnasium, linked by a central entryway, which includes an enclosed area between the new and old portions of the building.

Honor Award for Design Excellence, AIA Kentucky, 1965

212. NUNNLEA
(Harriet Funk Hise House)
9316 Hurstbourne Lande, Hurstbourne Acres
Harriet and Alfred Hise
Landmark designation: NRHP, 1980
1820s–1860s

Shortly after the Civil War, Harriet Funk Hise inherited 100 acres of land from her parents and built a house akin to the French Creole subtype, a mix of French, Caribbean, Spanish, African, and English building traditions, seen frequently along the Gulf Coast between Biloxi, Mississippi, and New Orleans and much of Louisiana. Only five examples of this type have been identified in Jefferson County.

Nunnlea is a brick, square, five-bay, hipped-roof dwelling, set on a limestone basement that creates a podium for a Georgian central-hall plan. The gallery, reached by four broad stone steps, covers the front facade and is held by four out-of-scale Doric columns and an entablature. E. T. Hutchings designed a new gallery after the flood of 1937 destroyed an earlier gallery, which was similar to the one at Beech Lawn on Six Mile Road. The new gallery creates a cool outdoor space for socializing. On the front elevation, floor-to-ceiling windows, with tall shutters on each side of the door, give ample light and shelter to the formal rooms inside. In Louisiana's hot, wet climate, the tall French windows under the gallery would open to ventilate the rooms. The columned gallery, the symmetrical facade, and the entrance with sidelights and double fanlight create the Greek revival style that is also frequently associated with the house type in the Deep South.

Additions to this house type in Kentucky usually involve side wings and telescoped ells. Nunnlea received a side wing after 1937, but its gabled ells are earlier additions. Brick outbuildings include a summer kitchen, a double-pen tenant house, and a smokehouse with a brick diamond-shaped vent much like the detail on the smokehouse at Beech Lawn that was built about the same time. Nunnlea now houses the Beautification League.

213. ANCHORAGE PRESBYTERIAN CHURCH
11403 Park Road, Anchorage
W. H. Redin, W. D. Evans
Landmark designation: NRHP, 1980
1869

W. H. Redin emigrated from England to the U.S. in 1826 with his family, who settled in Louisville by 1834. He studied art at the National Academy of Design in New York City in the 1840s and by 1860 advertised himself as an architect in Louisville. He designed several churches in the vicinity, including his stone Gothic revival Presbyterian edifice (1866) in nearby Pewee Valley, where he was senior warden of the vestry. His brick Gothic revival church (1869) for the Anchorage congregation, established in Kentucky in 1799, is an example of a country parish church that many architects, such as Richard Upjohn of New York, designed throughout the eastern U.S. more or less according to the rules set down by the Pugins in the 1830s. The buttressed bell tower is set on the side of the buttressed nave, giving the church an asymmetrical entry and imbuing it with the dynamic organic nature that the Pugins considered appropriate for a small congregation of 300 persons. The nave ends with a transverse chapel and recitation wing. The interior has been extensively renovated several times; however, the cherry pews are original, as are the wood wainscoting and stained-glass windows. An educational and office wing was added in 1956. Recently, a new organ was installed, once again significantly changing the chancel from its original condition.

214. ANCHORAGE INDEPENDENT SCHOOL
(Anchorage Public School)
11318 Ridge Road, Anchorage
D. X. Murphy & Brothers, Luckett & Farley, Nolan & Nolan,
Bickel Gibson, Gibson & Mason
1913–1915

Anchorage Independent School is situated at the edge of the Olmsted-designed village of Anchorage. The original design by D. X. Murphy & Brothers remains intact despite a total of eight additions and renovations.

In 1913, an eight-acre plot of land at Ridge and Bellewood Roads was purchased from Harry H. Warren to build a modern school for the citizens of Anchorage. The original Anchorage Public School, a six-classroom structure built in 1915, is now the east wing. The many early additions to the school were financed by taxes and revenue from the Southern Pacific Railroad, which moved its franchise from downtown Louisville to Anchorage in 1916. Murphy's west wing (1921) includes a symmetrically placed front entry and auditorium, and the gymnasium (1923) forms the central core for the Spanish revival complex. The 1921–23 configuration remains intact despite several interior classroom updates.

A school consolidation in neighboring Middletown in 1950 and the 1952 completion of Eastern High School threatened the school's existence. However, the citizens of Anchorage voted to remain independent and continued to offer instruction from kindergarten through the ninth grade. By 1959, it was the only remaining independent school district in the Louisville area.

The 1982, 1986, and 1998 additions use the vocabulary of the original building, while the 1989 and 1991 additions offer modern variations on the Spanish revival aesthetic.

215. WETHERBY HOUSE
(Davis Tavern)
11803 Shelbyville Road, Middletown
William White
Landmark designation: NRHP, 1983
c. 1796

Millions of dollars were transacted in the slave trade at this important stage stop and tavern, which served travelers on Shelbyville Road. Originally a brick, five-bay, central-hall I-house, Davis Tavern was expanded by three bays, a shed, and an ell addition. It was further altered with a second door in the 1840s to accommodate the frequent travel and tavern traffic between Louisville, Shelbyville, and Frankfort.

216. HEAD HOUSE ANTIQUES & UNIQUES
(Benjamin Head House)
11601 Main Street, Middletown
Benjamin Head
Landmark designation: NRHP, 1974
1812–1815

This detached stone dwelling, with its side entry–hall plan and kitchen ell, is an excellent example of the federal townhouse found frequently in cities and towns throughout the original colonies and in Kentucky. Finely laid two-foot-thick stone walls, an expressive arch of voussoirs and keystone over the front door, and jack arches over the windows give this house a robust muscularity that contrasts with the delicacy of the beaded elliptical fanlight over the front door and its sidelights. The two large stone end chimneys add to the powerful asymmetry of the two-thirds Georgian facade. In plan, the side hall has doors that lead into the parlor and dining room and a stair with a quarter turn to a landing that leads to three rooms on the second floor. From there, a stairway opens to a loft and storage room in the garret where slaves and servants slept. The large stone kitchen ell is two steps lower than the main floor.

The slope of the site provides space in the back for an outside door into a basement kitchen, which servants and slaves may also have used. A detached summer kitchen with a full cellar, a livery stable, a servant's quarters, and a frame chicken house are original outbuildings. Outbuildings transplanted from other places to the site include the first doctor's office in Middletown, the first barbershop in Eastwood, and a log grocery store from Pewee Valley. The interior was heavily restored in 1930 and 1974 and has been adaptively reused by Head House Antiques & Uniques since 1996.

217. THORPE COMMERCIAL GROUP
(Joseph Abell House)
12210 Old Shelbyville Road, Middletown
Joseph Abell
Landmark designation: NRHP, 1980
1804

In about 1803, Joseph Abell migrated from Maryland to Kentucky, where he established a 600-acre plantation and built a main house and dependencies, now mostly gone. This Flemish-bond brick I-house (one-room deep, two rooms and a central hall wide, and two stories high) was similar in plan and construction to many houses in the Tidewater region of Maryland and Virginia. Although it was considered a substantial dwelling at the time, it is relatively small in scale and typical of early-nineteenth-century country houses on large estates near Louisville, such as Oxmoor, which was also a small house originally. In 1806, Abell added a wing that served as his medical office, and at that time the summer kitchen was lengthened to an ell that stretched into the backyard. A modest porch, though probably not the original one, protects a double-door entrance with a five-light transom and two sidelights bracketed by engaged pilasters. All the mantels except one are original, as are the stair, window glass, ash flooring on the first level, poplar flooring on the second, and most of the other interior woodwork. The insistent symmetry of the front elevation presents a formal and ordered Georgian aesthetic, which contrasts strongly with the organic, asymmetrical rear elevation, reserved for the eyes of family and servants. The current owner renovated and restored the house in 2001 with the help of a historic-preservation tax credit. An unusual hexagonal smokehouse and stone well also remain from the early nineteenth century.

Descendants who followed Joseph Abell's early medical profession include Dr. Irvin Abell, professor of surgery at the University of Louisville around the turn of the twentieth century, and Dr. Irvin Abell Jr., also a leading surgeon in Louisville during the mid-twentieth century. Helen Edwards Abell married Irvin Abell Jr. in 1940 and later became one of Louisville's most effective and well-known preservationists. In 1982, she received the National Trust for Historic Preservation's highest award, the Louise du Pont Crowninshield Award. In her honor, the Helen Edwards Abell Chair in Historic Preservation was established at the University of Kentucky.

218. NOTRE RÊVE
(Beech Lawn)
8000 Six Mile Road, South End
John Edward Bryan
Landmark designation: NRHP, 1980
1866

Beech Lawn, renamed Notre Rêve by the current owner, is a relatively rare penetration into Kentucky of a house type seen frequently in the Deep South, from Biloxi, Mississippi, to New Orleans and Baton Rouge, Louisiana, where French colonists began to settle during the late seventeenth century. In response to the hot, humid climate, French builders mixed their traditions with Caribbean, Spanish, African, and English forms to produce a hybrid dwelling that was superbly adapted to its new place. Built in about 1866, Beech Lawn, like Nunnlea and at least three other examples in Jefferson County, is a square, brick, five-bay, single-story house with a low-hipped roof, ending in a widow's walk. A broad gallery, held by thin, fluted columns, capitals, and a plain entablature, stretches across the front facade, providing an outdoor room for sitting and protection from the sun for the floor-to-ceiling windows and the tall, thin door, its sidelights, and fanlight. The house sits on a basement, creating a pavilion base for a Georgian plan that includes a central hall with four flanking rooms, hearths, doors to the hall in each room, and doors between contiguous rooms. In Jefferson County, extensions to these houses tend to be telescoped gable additions, wings, and carbuncles. Brick outbuildings include a summer kitchen, double-pen tenant house, and smokehouse. A frame barn and sheds also stand. An extensively landscaped parcel with a wide variety of trees and plants displays John Edward Bryan's interest in horticulture, one of the serious pastimes of gentleman farmers during most of the nineteenth century in Kentucky. Bryan was also a wood carver and furniture maker. He carved the wood parlor mantel with a lily and rose motif.

219. ST. GABRIEL THE ARCHANGEL
5505 Bardstown Road, Fern Creek
Al J. Schneider, Omni Architects (Lexington)
1953–2003

St. Gabriel the Archangel church and school was founded in Fern Creek, outside of downtown Louisville, in 1953. Longtime builder and developer Al J. Schneider built the original church. With increased suburban expansion, the growing Catholic parish needed to enlarge its existing sanctuary and create additional classroom space within its school. Omni Architects, in conjunction with the parish, developed a four-phase master-plan expansion. The first

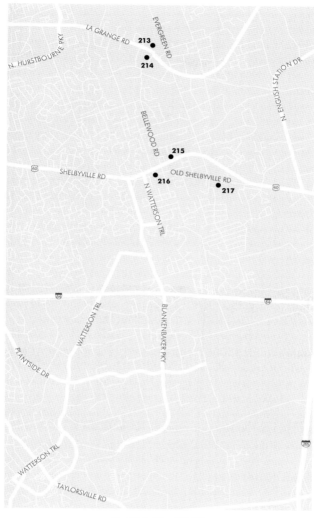

Map 10: Buildings 213–217

phase included the construction of a new church and multipurpose activities building, while phase two was a renovation of the existing church into administrative offices. Both phases were completed in 1994. Phase three was completed in 2001, when a school and media center were built. Phase four has yet to be realized but will allow for further expansion of the classroom building.

Located in a single-family suburban neighborhood, the new church uses brick and precast concrete to reflect the quality and characteristics of the surrounding community. A long gabled roof spans the sanctuary space. Two doors separate the narthex from the sanctuary. During Christmas and Easter services, these doors open to provide overflow seating for as many as 200 more parishioners. A circular stained-glass window, designed by Father Peter Gray of Philadelphia, creates a focal point above the altar at the south end of the chancel space, while clerestory windows in the gable allow north light to enter above the narthex. Omni's phase-two renovation transformed the original church into a light-filled two-story office and classroom space. By extending the choir balcony into the main chancel, a second-story loft pulls away from the building's walls to create two continuous light wells at either side of the loft. These wells allow light to penetrate deep into the former sanctuary space.

To meet the needs of the largest parochial school in the Louisville metropolitan area, Omni designed a contemporary three-story addition to the existing educational complex. The school and media center has three programmatic elements in its three levels. A preschool with an outdoor play area is at the lower level, as well as a technology center and curved library and reading area, and computer classrooms at level one, and the seventh- and eighth-grade classrooms at level two. The facade of the curved form, referred to as the "kiva," is composed of translucent fiberglass panels, which allow a soft, diffuse light to illuminate the reading area. The classrooms above are organized into two clusters, to facilitate team teaching, with an extended learning center in each cluster. A terraced landscape unifies the complex.

Church: Citation Award, AIA Kentucky; Merit Honor Award, Kentuckiana Masonry Institute, 1995.

School: Citation Award, AIA Kentucky; Merit Honor Award, Kentuckiana Masonry Institute, 2002.

220. TRIAERO
(Irma Bartman Residence)
8310 Johnson School Road, Fern Creek
Bruce Goff
Landmark designation: NRHP, 1980
1940–1942

Nationally known architect Bruce Goff designed this house, known as Triaero, as a small weekend cottage for Irma Bartman and her son, Kenneth, who at the time of the commission was a student of Goff at the Chicago Academy of Fine Arts.

Triaero reflects Frank Lloyd Wright's influence on Goff, who had studied with Wright in the 1930s, and encompasses Goff's modernist attitude: the desire to integrate industrially produced building materials. Goff characterized the structure as "the first minimum-space home in America to carry through consistently an individual expression of design to the smallest detail." The crystalline appearance of the Bartman Residence represents an approach that he would continue to explore throughout his career.

The house is essentially one large, continuous triangular shell. A steel frame consisting of three columns holds up a triangular collar truss, with purlins cantilevered to the edge of the overhang. An external system of bracing and the central core (fireplace, bath, and kitchen) support the triangular roof, allowing it to cantilever from the core and stand free of all other walls. The carport was originally within the volume of the house and interrupted the home space. However, it has been replaced with an architect's studio, unifying the plan. Two corners of the main triangle are truncated to form reflecting pools. At the edge of the pools and under the roof overhangs, Goff incorporated large glazed openings that visually extend the interior, particularly through the reflection of the distant sky and trees.

The design uses a triangular motif throughout, including large twelve-foot-wide planes of glass, a guy-wired chimney flue, and a sweeping wingspread roof, which extends into overhangs of latticed redwood that seem to float above the walls below. The walls are sheathed in copper and secured with narrow vertical battens of redwood. The project is reminiscent of Buckminster Fuller's Dymaxion House of 1927. The triangular motif extends to the site, where V-shaped landscape wedges terrace the hillside, echoing the reflecting pools at the building's corners. Goff also designed the original furniture for the house.

The house was severely damaged by fire in 1959 but was rebuilt. A complete restoration, using Goff's original drawings, continues under Louisville architect Jack Neuschwander.

221. CANDLEWOOD
(Robert Hord House)
15903 Shelbyville Road, Eastwood
Robert Hord
Landmark designation: NRHP, 1983
1847–1848

Candlewood still exudes a powerful presence on the landscape, even though it is no longer the center of a 2,000-acre plantation. It sits far back on its site but is visible through stately trees, which add to the dignity and grace of the house. The front facade is symmetrical and has five bays, separated by six engaged pilasters that enhance the verticality of the dwelling and lend it heaviness. The pilasters carry flat, square capitals, an entablature, and an overhanging cornice. The house has a classic Georgian plan, with a large central hall flanked by two rooms on each side, which functioned as a parlor, dining room, drawing room, library, and later a bedroom. Hearths in each of the main rooms lead to interior end chimneys. Broken roof pediments on the gable ends, with an arch and fanlight in the tympanum, add to the dwelling's Greek revival expression. The dormers are twentieth-century additions.

222. BLAND RESIDENCE
7521 Fisherville Woods Drive, Fisherville
Michael Koch and Associates, Architects and Planners
2001

The Bland Residence steps up the hillside of a narrow four-and-a-half-acre meadow in Fisherville, Kentucky, located along the Jefferson and Shelby County border just east of I-265. Arranged as a space for both living and working, the house has four linked but distinctly different pavilions: a living pavilion, a sleeping pavilion, and two support pavilions (garage and workshop). A screened-in porch separates the two-car garage and large workshop.

The building's angled shapes and complicated geometric forms are unique to Louisville. The house has concrete foundation walls, protruding V-shaped Brazilian-mahogany decks, and an exterior envelope clad in gray-green cement board and yellow Parklex (composite Spanish plywood), punctuated by large expanses of

glass. These openings allow views toward the heavily wooded surrounds in all directions. Inside the house, the pavilions unite to
form a continuous living environment, accented by rough-textured
concrete walls and smooth Parklex surfaces. The resulting space
is a collage of materials, skillfully constructed by Ross Arterburn
Builders. Kenneth von Roenn of Architectural Glass Art designed
the glass sculpture near the open fireplace that separates the living
and dining areas.

Merit Award for Design Excellence, AIA Kentucky, 2002

223. FARNSLEY-KAUFMAN HOUSE
3400 Lee's Lane, Shively
David Farnsley
Landmark designation: NRHP, 1983
1811

David Farnsley moved with his parents to Kentucky in 1796, and
in 1811 he purchased 300 acres of land along the Ohio River and
built a log cabin chinked with stones, mud, and animal hair. His
cabin had a stone chimney at one end, which created a large heating and cooking fireplace in the first-floor common space, comprising a kitchen, bedroom, storage area, family room, and place for
entertaining guests. A side stair led to an unheated sleeping loft,
which was covered by a roof shingled with wood. Farnsley also built
numerous other outbuildings to support his mixed, middling farming operation, driven by slave labor and market demands. To make
his house more spacious for his family in 1831, he attached a two-
story brick addition to the log structure, which he increased to two

stories. Through this accretion, he created a central-hall I-house, one of the symbols of nineteenth-century agricultural success. The agricultural complex remained in operation and intact for more than 180 years.

The Friends of the Farnsley-Kaufman House rescued it from demolition in 1997, and, in conjunction with the Farnsley Middle School, Restoration Group Incorporated, the Center for Historic Architecture and Preservation and the Kentucky Archaeological Survey at the University of Kentucky, and the Kentucky Heritage Council, they are gradually restoring the house, the remaining out-buildings, and the landscape without romanticizing them. In 2004, the Friends received a Save America's Treasures grant from the fed-eral government, not "to perpetuate a historical myth of a grandiose past," but to preserve the physical evidence of how changes in the property were registered over time and to restore the property "as resource for educational and community activities."

224. FARNSLEY-MOREMAN HOUSE
(Riverside)
7410 Moreman Road, Bethany Oaks
Gabriel Farnsley
Landmark designation: NRHP, 1979
1837–1839

Gabriel Farnsley built this handsome central-hall house on the Ohio River, a most convenient transportation route for ensuring the suc-cess of his growing agricultural enterprise. Sited in the tradition of Virginia plantations to face the river with a landing where riverboats could stop to take on boiler wood and food, Farnsley's farm also catered to weary visitors, who would stay the night in the traveler's room in the back ell. The interior appointments, including the hearths and window and door surrounds, are all in the plain style, but the reeded pilasters at the door have federal origins. Farnsley eventually put together a mixed farming operation more than 400 acres and thirteen slaves at the time of his death in 1849. Numerous outbuildings, such as slave quarters, a summer kitchen, and barns, no longer exist. The Moreman family bought the house in 1860, expanded the farm to 1,500 acres, and renamed it Riverside in 1879. The U.S. Army Corps of Engineers rebuilt the landing in 1974–78, and the *Spirit of Jefferson* still lands there to take passengers on cruises. The Farnsley-Moreman House purchased the property in 1989 with CDBG funds, restored it, and built a visitor's center.

Open Wednesday through Saturday, 10 A.M. to 4:30 P.M. and Sunday, 1 P.M. to 4:30 P.M. For a cruise schedule call 502-574-2355.

225. LAWRENCE RESIDENCE
8618 Lakeridge Drive, Waverly Hills
Design Environment Group Architects (DEGA)
1969–1971

James Lee Gibson of Design Environment Group Architects (DEGA) designed this three-story modern house in Waverly Hills for Celia and Dr. Robert Lawrence and their three children in 1969. While all of the neighboring houses front the street, Gibson's design takes advantage of the deep triangular-shaped five-acre plot of land adjacent to Waverly Park. Completed in 1971, the vertical cedar-sided house sits back on the lot, high above the street, engaging the crest of the steep slope, while maintaining the densely forested site.

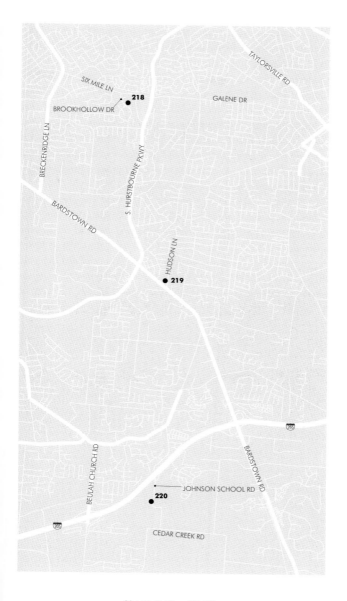

Map 11: Buidlings 218–220

A staircase extends from the ground level to a first-floor entry deck and leads into the main space of the house. A two-story entry foyer, with bridges above, separates the living spaces of the house: the living room and master bedroom to the west and the kitchen, dining room, and bedrooms to the east. There is a windowless entertainment room immediately to the left of the entry. As a focal point of the entry sequence, the wood-clad kitchen floats between the entry foyer and the dining area. Open voids carved into the kitchen volume create spaces for dish or pantry storage or for object or art exhibition, while glazed windows and other voids allow light to penetrate deep into the house's interior.

Similar to other DEGA projects of the time, the primary programmatic elements of the house are clearly legible in the treatment of the facade. The dining room extends beyond the front facade onto a triangular patio that cantilevers twelve feet over the walkway below (a four-by-four column is a recent addition). The four bedrooms on the southeast side of the house project from the vertical plane of the facade, revealing a built-in seating area at each window.

226. SOUTHERN LEADERSHIP ACADEMY
(Southern Junior High School)
4530 Bellevue Avenue, Beechmont
J. Meyrick Colley, addition by Design Environment Group
Architects (DEGA)
1927

The original design by J. Meyrick Colley is an impressive three-story art deco building with a symmetrical tripartite bay structure at the top of a steeply sloping site. A three-story central archway emphasizes and punctuates the rhythmic undulations of the rest of the primary facade. A terraced and bermed landscape master plan was never realized. In 1969, the Louisville architecture firm DEGA designed an addition that doubled the size of the existing building. Given the constraints of the long, narrow site, the design team, led by James Lee Gibson, proposed an L-shaped plan that would wrap the northern facade of the building and expand the western facade to form two enclosed central courtyards. The volumetric delineation and use of concrete formwork are reminiscent of Le Corbusier's Dominican Friary at La Tourette (1957–60). This award-winning project is a successful blend of old and new structures. In 1993, Nolan & Nolan upgraded the building to comply with the Americans with Disabilities Act (ADA standards).

DEGA addition: Honor Award for Excellence in Architecture, AIA Kentucky, 1973

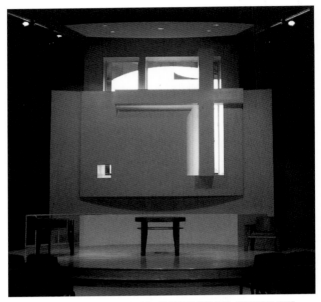

227. ST. JEROME'S CATHOLIC CHURCH
903 Fairdale Road, Fairdale
Nolan & Nolan, renovation by David Biagi
1968

The original St. Jerome's Catholic Church was a glue-laminated structure with a brick veneer exterior and two shed volumes placed back to back. The smaller volume was the entry vestibule, and the larger one was the worship space with an altar on its short axis and stained-glass windows on the sidewalls. In 2000, to accommodate its 400-member congregation, St. Jerome's hired David Biagi of Shelbyville, Kentucky, to renovate the existing structure with an identifiable quality.

The Biagi design inserts a copper cross and bell cage into an existing tower-like volume and adds two entry canopies and new front doors as the transition between parking lot and lobby. A new immersion-scale baptismal font, located in the center of the expanded, light-filled lobby, symbolizes the entrance to the church community through baptism. A suspended counter-curved canopy mediates the space between the lobby and nave, extending 30 feet overhead. The sanctuary is a round dais with a circular altar, on axis with the baptismal font. A new backdrop behind the altar uses an asymmetrical cross-shaped cobalt blue–paneled window, designed by Kenneth von Roenn of Architectural Glass Art to create a focal point for the ambo and to extend the primary axis upward. Two of the existing stained-glass panels were relocated to the entry vestibule, with one panel relocated to a window in a new "reservation" chapel to the side of the sanctuary space. A curved wall, housing the stations of the cross, masks the new sacristy, meeting room, and bathrooms behind.

228. OKOLONA ELEMENTARY SCHOOL
7606 Preston Highway, Okolona
Jasper D. Ward
1974

Public-school design in the 1960s and 1970s was driven by concerns about construction, maintenance costs, and vandalism, far outstripping the opportunities to use the building's architecture to support educational goals. Architects who ventured to work in these conditions—and a number of leading firms in Louisville chose not to—had to be almost subversive to include features of architectural merit in their designs. The school board mandated concrete buildings with no windows, which is what they got. But Jasper D. Ward was one of the designers willing to work within such constraints. His design for the Okolona Elementary School demonstrates his creativity as well as the limitations of the school commission at the time.

The interior of the building is a series of teaching areas, irregular in plan. Of more interest is the truss roof system Ward used, which is carried on a series of concrete columns. It is most visible within the canopy at the entrance of the building, where diagonal

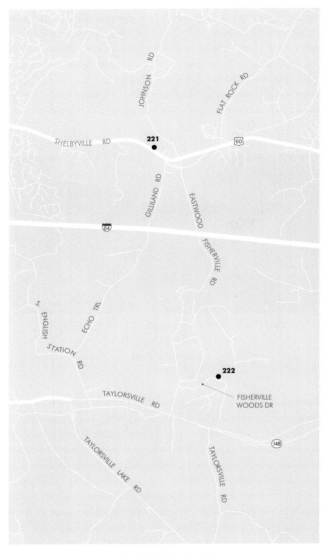

Map 12: Buildings 221–222

steel brackets attach to the top of each column, supporting the roof as well as a globe light nestled in the brackets themselves. The cafeteria and gymnasium (one large shared space) use the same system in a double-height space. Ward detailed the concrete so that the name of the school was cast into the wall adjacent to the entrance, a particularly nice touch.

229. DAULTON RESIDENCE
11602 Chapel Hill Road, Prospect
Bickel Gibson
1991–1992

Located in the conservative Covered Bridge Crossing subdivision in Oldham County and developed by architects Bill Martin and Don Langan, the Daulton Residence is a uniquely modern house designed by James Lee Gibson of Bickel Gibson. The arc-shaped structure steps down the hillside of a densely forested site of four and a half acres and is a hundred yards southwest of the Chapel Hill Road cul-de-sac. The volume of the house responds to the curving contours of the site. A graceful curving stonewall becomes an organizing element of the plan, making a strong relationship between inside and outside. The facade at the rear of the house has two balconies topped with metal handrails. These balconies create voids in the rear elevation that provide covered platforms with views extending to the terraced landscape beyond.

Of interest is the two-and-a-half-story thirty-foot-tall living room, located a half level below the first floor. A two-story cylinder, at the same level as the living room, contains a glazed conservatory. The exterior of the building is a bleached vertical Western red cedar and rough limestone.

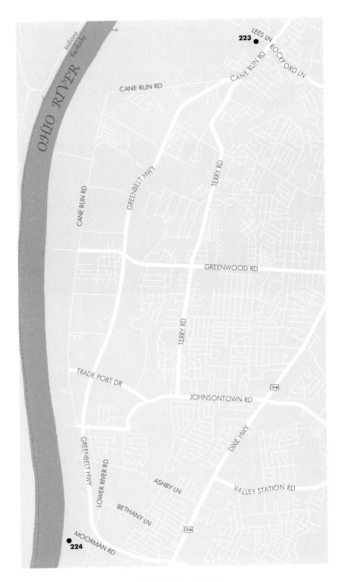

Map 13: Buildings 223–224

Map 14: Buildings 226–227

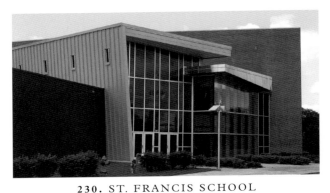

230. ST. FRANCIS SCHOOL
11000 US Highway 42, Goshen
Jasper D. Ward, expansion and renovation by Bravura
1970

From its 1948 origins in nearby Harrods Creek, St. Francis School moved to a 70-acre site in Goshen in 1970. Jasper D. Ward, who had experience with a number of public educational buildings in Louisville (Okolona Elementary School), was the architect. His design demonstrates similarities with those projects, such as clustered work areas and the extensive use of poured concrete construction. Ward chose a hexagonal form as the basis for his open classrooms. The areas between the hexagons provided free-flowing spaces, both on the interior and exterior of the school, for circulation and other kinds of activity. Two additions accommodated a gymnasium, science classrooms, and art room in 1974, and a library, computer center, and foreign-language classrooms in 1982.

In 1996, the school expanded its grounds and a year later began a series of renovations to the existing building and additions. Jim Walters of Bravura designed the project. Ward's strong geometry was treated respectfully yet playfully by Walters: while echoing the hexagonal forms, his design is more open, reinforcing an awareness and engagement with the broader world. A "curving main street" connects old and new portions of the school. The new multipurpose room opens to the landscape far more than the original building, taking advantage of the rural setting. One departure from Ward's methods is in the materials: Walters utilized a series of different colors of brick, metal, and screen to highlight different architectural intentions.

231. WOODLAND FARM
(Clifton)
4801 Greenhaven Lane, Oldham County
Thomas Barbour
Landmark designation: NRHP, 1997
1793

The importance of the Ohio River in Louisville's early history extended far from the Falls of the Ohio and the portage around them. Just as plantation houses faced rivers in Virginia, many early Kentucky plantation houses faced the Ohio, lending them a power of place and positioning them to assume prominence in many aspects of life during the first half of the nineteenth century. Once a 2,500-acre tract, which Thomas Barbour surveyed in 1782, Clifton, now Woodland Farm, is a significant example of an early upland plantation. The oldest extant building, a summer kitchen, dates from 1793. The land has been continuously cultivated since 1813.

Barbour, a founding father of Oldham County, built the main residence in 1835. In 1855, Colonel Richard Jacob purchased the property; eight years later, Jacob was elected Kentucky's seventeenth Lieutenant Governor. After the Civil War, the owners of Clifton specialized in livestock farming, and the current owners have a nationally recognized breeding farm for American buffalo. The main house is a symmetrical brick Georgian structure. A central hall divides the plan, and a service wing has been added on the east side. The house is magnificently sited on a bluff overlooking the Ohio River. A kitchen and herb garden are located just behind the house. Woodland Farm, about a 1,000 acres, is the largest single Kentucky property on the National Register.

232. SHANDS HOUSE
8915 Highway 329, Crestwood
David Morton (San Francisco)
1994

San Francisco architect David Morton's finely crafted design for Reverend Alfred and Mary Shands responds to two spectacular landscapes: the rolling countryside of the Ohio River valley on the outside and the clients' fascinating collection of contemporary and folk art on the inside. The house's facades make two sweeping curves in deference to the landscape. The south elevation is on the front approach, drawing visitors into a small courtyard from which one enters the house. The western facade is even more expansive, with a great curving arc that frames views across the rural landscape of fields and forests. A pergola covered with wisteria curves in the opposite direction from the house, creating a courtyard.

A series of pavilions create distinct rooms for specific functions within the house. Yet these areas are secondary to the expanse of public open spaces that are used for the exhibition of art. The Shands have been major patrons of the arts, both nationally and in Kentucky; the house provides an elegant frame for the display of their private collection. Larger works, especially sculpture and craft, dominate the open spaces, while smaller works are placed in the pavilions. The quality of natural light is exceptional throughout the public areas; the two landscapes, interior and exterior, complement each other profoundly. An upstairs study has been transformed into a Sol Lewitt installation.

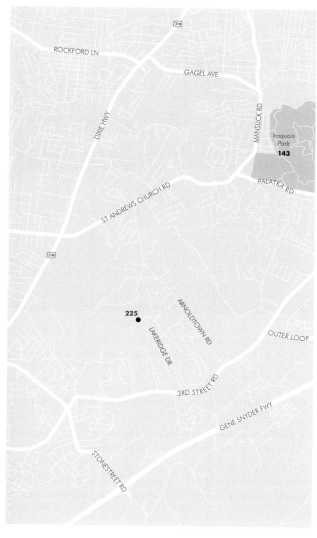

Map 15: Building 225

233. BIAGI HOUSE
4581 Aiken Road, Todd's Point
David Biagi
1994–1995

This small, ingenious house, just fourteen feet wide, still feels quite spacious because its four levels interconnect; the effect is much like Adolf Loos's Raumplan. Built in 1994 for $45,000, the design demonstrates the principle beliefs of the architect, most notably the control of light as a dynamic expression, a three-dimensional proportioning system with a corresponding volumetric and spatial relationship, and the artful use of conventional materials in unconventional ways. The house has been featured in a number of popular journals and home television shows and has elicited much interest: architect Biagi received more than 300 calls from prospective clients after one broadcast.

The geometries of the design, both internal and external, are rigorous, yet they provide a foil for the quintessential Kentucky landscape of fields and forests around the house. Within the clear openings, conventional windows are grouped to form abstract designs, which in turn frame views of the surrounding landscape.

The original design was intended to evolve and respond to the changing criteria of its inhabitants. With the addition of a rectangular pavilion sited near the original structure, the new center of the house has become the spatial void on the terrace between the two structures. The spatial organization of the completed house is a three-dimensional spiral, moving upward in the original house and downward in the addition. The new portion has two levels: an upper level that serves as a formal entry and dining room and a lower level that serves as both a guest room and living room.

Map 16: Building 228

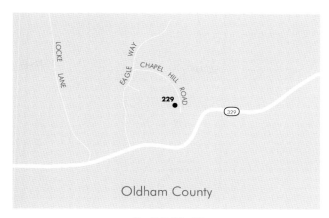

Map 17: Building 229

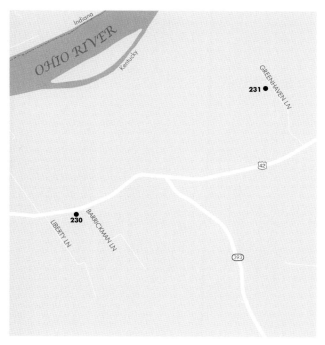

Map 18: Buildings 230–231

Map 19: Building 232

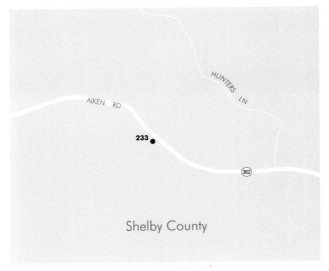

Map 20 Building 233

SUGGESTED TOURS

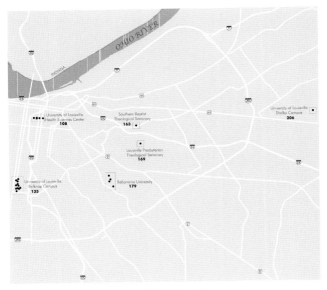

Map 21: College Campus Tour

College Campuses

This tour of universities and colleges includes six campuses. While only selected buildings are fully developed within the project descriptions, the primary role of the tours is to capture the breadth and uniqueness of each of the academic settings. These range from the urban surroundings of the University of Louisville Belknap and Health Sciences campuses to the suburban University of Louisville Shelby Campus (formerly Kentucky Southern College) to the more idyllic settings of the seminaries and Bellarmine University. In each case the larger context of campus orients the reader and links the landscapes and spaces between its buildings to the more fully developed building entries.

108.   University of Louisville Health Sciences Center
135.   University of Louisville, Belknap Campus
163.   Southern Baptist Theological Seminary
169.   Louisville Presbyterian Theological Seminary
179.   Bellarmine University
206.   University of Louisville, Shelby Campus

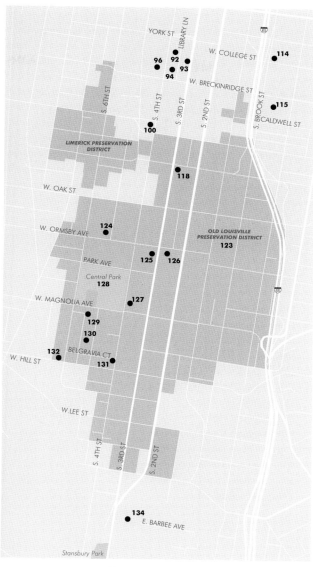

Map 22: Old Louisville Tour

Old Louisville

Old Louisville's boundaries extend roughly from Kentucky Street to the University of Louisville, from Floyd to Sixth Streets. Known as the "Southern Extension" and developed between the 1870s and early 1900s, it was Louisville's first suburb. The term "Old Louisville" was first applied during the 1950s, a time during which the area fell into decline and neglect. In the last decade the area has undergone significant revitalization. Our tour leads the reader through the most significant stately mansions, churches, parks, schools, and museums which together, demonstrate the qualities and diversity of the district. The boulevards, streets, and alleys of Old Louisville comprise the third largest National Preservation District and the largest Victorian district in the United States.

Olmsted Parks

Fredrick Law Olmsted, known for his designs of Central Park in New York City, the Biltmore Estate, and the U.S. Capitol Grounds, designed a system of parkways comprising three major parks—Iroquois, Shawnee, and Cherokee—that, with the smaller parks and parkways, create an "emerald necklace" across the city. Seen as the ultimate park system of Olmsted's career, it is listed on the National Register of Historic Places. The parks and parkways serve many purposes: as places for reflection, relaxation, recreation, and socializing. Of particular note are the rolling hills of Seneca Park; Hogan's Fountain and a 9-hole golf course at Cherokee Park; the panoramic overlook of downtown at Iroquois Park; and the 18-hole golf course at Shawnee Park. In addition to the eighteen parks and six parkways, the Olmsted firm worked on more than 150 projects in the Louisville area. These include the Brown-Forman and University of Louisville campuses, Gardencourt, and the Bernheim Arboretum and Research Forest.

128.   Central Park
143.   Metro Parks:
        Shawnee Park
        Chickasaw Park
        Boone Square
        Elliott Square
        Victory Park
        Algonquin Park
        Exeter Square
        Stansbury Park
        Wayside Park
        Iroquois Park
        Shelby Park
        Churchill Park
        Tyler Park
        Willow Park
        Bingham Park
        Cherokee Park
        Seneca Park

(See also Susan Rademacher's essay on Olmsted's Louisville parks, page 45.)

Map 23: Olmsted Park Tour

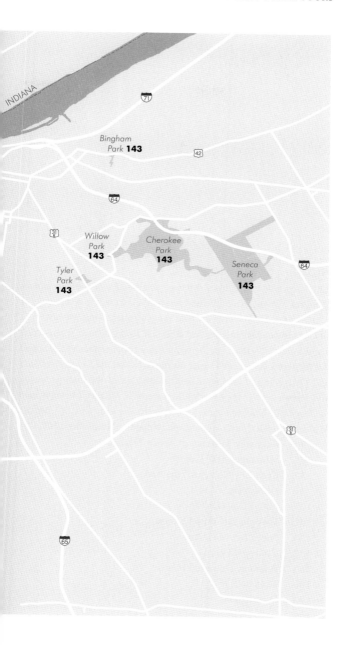

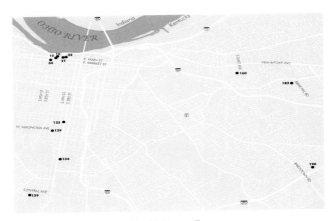

Map 24: Museums Tour

Museums

This tour links the cultural heritage and history of the city and its founders with the exhibition and production of the fine arts and crafts of the world. The focus of the tour ranges from the historic homes of Locust Grove, Farmington, and Whitehall to the history of horse racing at Churchill Downs to the significant art collections at the Speed Art Museum, Kentucky Center for the Arts, and the Museum of Arts and Design to the exhibition and production of the arts, products, and sciences at the Glassworks, the Louisville Slugger Museum, and the Louisville Science Center, respectively. The tour also includes the Muhammad Ali Center, anticipated to open in November 2005.

<table>
<tr><td>16.</td><td>Kentucky Museum of Arts + Design</td></tr>
<tr><td>21.</td><td>Muhammad Ali Center</td></tr>
<tr><td>22.</td><td>Kentucky Center for the Arts</td></tr>
<tr><td>34.</td><td>Glassworks</td></tr>
<tr><td>125.</td><td>Filson Club Historical Society</td></tr>
<tr><td>129.</td><td>Theophilus Conrad House</td></tr>
<tr><td>134.</td><td>Speed Art Museum</td></tr>
<tr><td>139.</td><td>Churchill Downs</td></tr>
<tr><td>160.</td><td>Peterson-Dumesnil House</td></tr>
<tr><td>182.</td><td>Whitehall</td></tr>
<tr><td>190.</td><td>Farmington</td></tr>
<tr><td>199.</td><td>Locust Grove</td></tr>
<tr><td>223.</td><td>Farnsley-Moreman House
Louisville Science Center</td></tr>
</table>

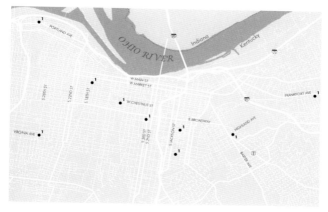

Map 25: Carnegie Libraries Tour

Carnegie Libraries

Nine free public library branches were built in the Louisville area between 1906 and 1914, with financial assistance from the industrialist and philanthropist Andrew Carnegie. These libraries represent some of the best examples of Louisville's architects of the time and act as focal points for each of the communities within which they are located. At the time, they served a range of neighborhoods across the city. The Main Library, the Western Colored, the Crescent Hill, and the Portland Library are still in operation today, while the others have been adaptively reused for a variety of purposes.

1. Carnegie Libraries
   - Portland
   - Jefferson
   - Crescent Hill
   - Western Colored
   - Highland
   - Shelby Park
   - Main Branch
   - Eastern Colored
   - Parkland

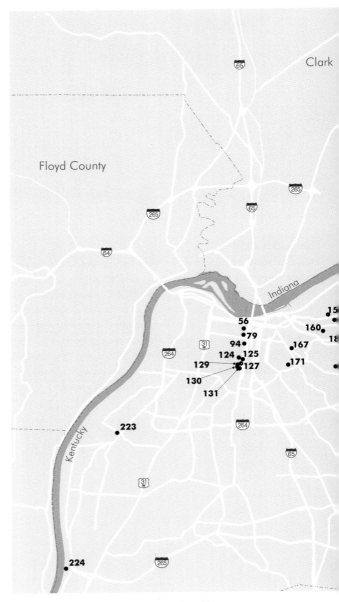

Map 26: Historic Houses Tour

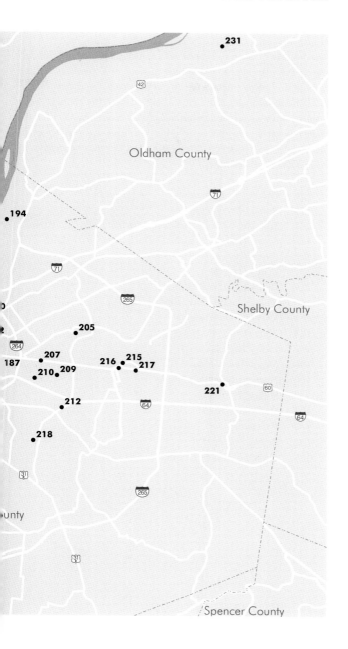

Historic Houses

The historic house tour represents a critical cross-section through the estates, plantations, and houses of many of Louisville's leading citizens that helped define the character, quality, and direction of the cultural heritage of the city. Many of these houses have been restored or preserved and currently serve as museums. Others have been renovated into offices or other uses and many still remain active as private residences. Please note that fees may be charged to visit some of the structures.

56.   Old House Restaurant
79.   Ronald-Brennan House
94.   Spalding College (Tompkins-Buchanan-Rankin House)
124. Speed House
125. Filson Club Historical Society
127. Landward House
129. Conrad-Caldwell House
130. William James Dodd Residence
131. Joseph Werne House
149. Merriwether House
157. Henry Reed House
158. Milam Tandy House
160. Peterson-Dumesnil House
167. Hillard House
174. Humphrey-McMeekin House
182. Whitehall
183. Spring Station
187. Theodore Brown House

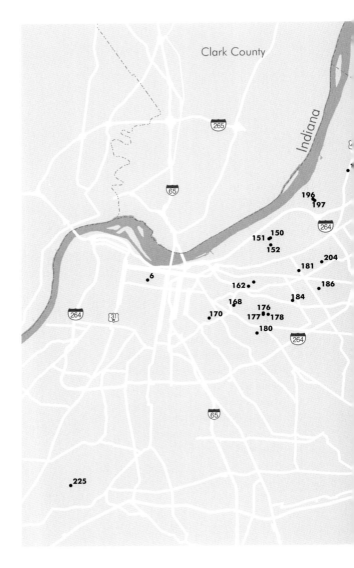

Map 27: Modern Houses Tour

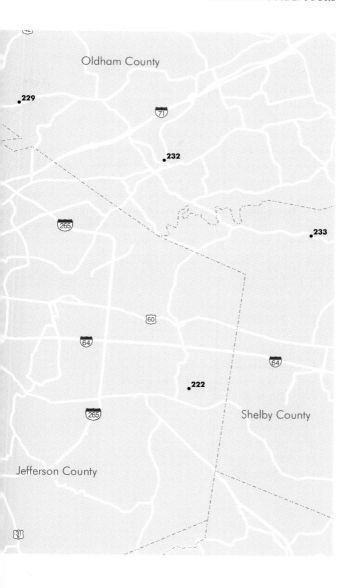

Modern Houses

The projects included here span a range of idioms—International Style to contemporary—of many of the leading figures of the modernist era. Of particular interest are projects designed by the nationally known architects Bruce Goff, William Wesley Peters (Taliesin Architects), Keck and Keck, Herb Greene, and Samuel Mockbee and include critical regionalists John H. Bickel III, Norman Sweet, Jasper Ward, DEGA—Donald L. Williams, James Lee Gibson, and H. Stow Chapman. All responded to the challenges of Louisville's burgeoning suburban landscape and issues of modern living from the late 1930s through the mid-1980s. Contemporary architects such as David Biagi and Michael Koch have continued the modernistic ethos into the 1990s and today. This tour represents several significant architectural investigations into single family and multi-family living spanning the last seventy years.

SELECTED BIBLIOGRAPHY

Anderson, James C., and Donna M. Neary. *Images of America-Louisville*. Charleston, S.C.: Arcadia Publishing, 2001.

Arieff, Allison. "An Old Kentucky Home." *Dwell* (April 2002): 38.

Brown, Theodore M. *Introduction to Louisville Architecture*. Louisville, Ky.: Chicago Spectrum Press, 2002.

Brown, Theodore, and Margaret M. Bridwell. *Old Louisville*. Louisville, Ky.: University of Louisville, 1961.

Cook, Jeffrey. *The Architecture of Bruce Goff*. New York: Harper & Row Publishers, 1978.

Courier Journal. *A Place in Time: The Story of Louisville's Neighborhoods*. Louisville: Courier-Journal and the Louisville Times Co., 1989.

Delong, David E. *Bruce Goff: Toward Absolute Architecture*. Cambridge, Mass.: MIT Press, 1988.

Graham, Anderson, Probst & White. *The Architectural Work of Graham, Anderson, Probst & White, Chicago: And Their Predecessors, D. H. Burnham & Co., and Graham, Burnham & Co*. London: B. T. Batsford, 1933.

Hall, Wade H. *High Upon a Hill: A History of Bellarmine College*. Louisville, Ky.: Bellarmine College Press, 1999.

Hedgepeth, Marty Lyn Poynter. "The Victorian to the Beaux-Arts: A Study of Four Louisville Architectural Firms, McDonald Brothers, McDonald & McDonald, Dodd & Cobb and McDonald & Cobb." Master's thesis, University of Louisville, 1981.

Jones, Elizabeth Fitzpatrick. "Henry Whitestone, Nineteenth-Century Louisville Architect." Master's thesis, University of Louisville, 1974.

Jones, Elizabeth Fitzpatrick, ed. *Jefferson County: Survey of Historic Sites in Kentucky*. Louisville, Ky.: Jefferson County Office of Historic Preservation and Archives, 1981.

Kees, Leslee F., and Donna M. Neary, eds. *Historic Jefferson County*. Louisville, Ky.: Jefferson County Historic Preservation and Archives, 1992.

Kleber, John E. *The Encyclopedia of Louisville*. Lexington, Ky.: University Press of Kentucky, 2001.

Klein, Maury. *History of the Louisville and Nashville Railroad*. New

York: MacMillan Company, 1972.

Lancaster, Clay. *Antebellum Architecture of Kentucky*. Lexington, Ky.: University Press of Kentucky, 1991.

Madsen, Jana J. "Louisville Greatest Legacy." *Buildings* (April 2001): 34–35.

Mahoney, Margaret H. *The Progress of the People: St. Francis of Assisi: 1886–1986*. Indianapolis, 1987.

Miller, Kelli Lorraine. "The Architecture of Jasper Ward: Catalogue Raisonne." Master's thesis, University of Louisville, 1999.

Morgan, William. Louisville: Architecture and the Environment. Dublin, N.H.: William L. Bauhan, Publisher, 1979.

Morris, Angela G. "Four Gothic Revival Churches by D. X. Murphy." Master's thesis, University of Louisville, 1995.

Mueller, William A. *A History of the Southern Baptist Theological Seminary*. Nashville, Tenn.: Broadman Press, 1959.

Newcomb, Rex. *Old Kentucky Architecture*. New York: William Helburn, Inc., 1940.

Oberwarth, C. Julian. *A History of the Profession of Architecture in Kentucky*. Louisville, Ky.: Gateway Press, Inc., 1987.

Rattenbury, John. *A Living Architecture: Frank Lloyd Wright and Taliesin Architects*. San Francisco: Pomegranate, 2000.

Riebel, Raymond Charles. *Louisville Panorama: A Visual History of Louisville*. Louisville Ky.: Gibbs-Inman Co.,1960.

Saliga, Paluine, and Mary Woolever, eds. *The Architecture of Bruce Goff, 1904–1982: Design for a Continuous Present*. New York: Prestel, 1995.

Sanders, Robert Stuart. *History of Louisville Presbyterian Seminary: 1853–1953*. Louisville, Ky.: Louisville Presbyterian Theological Seminary, 1953.

Scully Jr., Arthur. *James Dakin, Architect: His Career in New York and the South*. Baton Rouge, La.: Louisiana State University Press, 1973.

Sergeant, John, and Stephen Mooring. "Bruce Goff." *AD Profiles* 48, no. 10 (1978).

Thomas, Samuel W. *Cave Hill Cemetery: A Pictorial Guide and Its History*. Louisville, Ky.: Cave Hill Cemetery Co., 1985.
———. *Churchill Downs: A Documentary History of America's Most Legendary Race Track*. Louisville, Ky.: Kentucky Derby Museum, 1995.

————. *Crescent Hill Revisited*. Louisville, Ky.: George Rogers Clark Press, 1997.

————. *Louisville Since the Twenties: Views Two, A Sequel to Views of Louisville Since 1766*. Louisville, Ky.: Courier-Journal and the Louisville Times, 1978.

————. *Oxmoor: The Bullitt Family Estate near Louisville, Kentucky Since 1787*. Louisville, Ky.: Butler Books Publishing, 2003.

————. *St. Matthews: The Crossroads of the Beargrass*. Louisville, Ky.: St. Matthew's Historical Society, 1999.

————. Views of Louisville Since 1766. Louisville, Ky.: Courier-Journal Lithgraphing Co., 1971.

Thomas, Samuel W., and William Morgan. *Old Louisville: The Victorian Era*. Louisville, Ky.: Courier-Journal and the Louisville Times, 1975.

Thompson, Jennifer N. "Carrere & Hastings." Master's thesis, University of Louisville, 1997.

Weissbach, Lee Shai. *The Synagogues of Kentucky: Architecture and History*. Lexington, Ky.: University Press of Kentucky, 1995.

Wiser, Stephen A. *Louisville: Sites to See by Design*. Louisville, Ky.: Stephen A. Wiser, 2002.

Yater, George H. *Two Hundred Years at the Fall Ohio: A History of Louisville and Jefferson County*. Louisville, Ky.: Heritage Corporation of Louisville and Jefferson County, 1979.

————. "Edwin Hite Ferguson and the Ferguson Mansion." *Filson Club History Quarterly* 58, no. 4 (October 1984): 436–57.

Falls of the Ohio Metropolitan Council of Governments. Metropolitan Preservation Plan. Louisville, Ky., May 1973.

National Register of Historic Places. Kentucky Listings and Jefferson County Listings. Washington, D.C. U.S. Park Service.

CONTRIBUTORS

Edith Bingham is a long-time volunteer in preservation and urban issues. She has played a leadership role in many organizations including Preservation Kentucky, Louisville Landmarks Commission, Kentucky Heritage Council, Shaker Village at Pleasant Hill, and was a founding member of Louisville's Preservation Alliance. She has lobbied for preservation-minded town planning and development in Louisville, led efforts to preserve the historic Brennan House, and chaired an advisory committee and supported the Shaker Museum at South Union. She is member of the Pope Villa National Advisory Board. In addition, Bingham chaired an advisory committee that was instrumental in establishing a Historic Preservation Masters Program at the University of Kentucky. In 1999 she received the Louisville Historical League's Founder's Award, and an Honor Award from the National Trust for Historic Preservation.

Grady Clay has written about city design issues for more than five decades as the urban affairs editor of the Louisville *Courier-Journal* and as author of numerous books, including *Real Places: An Unconventional Guide to America's Generic Landscape, Right Before Your Eyes: Penetrating the Urban Environment* and *Close-Up: How to Read the American City.* He served as president of the American Society of Planning Officials and the National Association of Real Estate Editors, and was the first director of *Landscape Architecture* magazine. Harvard University named him as a Nieman Fellow. In 1999 Clay was awarded the Olmsted Medal by the American Society of Landscape Architects for his "outstanding contributions to the environment through action and policy." His weekly radio commentaries, heard on WFPL in Louisville, have been issued in a new book, *Crossing the American Grain.*

Dennis Domer is the Helen Edwards Abell Chair in Historic Preservation at the University of Kentucky and was the Clay Lancaster Distinguished Professor there from 2000 to 2003. He was the Associate Dean of the School of Architecture and Urban Design at the University of Kansas from 1980 to 1999. He received a B.A. degree in French and German from Baker University, an M.A. in German from the University of Kansas, a M.A. in American Civilization from the George Washington University, and a Ph.D. in

Higher Education from the University of Kansas. His books include *Alfred Caldwell: The Life and Work of a Prairie School Landscape Architect* and *Embattled Lawrence: Conflict and Community.*

Gregory A. Luhan, RA, is Assistant Professor of Architecture at the University of Kentucky, College of Design. He practiced architecture in New York City for Peter Eisenman and Charles Gwathmey after graduating from Princeton University (1998) and Virginia Polytechnic Institute (1991). He has written several articles and created digital models of Venice, Italy; Shanghai, China; Louisville, Kentucky; and New York City. His models of New York were the basis of the 1999 Canadian Center for Architecture-sponsored IFCCA-Design of Cities Competition. Luhan teaches a digital studio and seminars on design theory and computing, whose work has been exhibited worldwide. He is currently completing a book on modern architecture in Louisville.

David Mohney was raised in Michigan, attended Harvard and Princeton, and practiced architecture in New York City for fifteen years with his wife, Joan Chan. They completed projects for SPY Magazine, Liberty Travel, and numerous residential clients. Since 1994, he has been Dean and Professor of Architecture at the College of Design at the University of Kentucky. Mohney's previous books include *Seaside: Making a Town in America* (with Keller Easterling), which received a citation from the American Institute of Architects in 1992, and *The Houses of Philip Johnson* (with Stover Jenkins) in 2001.

Susan Rademacher is a Landscape Architect and President of the Louisville Olmsted Parks Conservancy. As the Assistant Director of Metro Parks in Louisville/Jefferson County, she is responsible for project review and approval for the entire Olmsted. She has lectured nationally, and was the Editor-in-Chief of *Landscape Architecture* and *Garden Design* magazines for ten years. She has written several books and articles on landscape planning and garden design including *Outdoor Living Spaces, Bold Romantic Gardens, and Garden Design: History, Principles, Elements, Practice,* and articles in *Process Architecture, Progressive Architecture, Landscape Architecture, Places, Landscape Journal,* and *Garden Design.* Rademacher was a Loeb Fellow in Advanced Environmental Studies at Harvard University in 1986-1987.

IMAGE CREDITS

Amy Bennett: 72, 145, 244, 302

Arrasmith Judd Rapp and Chovan, John Chovan: 245, 332

Bickel Gibson, James Lee Gibson: 125, 373

Chicago Tribune Competition: 24

David M. Biagi: Back cover (right), 380

David Modica: 304, 363

David Mohney: Back cover (center), 64, 83, 85, 86, 91, 92, 93, 96, 98, 99, 111, 116, 118, 121, 127, 130, 131, 152, 162, 202, 204, 206, 209, 210, 230, 249, 264, 265, 267, 279, 285, 310, 325, 327, 341, 371, 377, 378

DEGA, James Lee Gibson: 68, 273, 369

Dennis Domer: 14, 17, 18, 19, 66, 70, 78, 81, 87, 102, 106, 114, 136, 140, 143, 150, 163, 167, 188, 189, 195, 198, 205, 213, 217, 221, 224, 227, 233, 237, 238, 240, 243, 275, 278, 281, 282, 283, 289, 291, 298, 315, 319, 324, 328, 335, 338, 343, 345, 348, 351, 354, 355, 356, 357, 362, 364, 365

Feng Li: 306

Frank Döring, OMNI Architects, Michael Jacobs: 336, 358

Gregory A. Luhan: Back cover (left), cover spine, 26, 34, 61, 65, 67, 69, 73, 74, 82, 95, 104, 107, 108, 110, 112, 119, 120, 122, 123, 129, 132, 134, 135, 137, 139, 142, 147, 148, 149, 151, 154, 156, 157, 158, 160, 161, 164, 165, 168, 170, 172, 174, 175, 177, 179, 180, 182, 184, 186, 191, 194, 197, 199, 201, 203, 214, 215, 218, 220, 225, 228, 231, 232, 234, 236, 242, 246, 252, 254, 256, 257, 260, 261, 263, 269, 270, 271, 272, 284, 286, 288, 292, 294, 296, 297, 299, 300, 303, 305, 307, 312, 317, 318, 321, 322, 329, 330, 331, 339, 344, 346, 347, 353, 361, 366, 370, 376

Heather Greene: 75, 84, 100, 103, 192, 212, 277, 293, 314, 352

Impact Photography, OMNI Architects, Michael Jacobs: 193, 258

John H. Bickel III: 25

Mark O'Bryan: 316

McCulloch & Bickel, James Lee Gibson: 326, 350

Muhammad Ali Center, Barry Alberts: 89

Patrick Thrush: 333

Photographic Archives, University of Louisville: 2, 30, 32, 35, 36, 39, 41, 42, 52, 54, 55, 56

Quadrant, Ted Wathan: 262, 46–47, 48–49

INDEX

M

N

T

LIST OF MAPS

COLOPHON

This book, designed by Deb Wood, is set in the Plantin typeface. Designed by F. H. Pierpont in the early 1900s and admired for its classic letterforms and legibility, Plantin is named for Christophe Plantin, a sixteenth-century Antwerp printer. *The Louisville Guide* has been printed and bound by Friesens, in Altona, Manitoba (Canada). The contents of this book, along with additional information and color photographs, is also available online at www.citybase.us.

NOTES

NOTES